LEGION

SON OF X

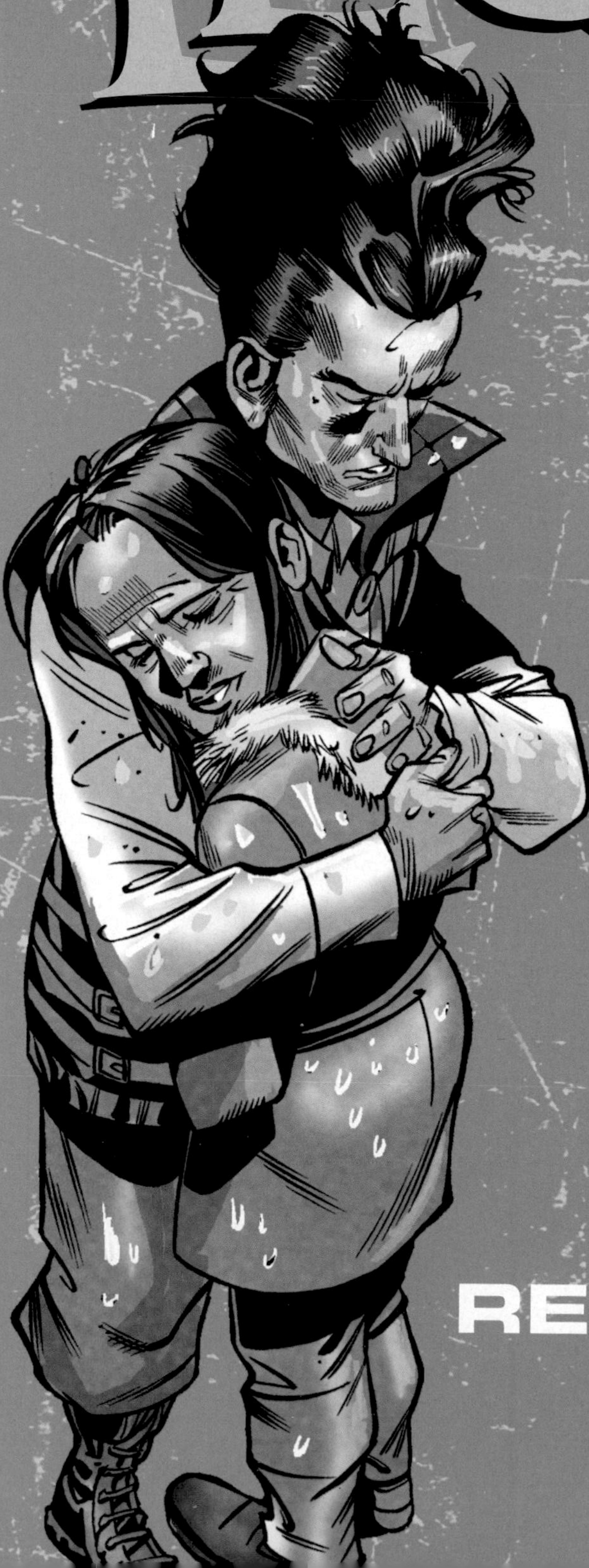

REVENANTS

REVENANTS

writer **SI SPURRIER**
pencilers **TAN ENG HUAT** (#13-15), **PAUL DAVIDSON** (#16) & **KHOI PHAM** (#17-18)
inkers **CRAIG YEUNG** (#13-15), **PAUL DAVIDSON** (#16) & **KHOI PHAM** (#17-18) with **JAY LEISTEN** (#18)
colorists **JOSÉ VILLARRUBIA** (#13-15) & **RACHELLE ROSENBERG** (#16-18)
letterers **VC'S CHRIS ELIOPOULOS** (#13) & **CORY PETIT** (#14-18)
cover artist **MIKE DEL MUNDO**
assistant editors **JENNIFER M. SMITH** & **XANDER JAROWEY**
editor **DANIEL KETCHUM**
x-men group editor **NICK LOWE**

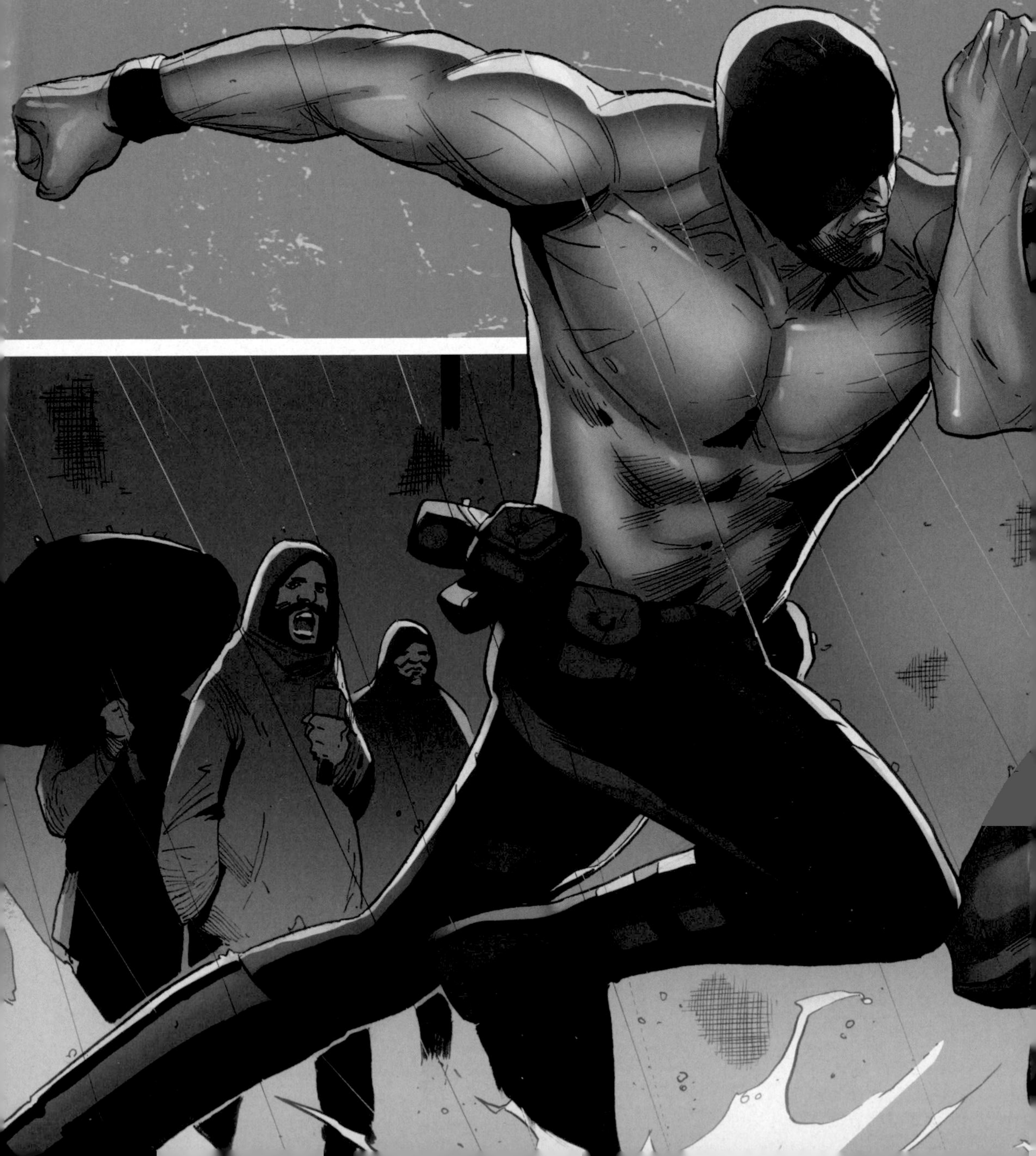

Collection Editor: Mark D. Beazley
Assistant Editor: Caitlin O'Connell
Associate Managing Editor: Kateri Woody
Senior Editor, Special Projects: Jennifer Grünwald
VP Production & Special Projects: Jeff Youngquist
SVP Print, Sales & Marketing: David Gabriel
Book Designers: Jeff Powell & Cory Levine with Adam Del Re

Editor in Chief: C.B. Cebulski
Chief Creative Officer: Joe Quesada
President: Dan Buckley
Executive Producer: Alan Fine

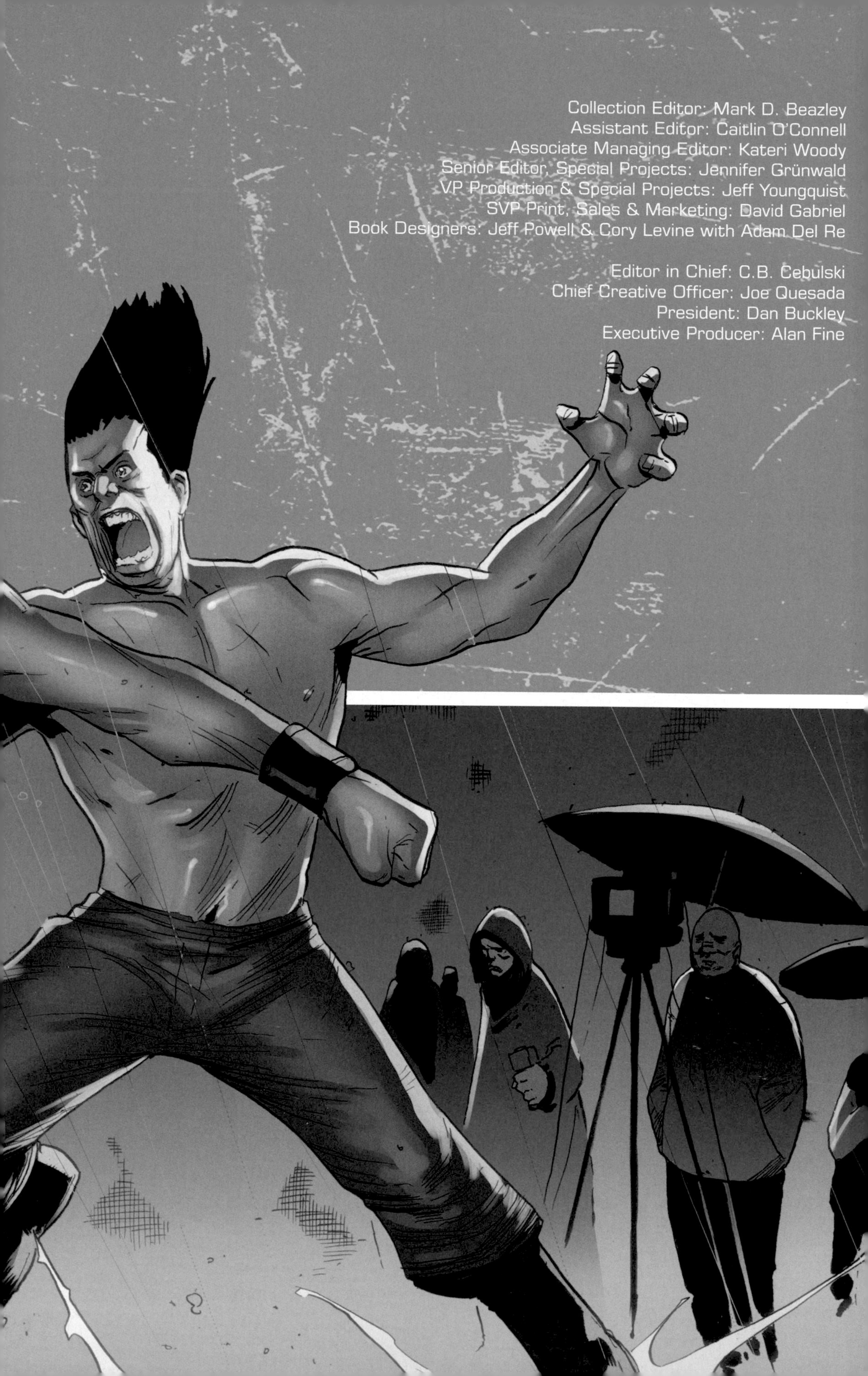

LEGION

SON OF X

CHARLES XAVIER'S MUTANT SON DAVID HALLER WOULD BE NEARLY OMNIPOTENT IF HE COULD LOCK HIS MULTIPLE PERSONALITIES AWAY IN AN EFFECTIVE MENTAL PRISON. BUT THAT TASK SEEMS INSURMOUNTABLE IN THE WAKE OF HIS FATHER'S UNTIMELY DEATH. NOW, DAVID FIGHTS TO KEEP HIS MIND AND POWERS UNDER CONTROL AS HE WORKS TO UPHOLD HIS FATHER'S LEGACY.

Previously

SINCE THE DEATH OF HIS FATHER, PROFESSOR XAVIER, DAVID HALLER HAS STRUGGLED TO ACHIEVE TWO LONG-TERM GOALS: CONTROL OVER THE MULTIPLE PERSONALITIES IN HIS MIND AND THE PROACTIVE, PREEMPTIVE PROTECTION OF THE MUTANT RACE. AFTER DEFEATING A SINISTER PERSONALITY IN HIS MIND THAT HAD WORN HIS FATHER'S FACE, DAVID FEELS MORE IN CONTROL OF HIS SCATTERED BRAIN THAN HE HAS IN SOME TIME — BUT HE STILL HAS PLENTY TO DO IN THE REAL WORLD. AND HIS NEXT MISSION WILL TAKE HIM BACK TO THE PLACE WHERE HE GREW UP — THE UNITED KINGDOM.

LEGION: SON OF X VOL. 3 — REVENANTS. Contains material originally published in magazine form as X-MEN LEGACY #13-18. First printing 2018. ISBN 978-1-302-91082-2. Published by MARVEL WORLDWIDE, INC., a subsidiary of MARVEL ENTERTAINMENT, LLC. OFFICE OF PUBLICATION: 135 West 50th Street, New York, NY 10020. Copyright © 2018 MARVEL No similarity between any of the names, characters, persons, and/or institutions in this magazine with those of any living or dead person or institution is intended, and any such similarity which may exist is purely coincidental. **Printed in Canada.** DAN BUCKLEY, President, Marvel Entertainment; JOHN NEE, Publisher; JOE QUESADA, Chief Creative Officer; TOM BREVOORT, SVP of Publishing; DAVID BOGART, SVP of Business Affairs & Operations, Publishing & Partnership; DAVID GABRIEL, SVP of Sales & Marketing, Publishing; JEFF YOUNGQUIST, VP of Production & Special Projects; DAN CARR, Executive Director of Publishing Technology; ALEX MORALES, Director of Publishing Operations; SUSAN CRESPI, Production Manager; STAN LEE, Chairman Emeritus. For information regarding advertising in Marvel Comics or on Marvel.com, please contact Vit DeBellis, Custom Solutions & Integrated Advertising Manager, at vdebellis@marvel.com. For Marvel subscription inquiries, please call 888-511-5480. **Manufactured between 3/2/2018 and 4/3/2018 by SOLISCO PRINTERS, SCOTT, QC, CANADA.**

10 9 8 7 6 5 4 3 2 1

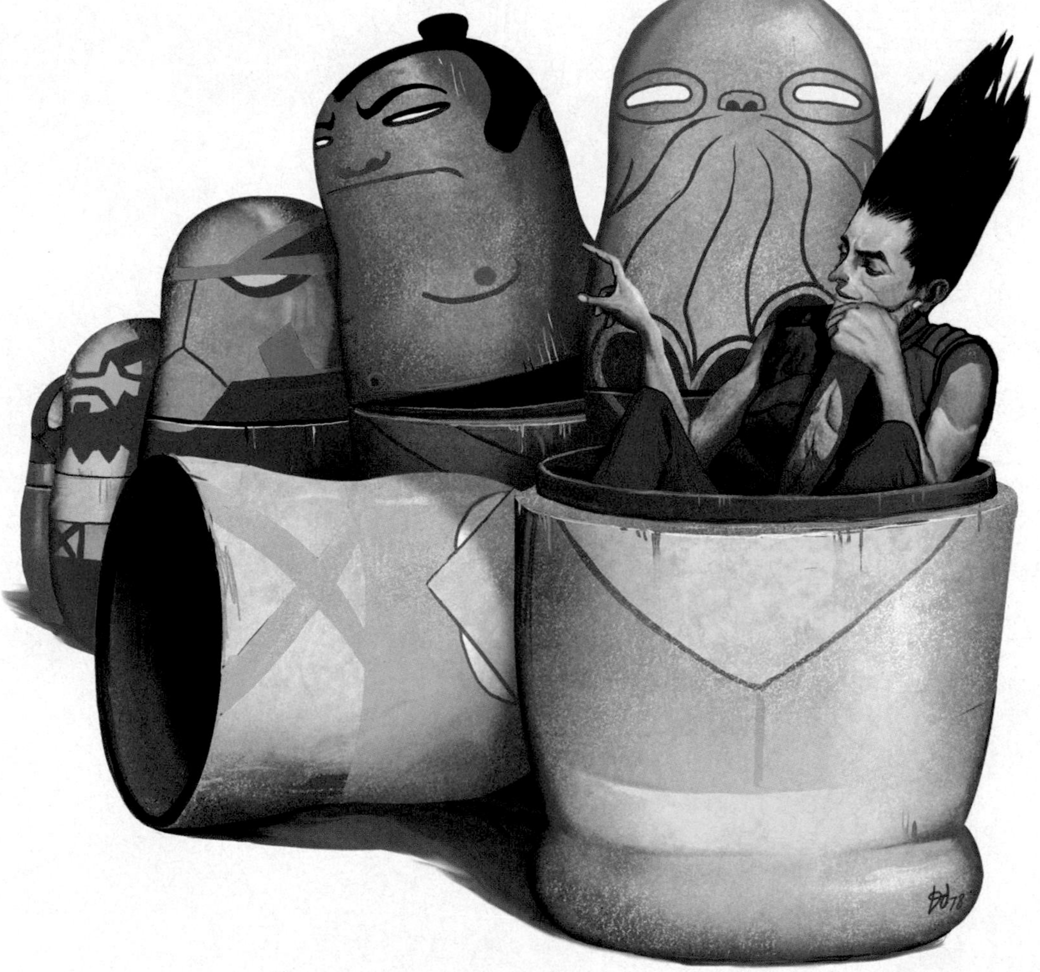

THIRTEEN

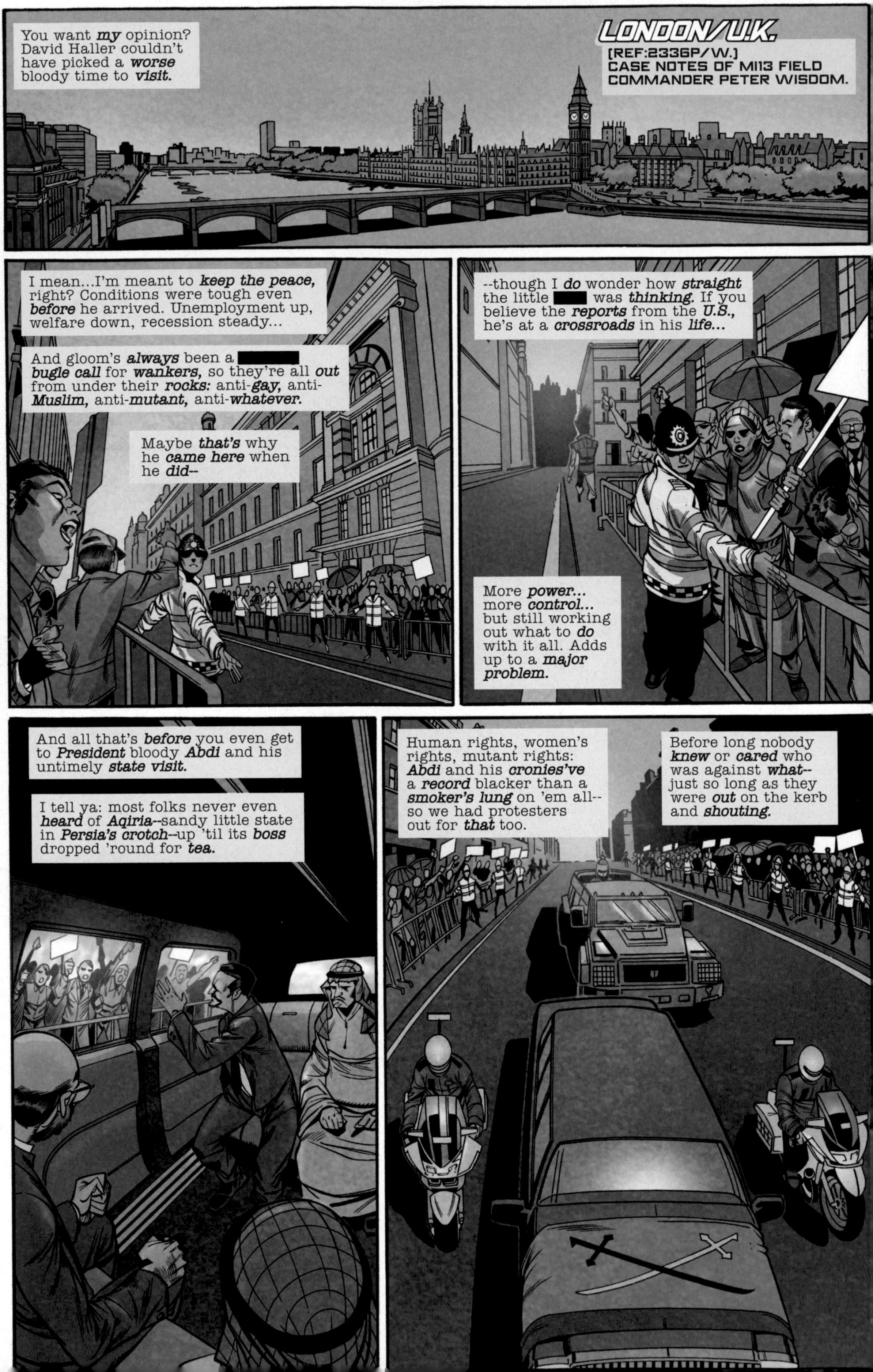
You want my opinion? David Haller couldn't have picked a worse bloody time to visit.
LONDON/U.K.
[REF:2336P/W.]
CASE NOTES OF MI13 FIELD COMMANDER PETER WISDOM.
I mean...I'm meant to keep the peace, right? Conditions were tough even before he arrived. Unemployment up, welfare down, recession steady...
And gloom's always been a [redacted] bugle call for wankers, so they're all out from under their rocks: anti-gay, anti-Muslim, anti-mutant, anti-whatever.
Maybe that's why he came here when he did--
--though I do wonder how straight the little [redacted] was thinking. If you believe the reports from the U.S., he's at a crossroads in his life...
More power... more control... but still working out what to do with it all. Adds up to a major problem.
And all that's before you even get to President bloody Abdi and his untimely state visit.
I tell ya: most folks never even heard of Aqiria--sandy little state in Persia's crotch--up 'til its boss dropped 'round for tea.
Human rights, women's rights, mutant rights: Abdi and his cronies've a record blacker than a smoker's lung on 'em all--so we had protesters out for that too.
Before long nobody knew or cared who was against what--just so long as they were out on the kerb and shouting.

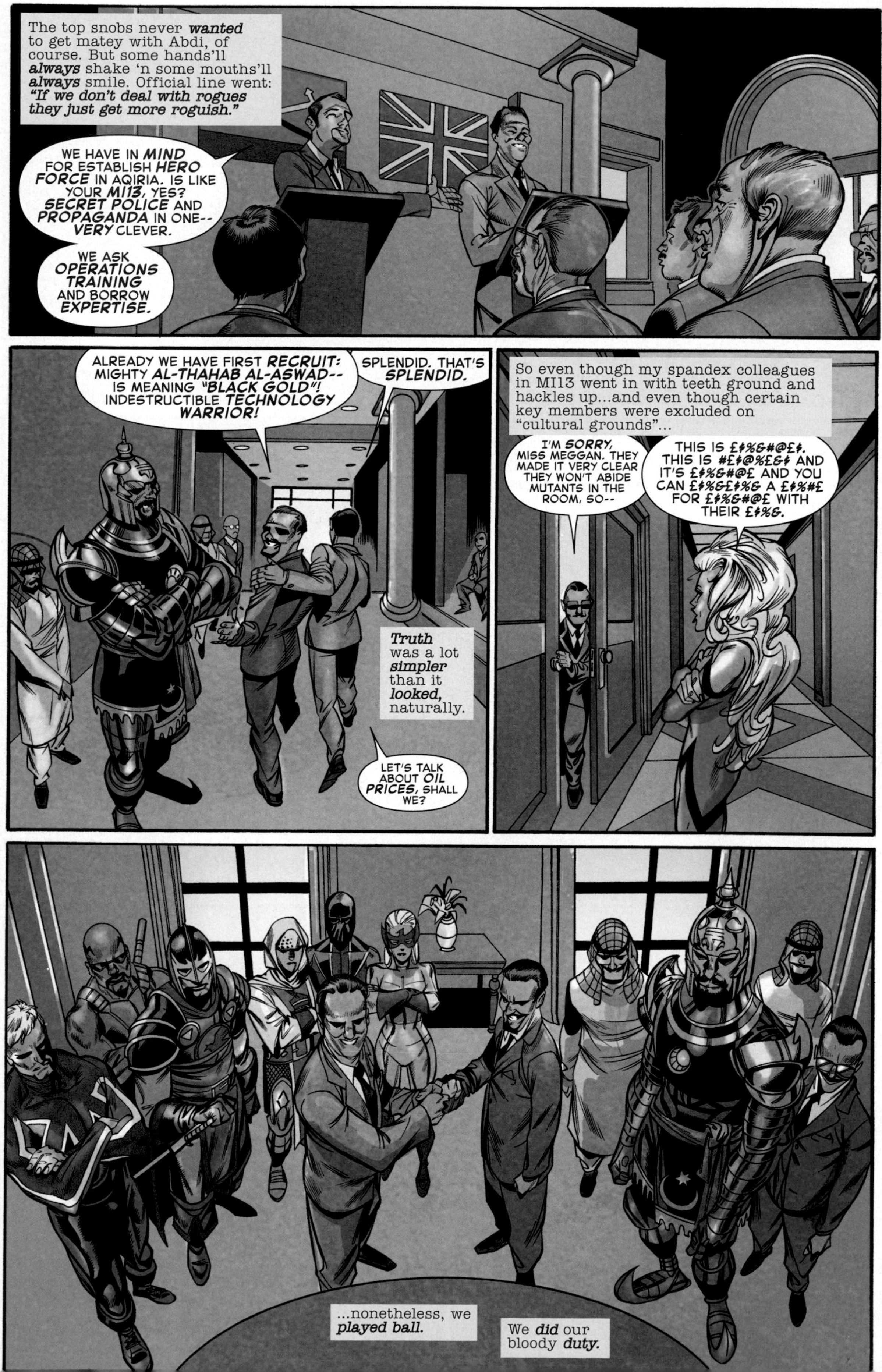

The top snobs never *wanted* to get matey with Abdi, of course. But some hands'll *always* shake 'n some mouths'll *always* smile. Official line went: *"If we don't deal with rogues they just get more roguish."*
WE HAVE IN *MIND* FOR ESTABLISH *HERO FORCE* IN AQIRIA. IS LIKE YOUR *MI13*, YES? *SECRET POLICE* AND *PROPAGANDA* IN ONE-- *VERY* CLEVER.
WE ASK *OPERATIONS TRAINING* AND BORROW *EXPERTISE.*
ALREADY WE HAVE FIRST *RECRUIT:* MIGHTY *AL-THAHAB AL-ASWAD*-- IS MEANING *"BLACK GOLD"*! INDESTRUCTIBLE *TECHNOLOGY WARRIOR!*
SPLENDID. THAT'S *SPLENDID.*
Truth was a lot *simpler* than it *looked,* naturally.
LET'S TALK ABOUT *OIL PRICES,* SHALL WE?
So even though my spandex colleagues in MI13 went in with teeth ground and hackles up...and even though certain key members were excluded on "cultural grounds"...
I'M *SORRY,* MISS MEGGAN. THEY MADE IT VERY CLEAR THEY WON'T ABIDE MUTANTS IN THE ROOM, SO--
THIS IS £$%&#@£$. THIS IS #£$@%£&$ AND IT'S £$%&#@£ AND YOU CAN £$%&£$%& A £$%#£ FOR £$%&#@£ WITH THEIR £$%&.
...nonetheless, we *played ball.*
We *did* our bloody *duty.*

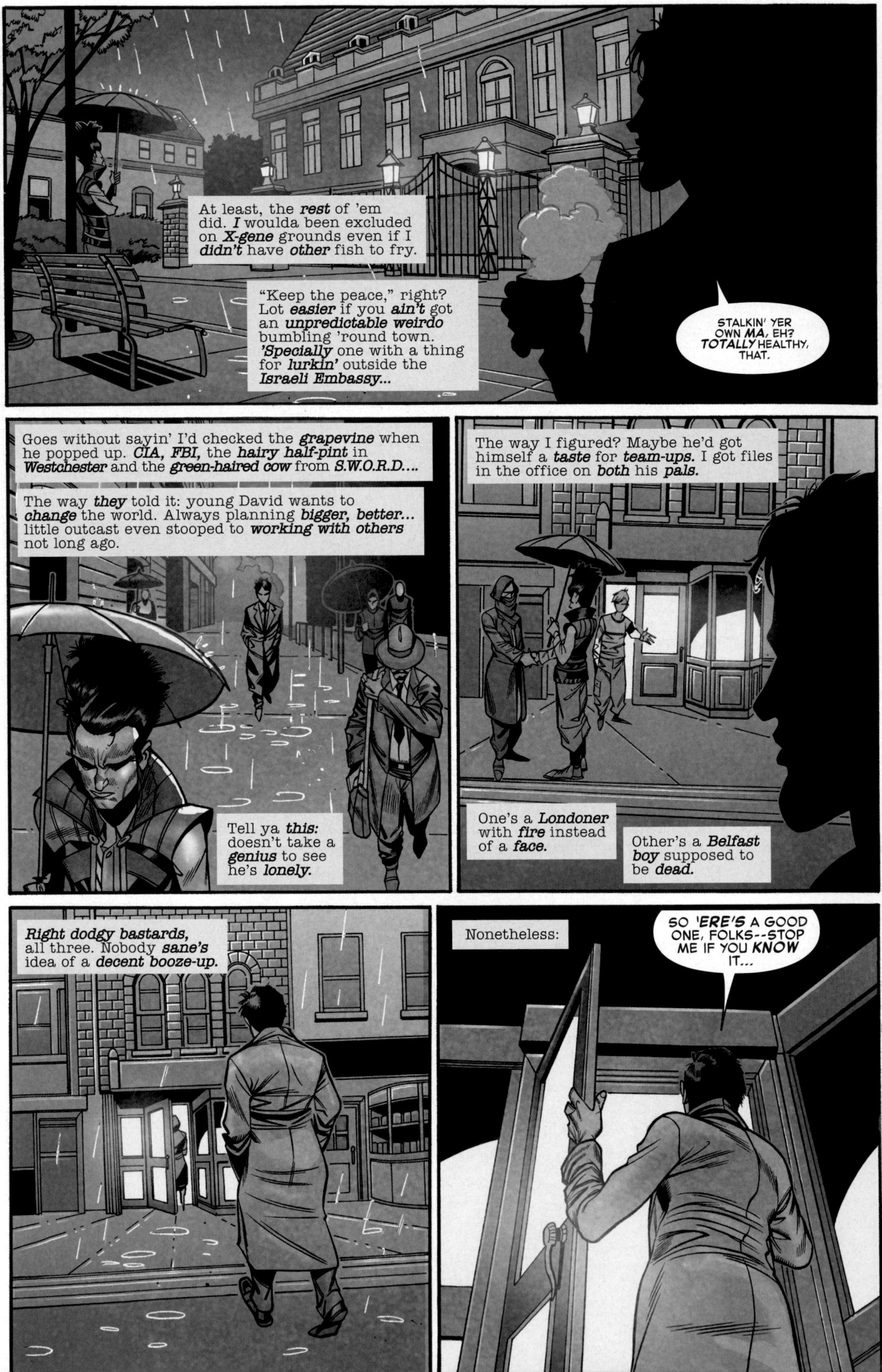
At least, the rest of 'em did. I woulda been excluded on X-gene grounds even if I didn't have other fish to fry.
"Keep the peace," right? Lot easier if you ain't got an unpredictable weirdo bumbling 'round town. 'Specially one with a thing for lurkin' outside the Israeli Embassy...
STALKIN' YER OWN MA, EH? TOTALLY HEALTHY, THAT.
Goes without sayin' I'd checked the grapevine when he popped up. CIA, FBI, the hairy half-pint in Westchester and the green-haired cow from S.W.O.R.D....
The way they told it: young David wants to change the world. Always planning bigger, better... little outcast even stooped to working with others not long ago.
Tell ya this: doesn't take a genius to see he's lonely.
The way I figured? Maybe he'd got himself a taste for team-ups. I got files in the office on both his pals.
One's a Londoner with fire instead of a face.
Other's a Belfast boy supposed to be dead.
Right dodgy bastards, all three. Nobody sane's idea of a decent booze-up.
Nonetheless:
SO 'ERE'S A GOOD ONE, FOLKS--STOP ME IF YOU KNOW IT...

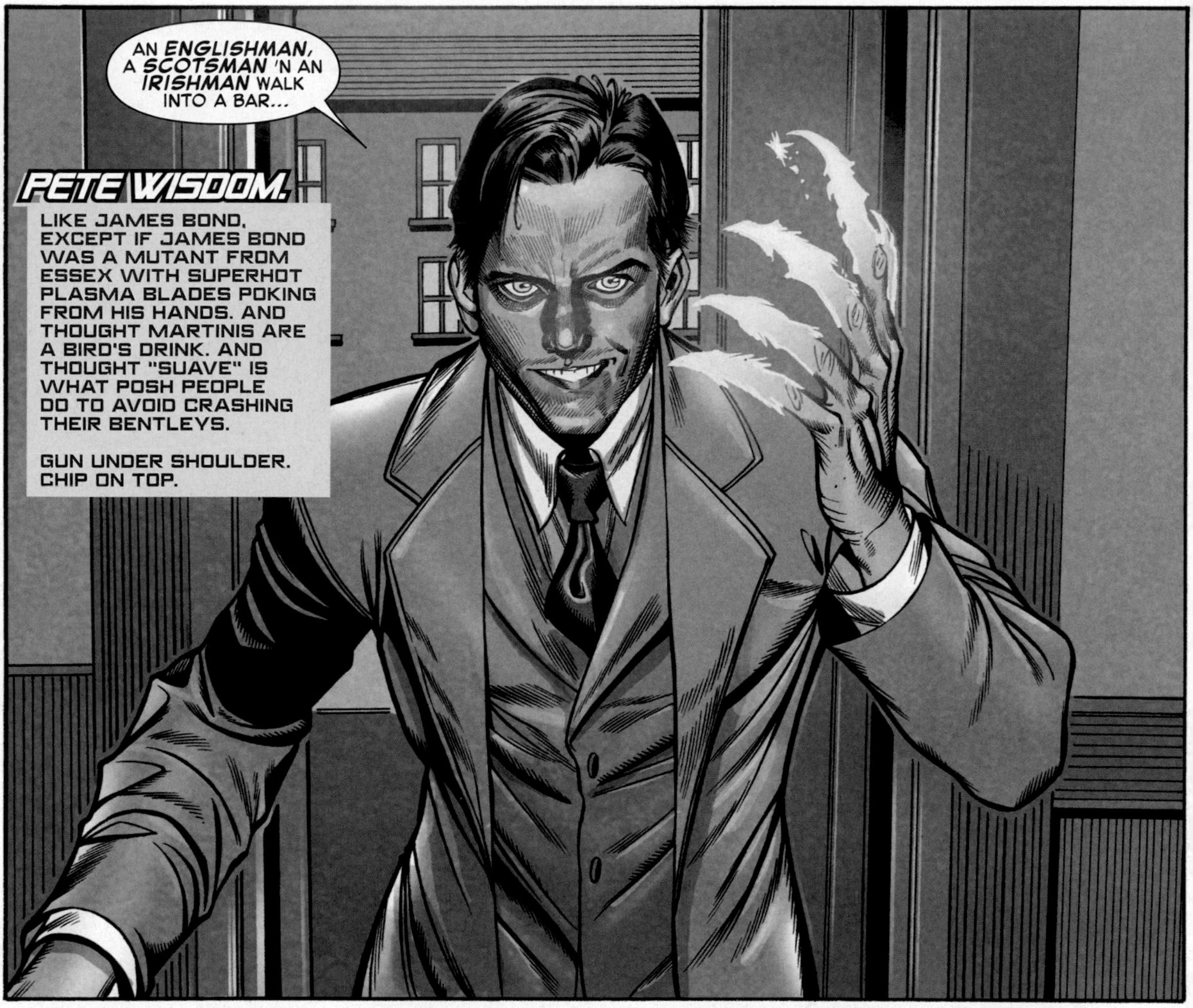
AN ENGLISHMAN, A SCOTSMAN 'N AN IRISHMAN WALK INTO A BAR...
PETE WISDOM.
LIKE JAMES BOND, EXCEPT IF JAMES BOND WAS A MUTANT FROM ESSEX WITH SUPERHOT PLASMA BLADES POKING FROM HIS HANDS. AND THOUGHT MARTINIS ARE A BIRD'S DRINK. AND THOUGHT "SUAVE" IS WHAT POSH PEOPLE DO TO AVOID CRASHING THEIR BENTLEYS.
GUN UNDER SHOULDER. CHIP ON TOP.

HOPE AND GLORY
PART 1

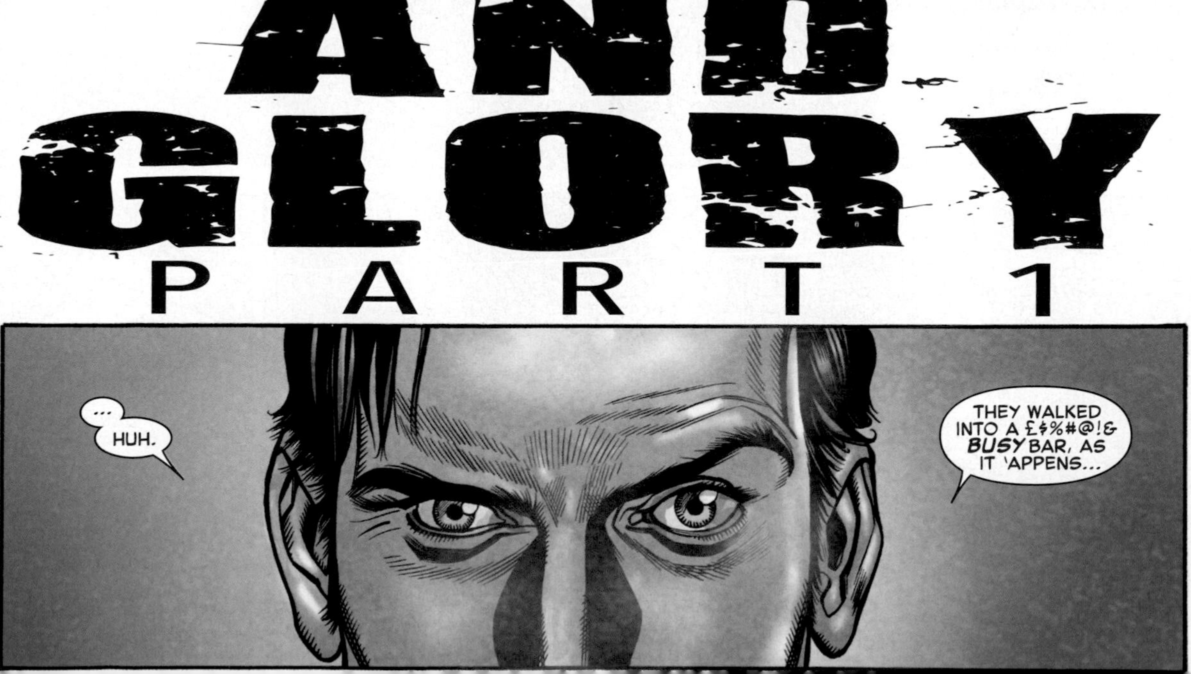
... HUH.
THEY WALKED INTO A £$%#@!& BUSY BAR, AS IT 'APPENS...

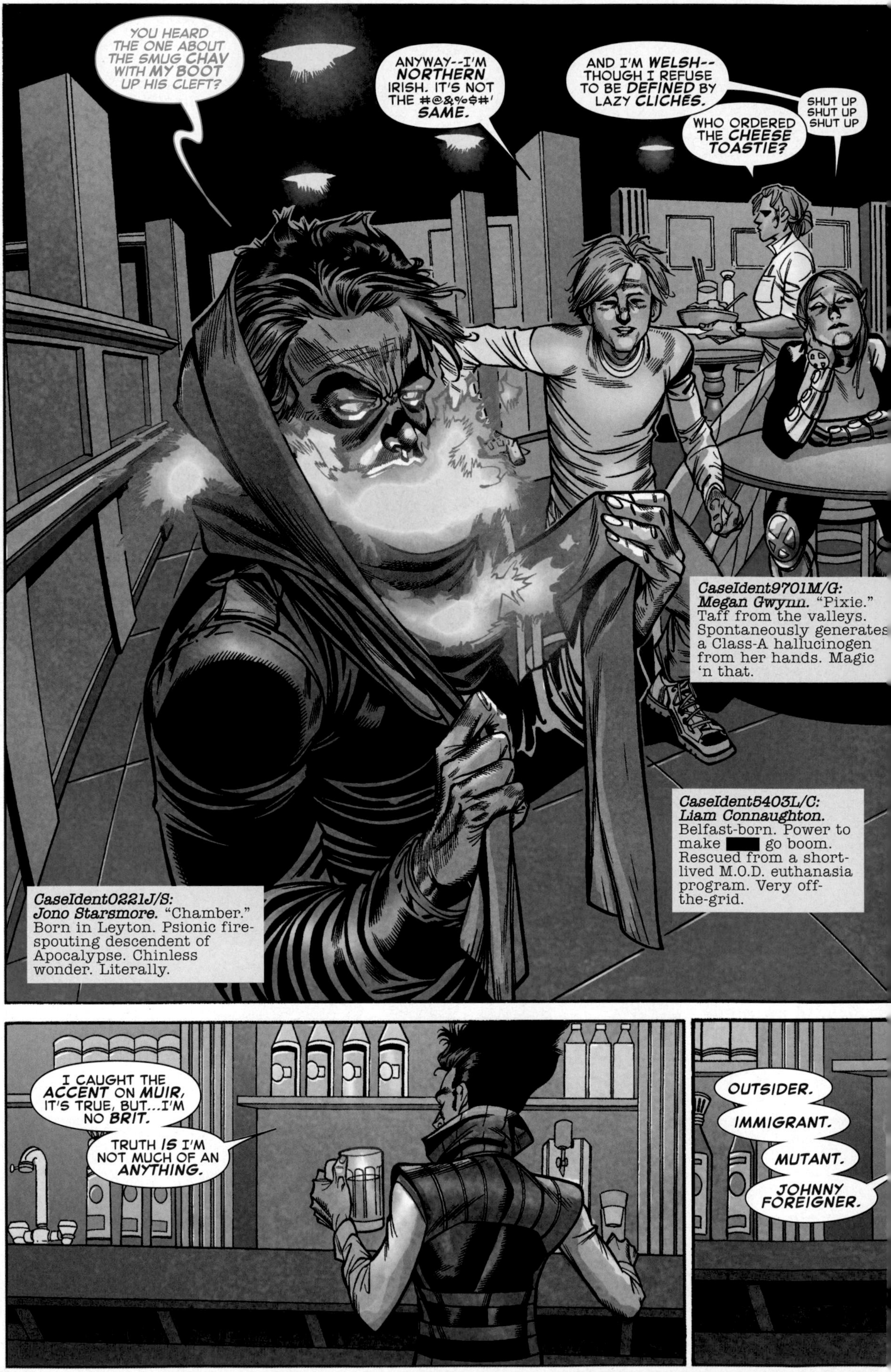
YOU HEARD THE ONE ABOUT THE SMUG CHAV WITH MY BOOT UP HIS CLEFT?
ANYWAY--I'M NORTHERN IRISH. IT'S NOT THE #@&%$#' SAME.
AND I'M WELSH--THOUGH I REFUSE TO BE DEFINED BY LAZY CLICHES.
SHUT UP SHUT UP SHUT UP
WHO ORDERED THE CHEESE TOASTIE?
CaseIdent9701M/G: Megan Gwynn. "Pixie." Taff from the valleys. Spontaneously generates a Class-A hallucinogen from her hands. Magic 'n that.
CaseIdent5403L/C: Liam Connaughton. Belfast-born. Power to make [redacted] go boom. Rescued from a short-lived M.O.D. euthanasia program. Very off-the-grid.
CaseIdent0221J/S: Jono Starsmore. "Chamber." Born in Leyton. Psionic fire-spouting descendent of Apocalypse. Chinless wonder. Literally.
I CAUGHT THE ACCENT ON MUIR, IT'S TRUE, BUT...I'M NO BRIT.
TRUTH IS I'M NOT MUCH OF AN ANYTHING.
OUTSIDER.
IMMIGRANT.
MUTANT.
JOHNNY FOREIGNER.

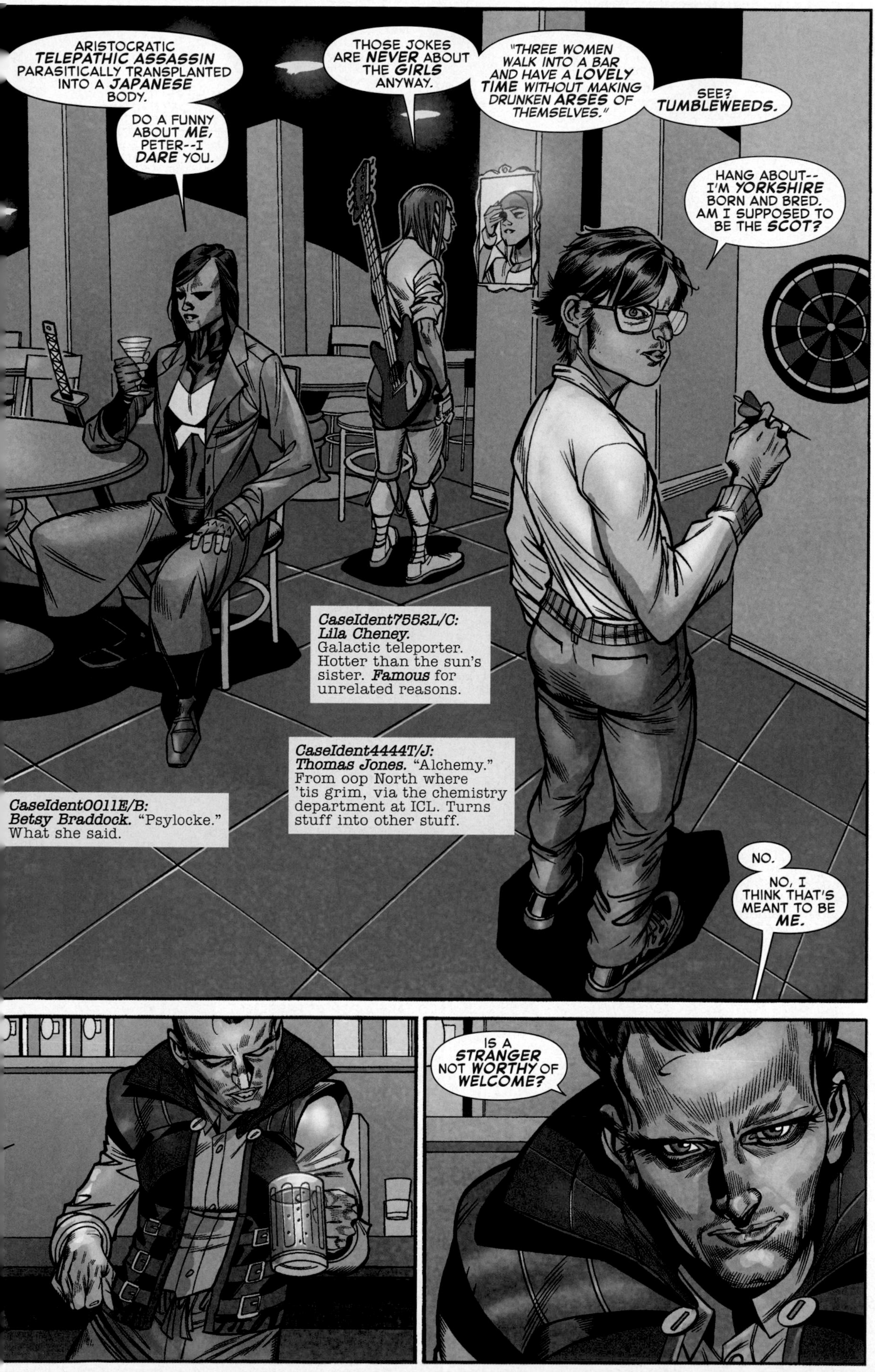

ARISTOCRATIC TELEPATHIC ASSASSIN PARASITICALLY TRANSPLANTED INTO A JAPANESE BODY.
DO A FUNNY ABOUT ME, PETER--I DARE YOU.
THOSE JOKES ARE NEVER ABOUT THE GIRLS ANYWAY.
"THREE WOMEN WALK INTO A BAR AND HAVE A LOVELY TIME WITHOUT MAKING DRUNKEN ARSES OF THEMSELVES."
SEE? TUMBLEWEEDS.
HANG ABOUT-- I'M YORKSHIRE BORN AND BRED. AM I SUPPOSED TO BE THE SCOT?
CaseIdent7552L/C: Lila Cheney. Galactic teleporter. Hotter than the sun's sister. Famous for unrelated reasons.
CaseIdent4444T/J: Thomas Jones. "Alchemy." From oop North where 'tis grim, via the chemistry department at ICL. Turns stuff into other stuff.
CaseIdent0011E/B: Betsy Braddock. "Psylocke." What she said.
NO.
NO, I THINK THAT'S MEANT TO BE ME.
IS A STRANGER NOT WORTHY OF WELCOME?

BLESS. ALL THE DEADLY *MENTAL* EVER WANTED WAS A *CRUMPET* AND A *CUDDLE*.

HA. *AYE*, FAIR ENOUGH. LET'S CUT TO THE *CHASE*?

YOU DON'T *WANT* ME HERE.

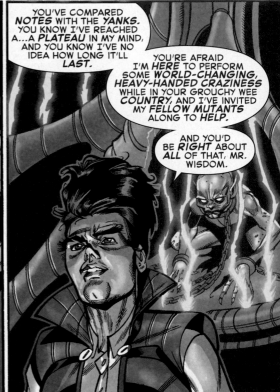

YOU'VE COMPARED *NOTES* WITH THE *YANKS*. YOU KNOW I'VE REACHED A...A *PLATEAU* IN MY MIND, AND YOU KNOW I'VE NO IDEA HOW LONG IT'LL *LAST*.

YOU'RE AFRAID I'M *HERE* TO PERFORM SOME *WORLD-CHANGING*, *HEAVY-HANDED CRAZINESS* WHILE IN YOUR GROUCHY WEE *COUNTRY*, AND I'VE INVITED MY *FELLOW MUTANTS* ALONG TO *HELP*.

AND YOU'D BE *RIGHT* ABOUT *ALL* OF THAT, MR. WISDOM.

HHH. IT'S FUNNY.

NOT LONG AGO I THOUGHT THE *ONLY WORDS* ANYONE *NEEDS* ARE "I *RULE* ME." BUT YOU KNOW *WHAT*?

I'M STARTIN' TO THINK *NO ONE* SHOULD HAVE TO *RULE ALONE*.

I'M CHASING MY FATHER'S *DREAM* THE ONLY WAY THAT *WORKS*, MR. WISDOM. MUTANTS MUST *WORK TOGETHER* TO *PREEMPTIVELY ANNIHILATE* THE *BIGOTRY* OF TH--

YEAHYEAH*YEAH*. JEEZ.

YOU WAS DOIN' *ALL RIGHT* UP 'TIL THE *CALL-TO-ARMS* BIT.

SEE...IF I WAS A *BETTING MAN* I'D SAY YOU'RE *HERE* TO TAKE A POP AT PRESIDENT *ABDI*. *PROPER* BUG UP HIS BUM ABOUT *X-PEEPS*, THAT ONE.

SOME SORT OF *DOUBLECLEVER SCHEME* TO ELIMINATE A *FUTURE THREAT*-- THAT'S YOUR *SHTICK* THESE DAYS, INNIT?

WELL:

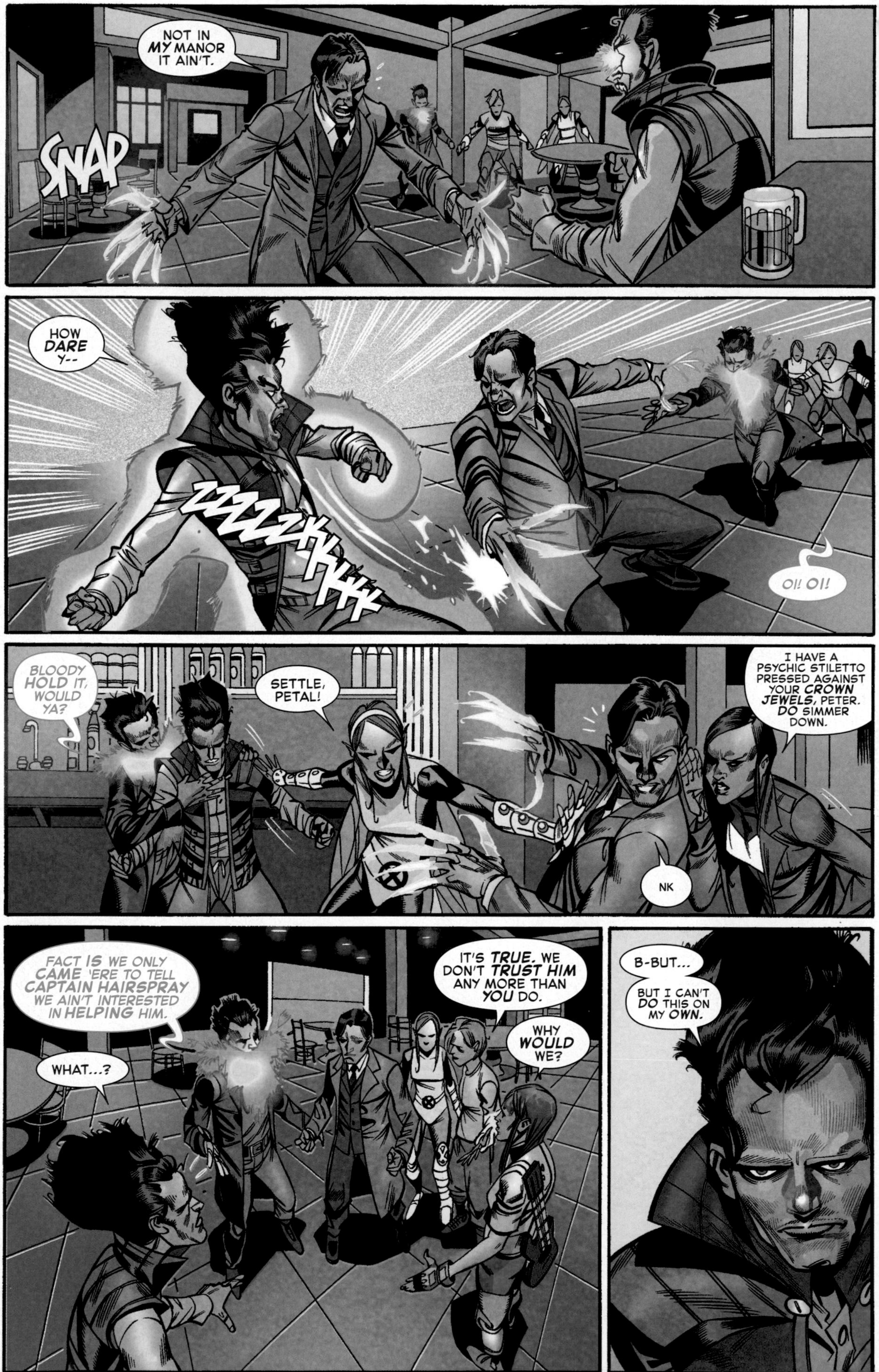
NOT IN MY MANOR IT AIN'T.
SNAP
HOW DARE Y--
ZZZZZKKKKKK
OI! OI!
BLOODY HOLD IT, WOULD YA?
SETTLE, PETAL!
I HAVE A PSYCHIC STILETTO PRESSED AGAINST YOUR CROWN JEWELS, PETER. DO SIMMER DOWN.
NK
FACT IS WE ONLY CAME 'ERE TO TELL CAPTAIN HAIRSPRAY WE AIN'T INTERESTED IN HELPING HIM.
WHAT...?
IT'S TRUE. WE DON'T TRUST HIM ANY MORE THAN YOU DO.
WHY WOULD WE?
B-BUT...
BUT I CAN'T DO THIS ON MY OWN.

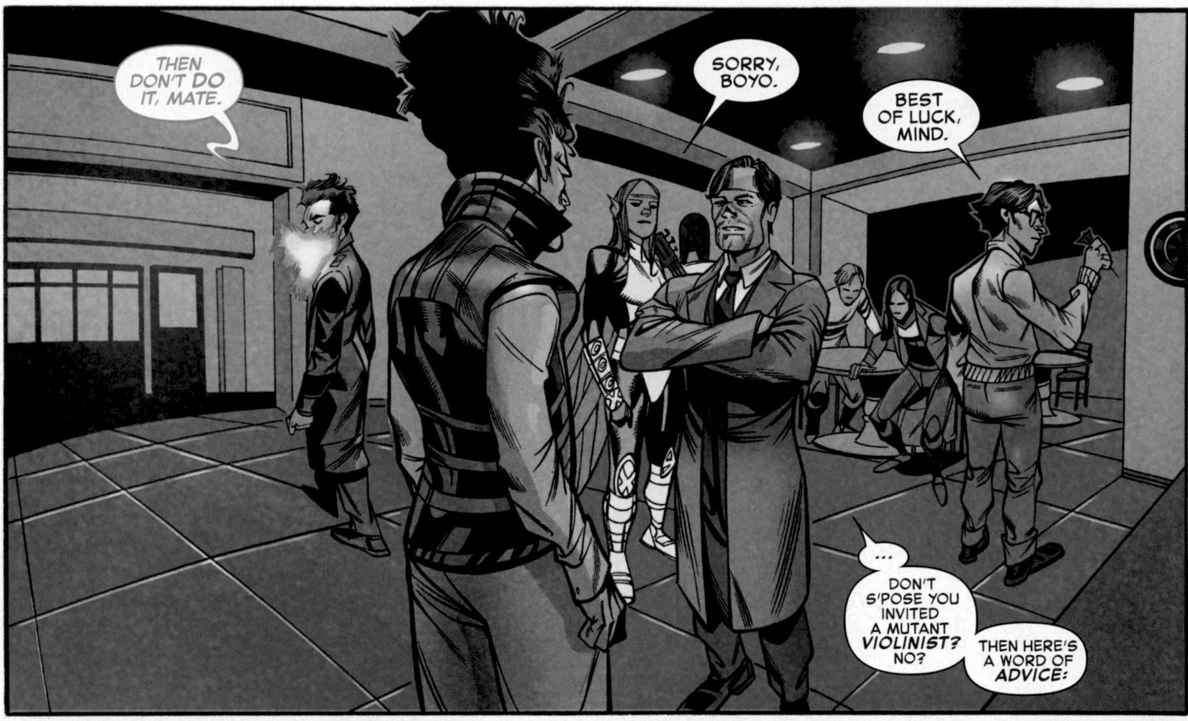
THEN DON'T DO IT, MATE.
SORRY, BOYO.
BEST OF LUCK, MIND.
...
DON'T S'POSE YOU INVITED A MUTANT VIOLINIST? NO?
THEN HERE'S A WORD OF ADVICE:

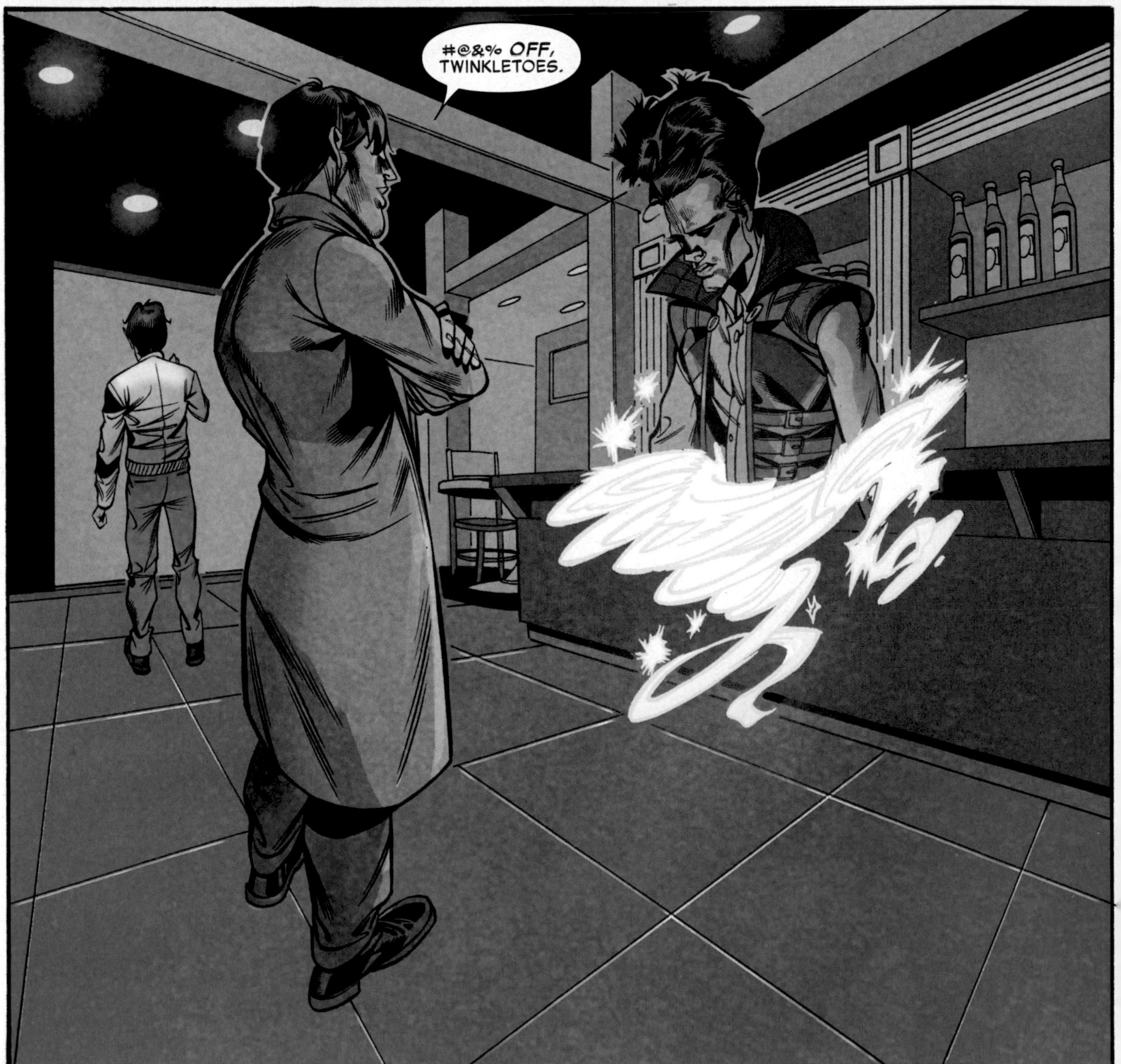
#@&% OFF, TWINKLETOES.

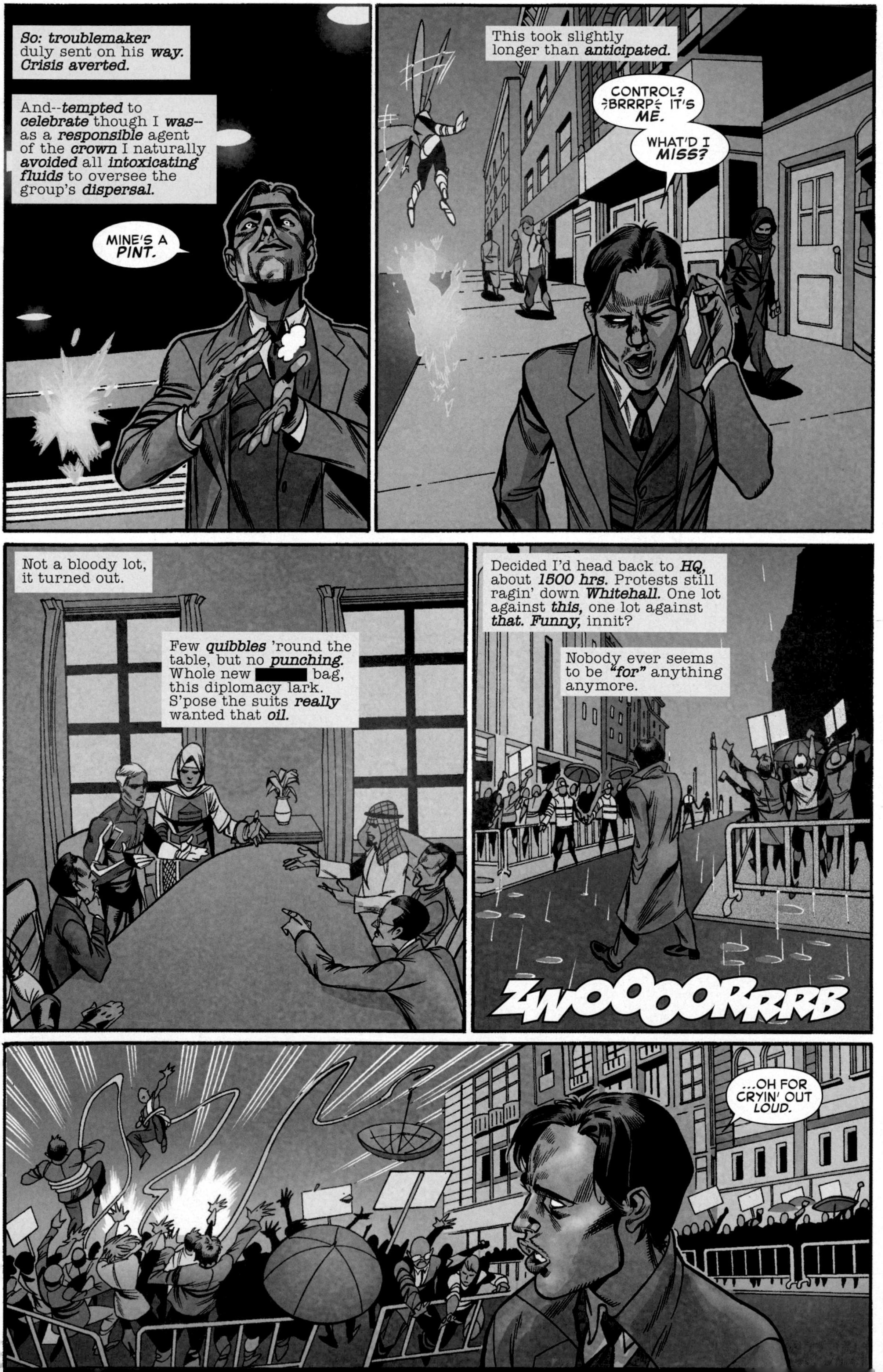

So: troublemaker duly sent on his way. Crisis averted.
And--tempted to celebrate though I was--as a responsible agent of the crown I naturally avoided all intoxicating fluids to oversee the group's dispersal.
MINE'S A PINT.
This took slightly longer than anticipated.
CONTROL? BRRRP IT'S ME.
WHAT'D I MISS?
Not a bloody lot, it turned out.
Few quibbles 'round the table, but no punching. Whole new [redacted] bag, this diplomacy lark. S'pose the suits really wanted that oil.
Decided I'd head back to HQ, about 1500 hrs. Protests still ragin' down Whitehall. One lot against this, one lot against that. Funny, innit?
Nobody ever seems to be "for" anything anymore.
ZWOOOORRRB
...OH FOR CRYIN' OUT LOUD.

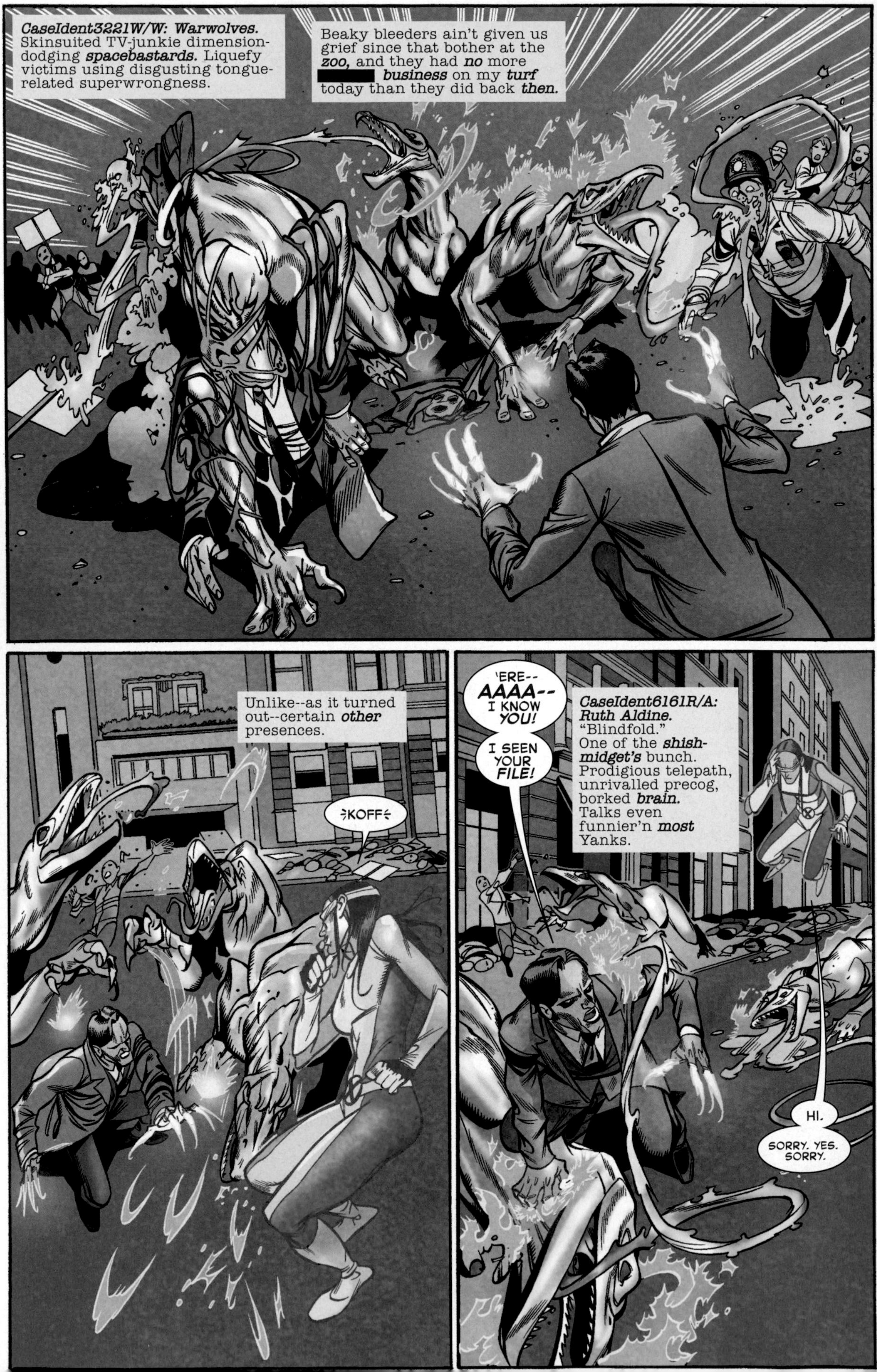
CaseIdent3221W/W: Warwolves. Skinsuited TV-junkie dimension-dodging spacebastards. Liquefy victims using disgusting tongue-related superwrongness.
Beaky bleeders ain't given us grief since that bother at the zoo, and they had no more [redacted] business on my turf today than they did back then.
Unlike--as it turned out--certain other presences.
KOFF
'ERE-- AAAA-- I KNOW YOU!
I SEEN YOUR FILE!
CaseIdent6161R/A: Ruth Aldine. "Blindfold." One of the shish-midget's bunch. Prodigious telepath, unrivalled precog, borked brain. Talks even funnier'n most Yanks.
HI.
SORRY. YES. SORRY.

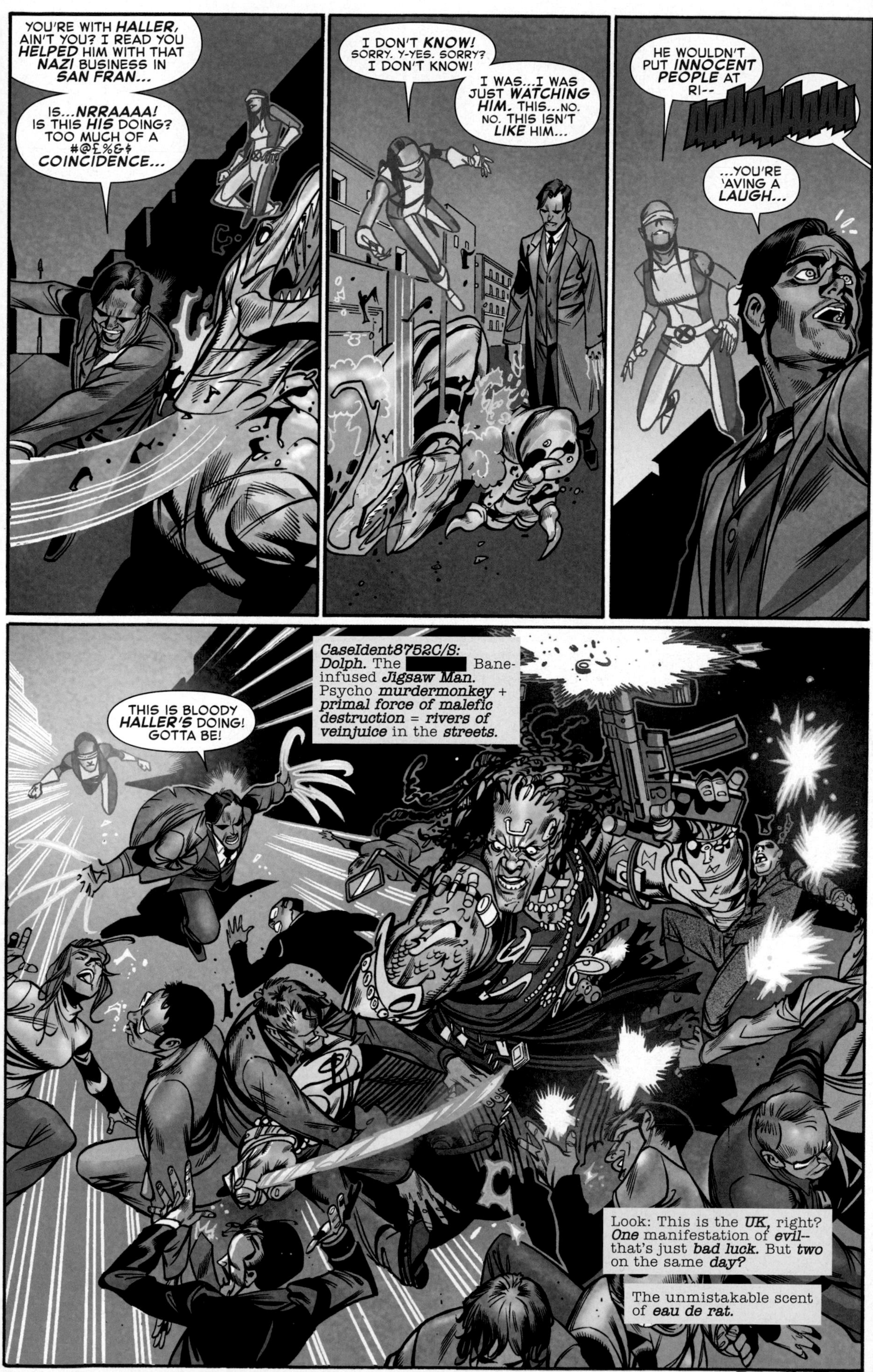
YOU'RE WITH HALLER, AIN'T YOU? I READ YOU HELPED HIM WITH THAT NAZI BUSINESS IN SAN FRAN...
IS...NRRAAAA! IS THIS HIS DOING? TOO MUCH OF A #@£%&$ COINCIDENCE...
I DON'T KNOW! SORRY. Y-YES. SORRY? I DON'T KNOW!
I WAS...I WAS JUST WATCHING HIM. THIS...NO. NO. THIS ISN'T LIKE HIM...
HE WOULDN'T PUT INNOCENT PEOPLE AT RI--
AAAAAAAAA
...YOU'RE 'AVING A LAUGH...
CaseIdent8752C/S: Dolph. The [redacted] Bane-infused Jigsaw Man. Psycho murdermonkey + primal force of malefic destruction = rivers of veinjuice in the streets.
THIS IS BLOODY HALLER'S DOING! GOTTA BE!
Look: This is the UK, right? One manifestation of evil--that's just bad luck. But two on the same day?
The unmistakable scent of eau de rat.

T-TRY TO *UNDERSTAND!* PLEASE. PLEASE?

HE'S...HE'S *LONELY.* HE'S *SO POWERFUL* A-AND HE'S...YES. PARDON? HE'S *FRIGHTENED* OF HIMSELF AND HE'S *HURTING--*

YOU'RE A CRAP *SALESMAN,* LOVE, YOU KNOW THAA*AAAA--*

--BUT ALL HE WANTS IS TO *HELP!*

I DON'T...SORRY. Y-YES...I DON'T *AGREE* WITH ALL THE THINGS HE *DOES.* NUH-UH. THE *MANIPULATION*...THE *CONTROLLING...*

B-BUT...*MR. WISDOM?*

HE'S NOT *EVIL.* SORRY. HE DOESN'T TAKE *RISKS.*

...WHAT YOU TRYNNA *SAY,* KID?

JOYYYYYY AND FFFEEEEEEAAAAR

HHH.

PLEASE TELL ME THAT'S NOT #@£%&#$ *PLOKTA* BEHIND ME.

CaseIdent0666A/A: *Plokta.* Venomous evil *megaprince* from an unpronounceable *armpit dimension* on the *cheap side* of Hell. Slightly less *welcome* than a *snotbubble* in your *sarnie.*

TH-THAT IS NOT PLOKTA BEHIND YOU.

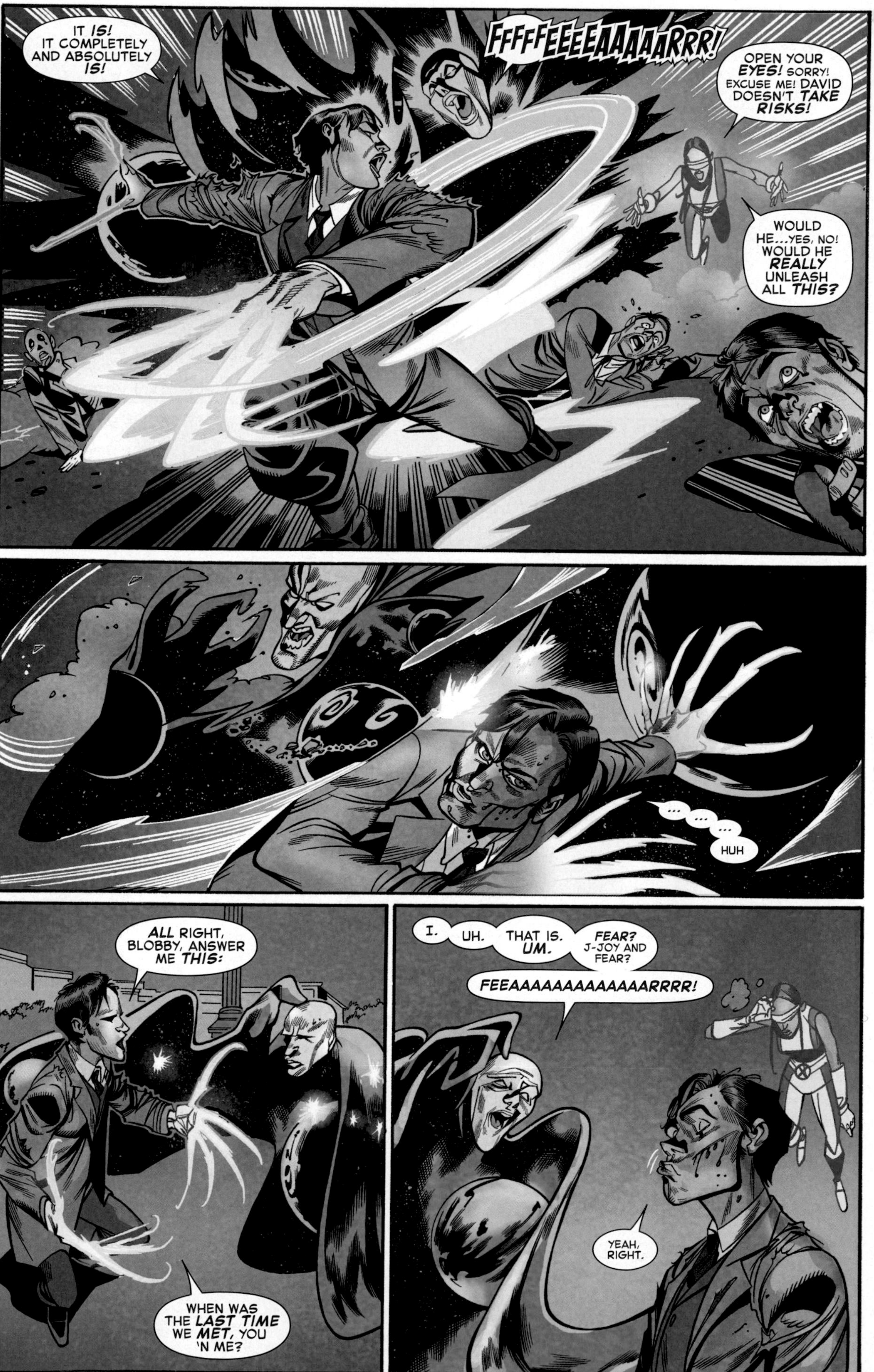
IT IS! IT COMPLETELY AND ABSOLUTELY IS!
FFFFFEEEEAAAAARRR!
OPEN YOUR EYES! SORRY! EXCUSE ME! DAVID DOESN'T TAKE RISKS!
WOULD HE...YES, NO! WOULD HE REALLY UNLEASH ALL THIS?
...
...
...
HUH
ALL RIGHT, BLOBBY, ANSWER ME THIS:
WHEN WAS THE LAST TIME WE MET, YOU 'N ME?
I.
UH.
THAT IS. UM.
FEAR? J-JOY AND FEAR?
FEEAAAAAAAAAAAAAARRRR!
YEAH, RIGHT.

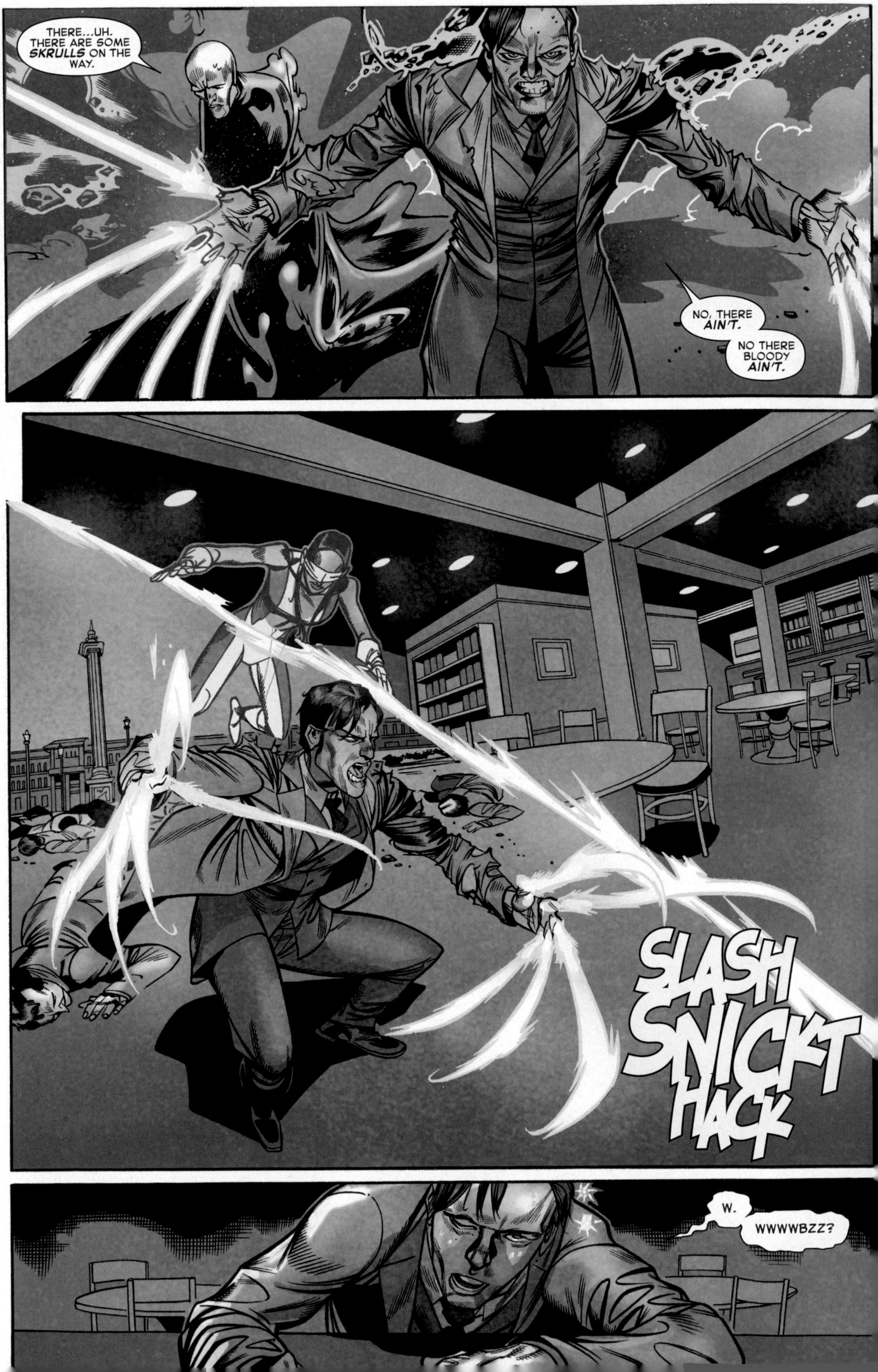
THERE...UH. THERE ARE SOME SKRULLS ON THE WAY.
NO, THERE AIN'T.
NO THERE BLOODY AIN'T.
SLASH
SNICKT
HACK
W.
WWWWBZZ?

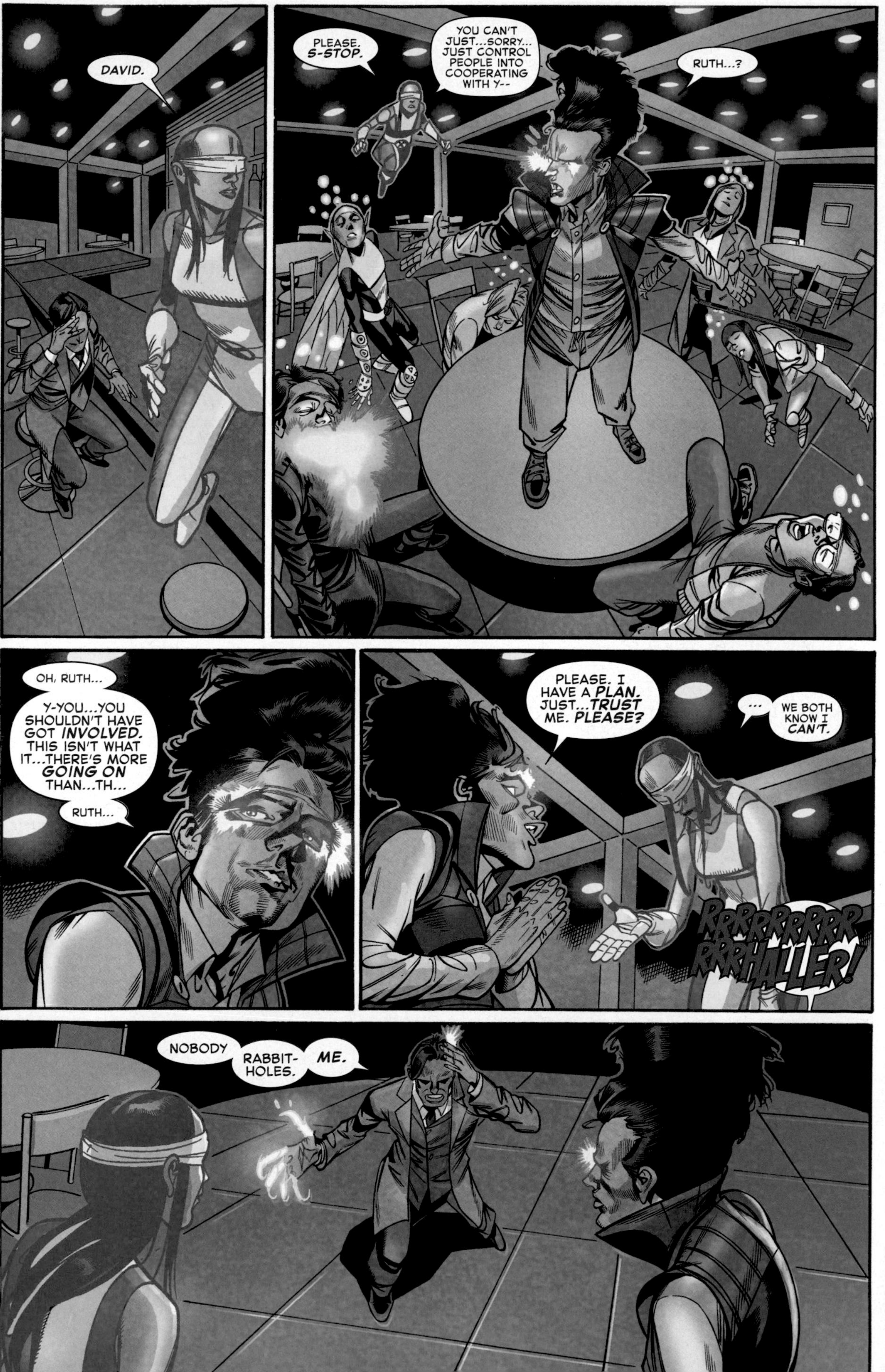
DAVID.
PLEASE. S-STOP.
YOU CAN'T JUST...SORRY... JUST CONTROL PEOPLE INTO COOPERATING WITH Y--
RUTH...?
OH, RUTH...
Y-YOU...YOU SHOULDN'T HAVE GOT INVOLVED. THIS ISN'T WHAT IT...THERE'S MORE GOING ON THAN...TH...
RUTH...
PLEASE. I HAVE A PLAN. JUST...TRUST ME. PLEASE?
...
WE BOTH KNOW I CAN'T.
RRRRRRRRRR RRRHALLER!
NOBODY
RABBIT-HOLES.
ME.

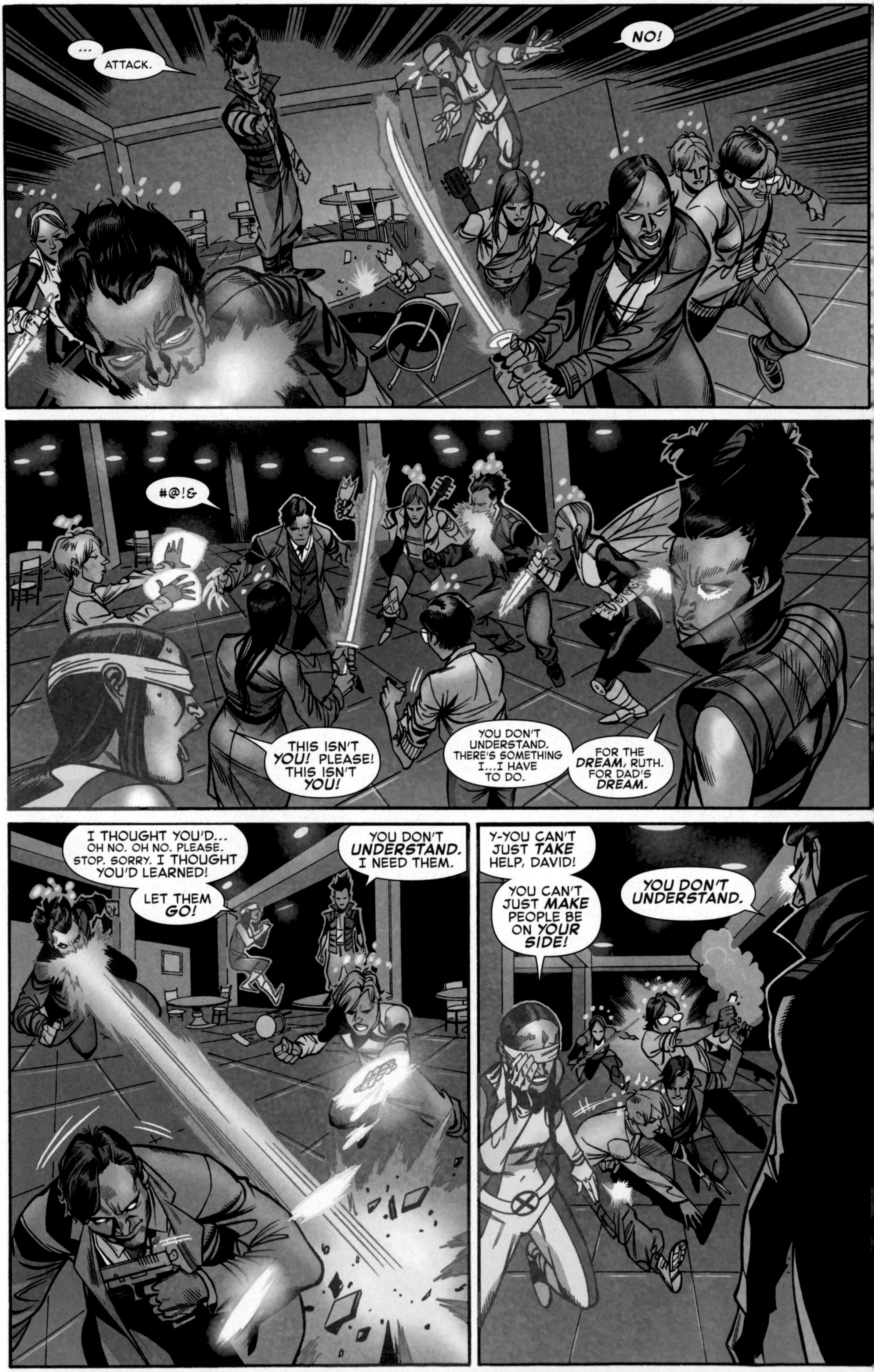
...
ATTACK.
NO!
#@!&
THIS ISN'T YOU! PLEASE! THIS ISN'T YOU!
YOU DON'T UNDERSTAND. THERE'S SOMETHING I...I HAVE TO DO.
FOR THE DREAM, RUTH. FOR DAD'S DREAM.
I THOUGHT YOU'D... OH NO. OH NO. PLEASE. STOP. SORRY. I THOUGHT YOU'D LEARNED!
LET THEM GO!
YOU DON'T UNDERSTAND. I NEED THEM.
Y-YOU CAN'T JUST TAKE HELP, DAVID!
YOU CAN'T JUST MAKE PEOPLE BE ON YOUR SIDE!
YOU DON'T UNDERSTAND.

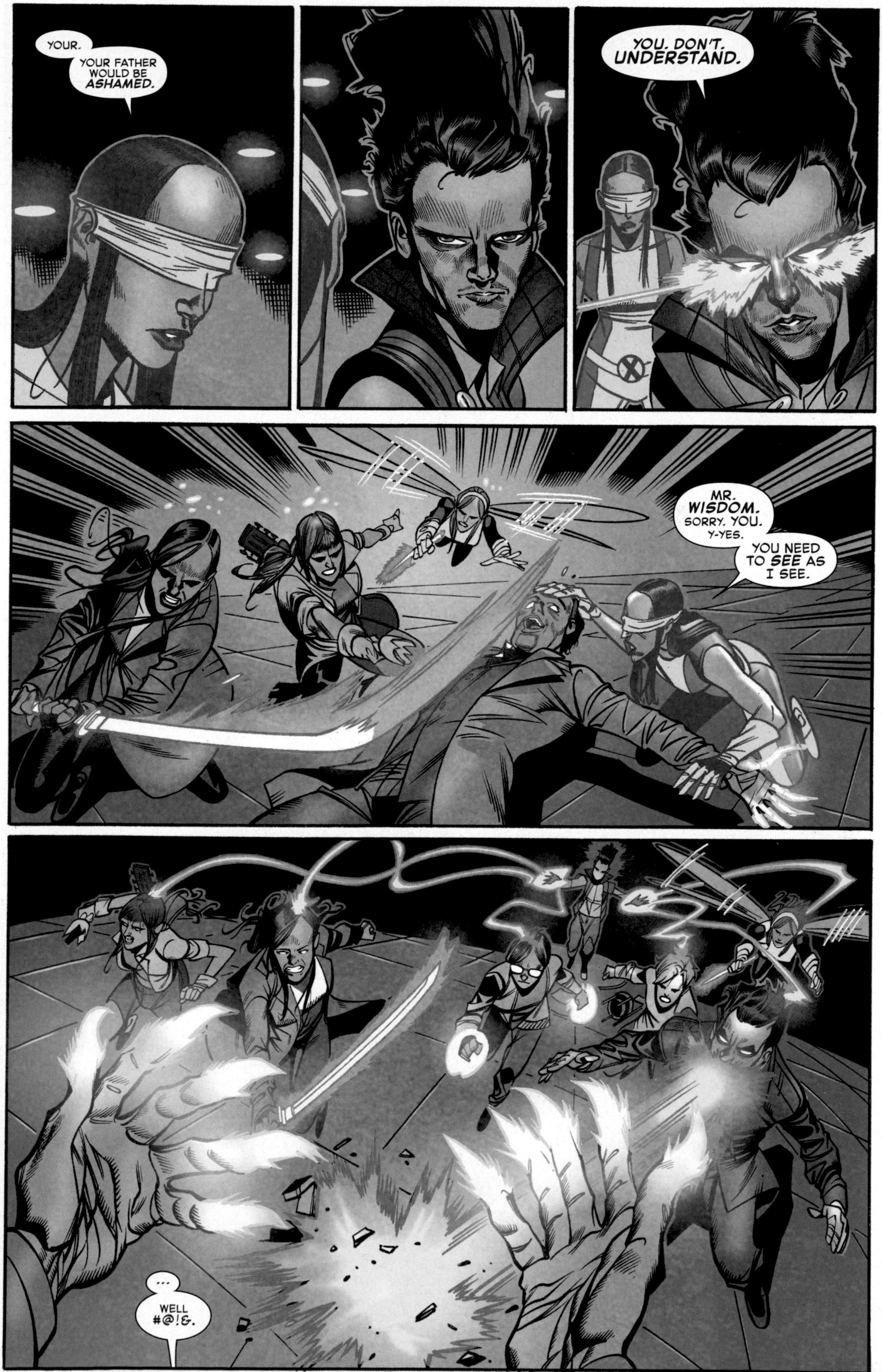
YOUR.
YOUR FATHER WOULD BE ASHAMED.
YOU. DON'T. UNDERSTAND.
MR. WISDOM. SORRY. YOU. Y-YES.
YOU NEED TO SEE AS I SEE.
...
WELL #@!&.

SNAKT

UUUUH

SNIP

HEH HEH HEH

N-NO!

SNAP

SNIP

NOT SO BLEEDIN' COCKY *WITHOUT* YER *MEAT PUPPETS,* ARE YA?

YOU!

DON'T!

UNDERSTAAAAAAAAAAAAND!

DON'T *HURT* HIM *PLEASE* DON'T *HURT* HIM *OH* DON'T *HURT* HIM *NO* DON'T *H*

SORRY, LOVE--

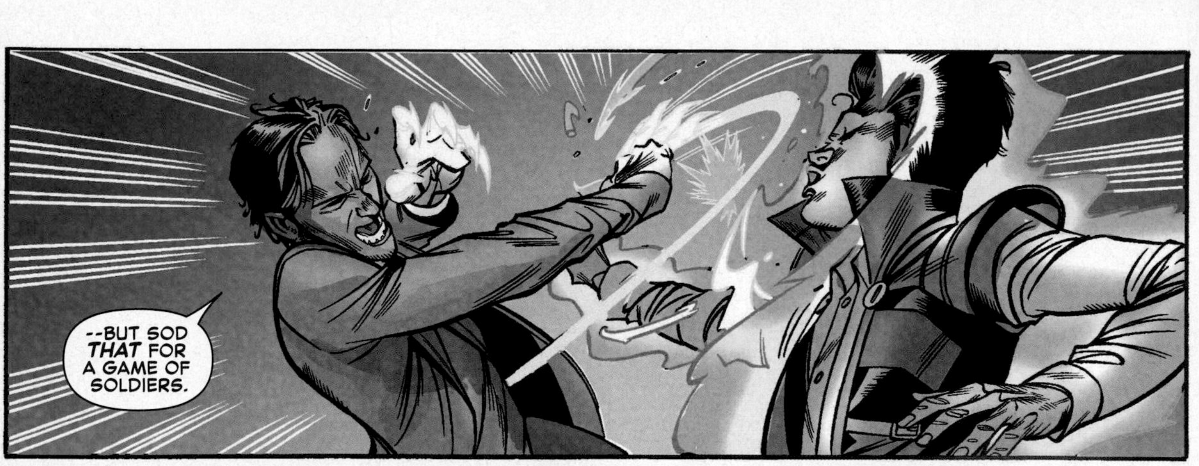
--BUT SOD *THAT* FOR A GAME OF SOLDIERS.

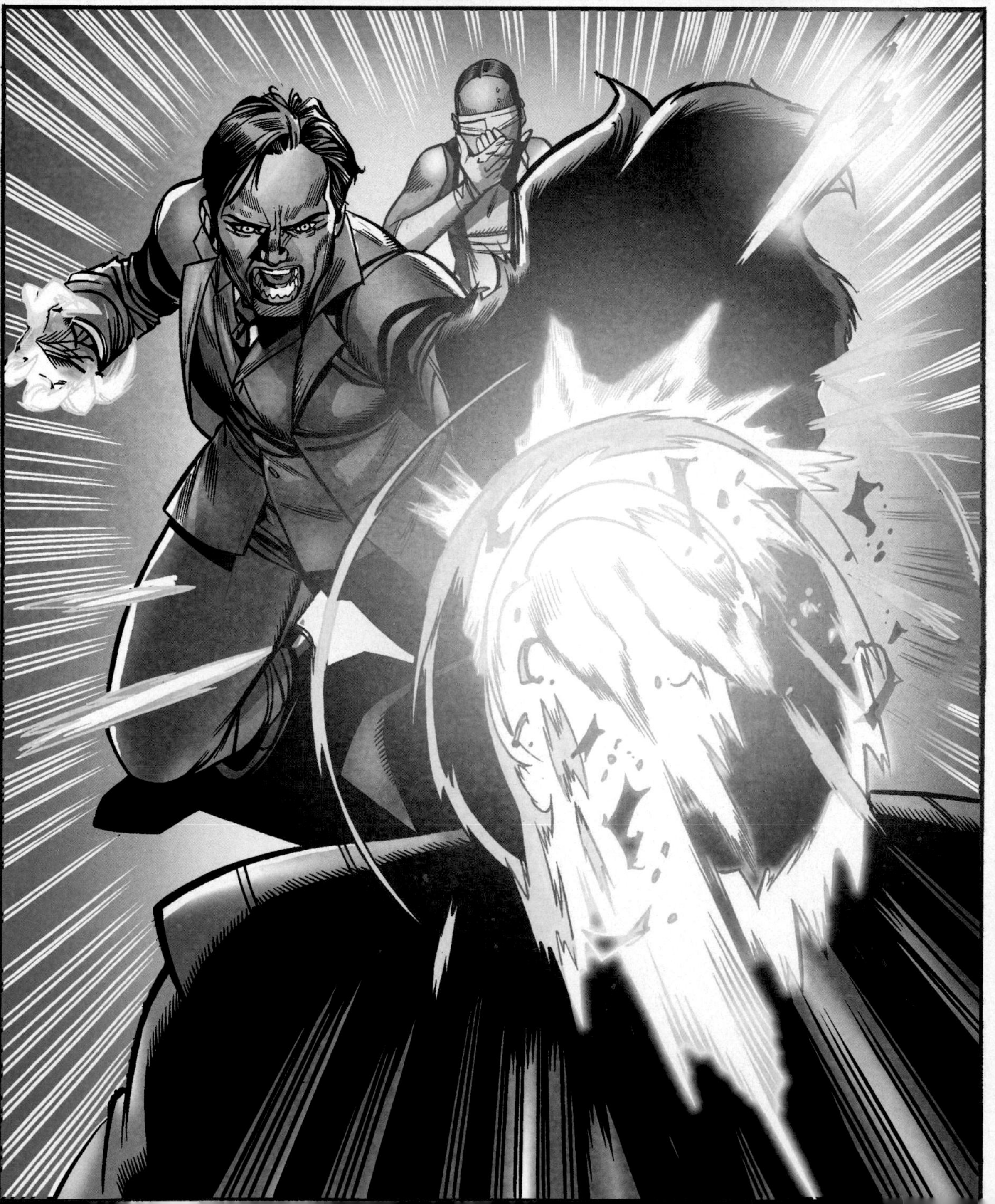

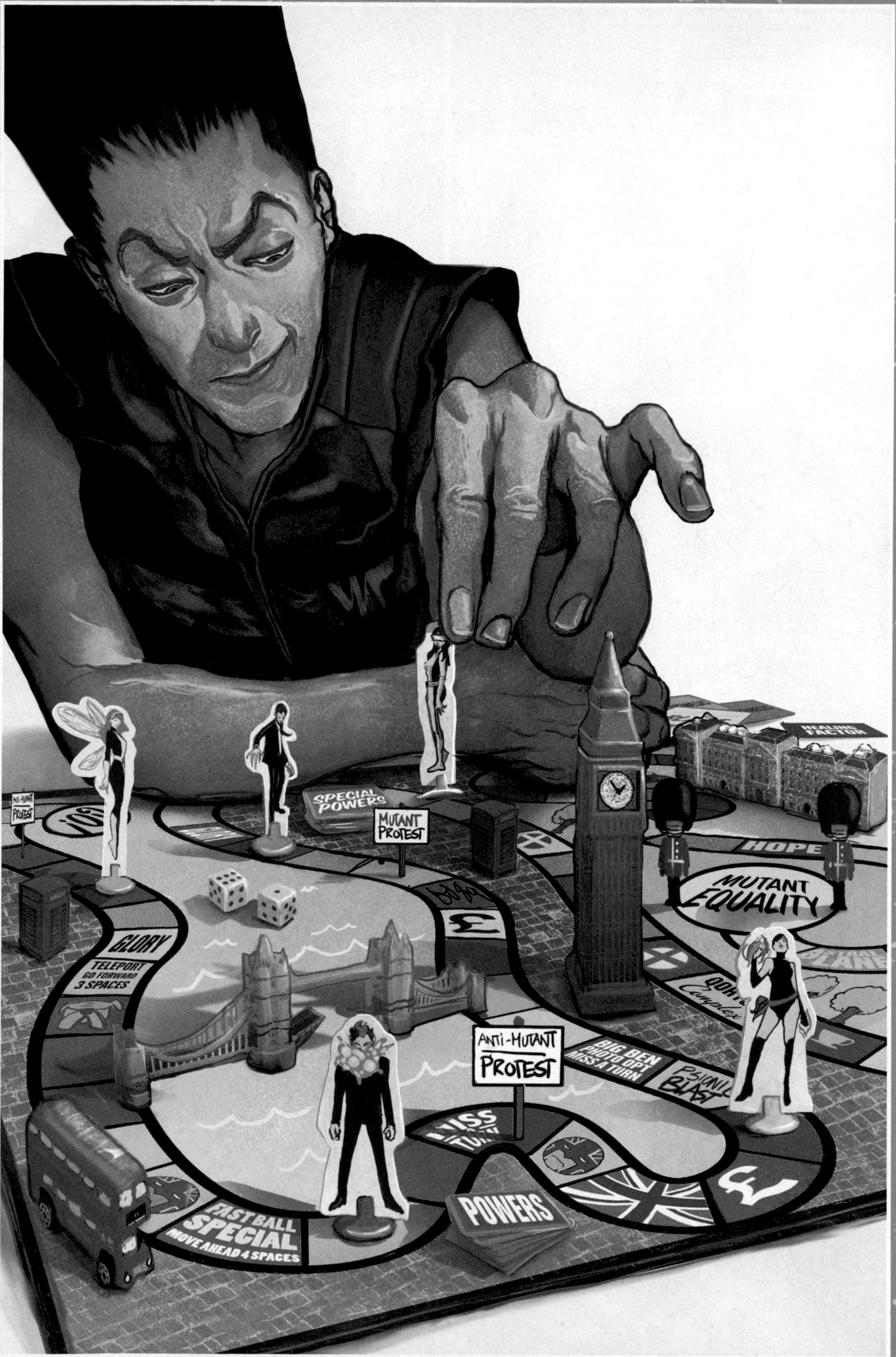
SPECIAL POWERS
MUTANT PROTEST
GLORY
TELEPORT GO FORWARD 3 SPACES
HOPE
MUTANT EQUALITY
ANTI-MUTANT PROTEST
BIG BEN PHOTO OPT MISS A TURN
FASTBALL SPECIAL MOVE AHEAD 4 SPACES
POWERS

FOURTEEN

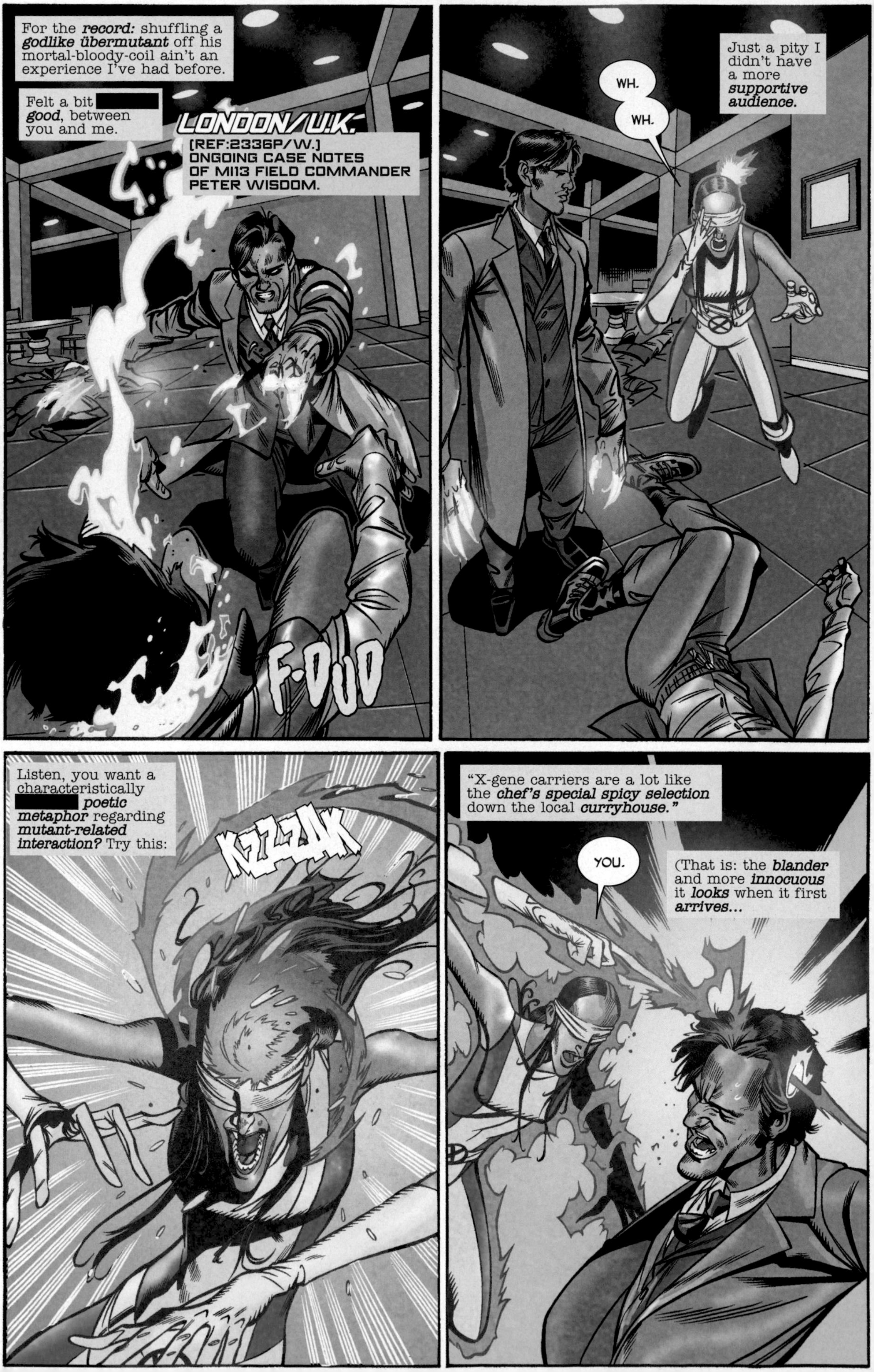
For the *record:* shuffling a *godlike übermutant* off his mortal-bloody-coil ain't an experience I've had before.
Felt a bit [redacted] *good*, between you and me.
LONDON/U.K.
[REF:2336P/W.] ONGOING CASE NOTES OF MI13 FIELD COMMANDER PETER WISDOM.
F-DUD
WH.
WH.
Just a pity I didn't have a more *supportive audience.*
Listen, you want a characteristically [redacted] *poetic metaphor* regarding *mutant-related interaction?* Try this:
KZZZAK
"X-gene carriers are a lot like the *chef's special spicy selection* down the local *curryhouse.*"
YOU.
(That is: the *blander* and more *innocuous* it *looks* when it first *arrives...*

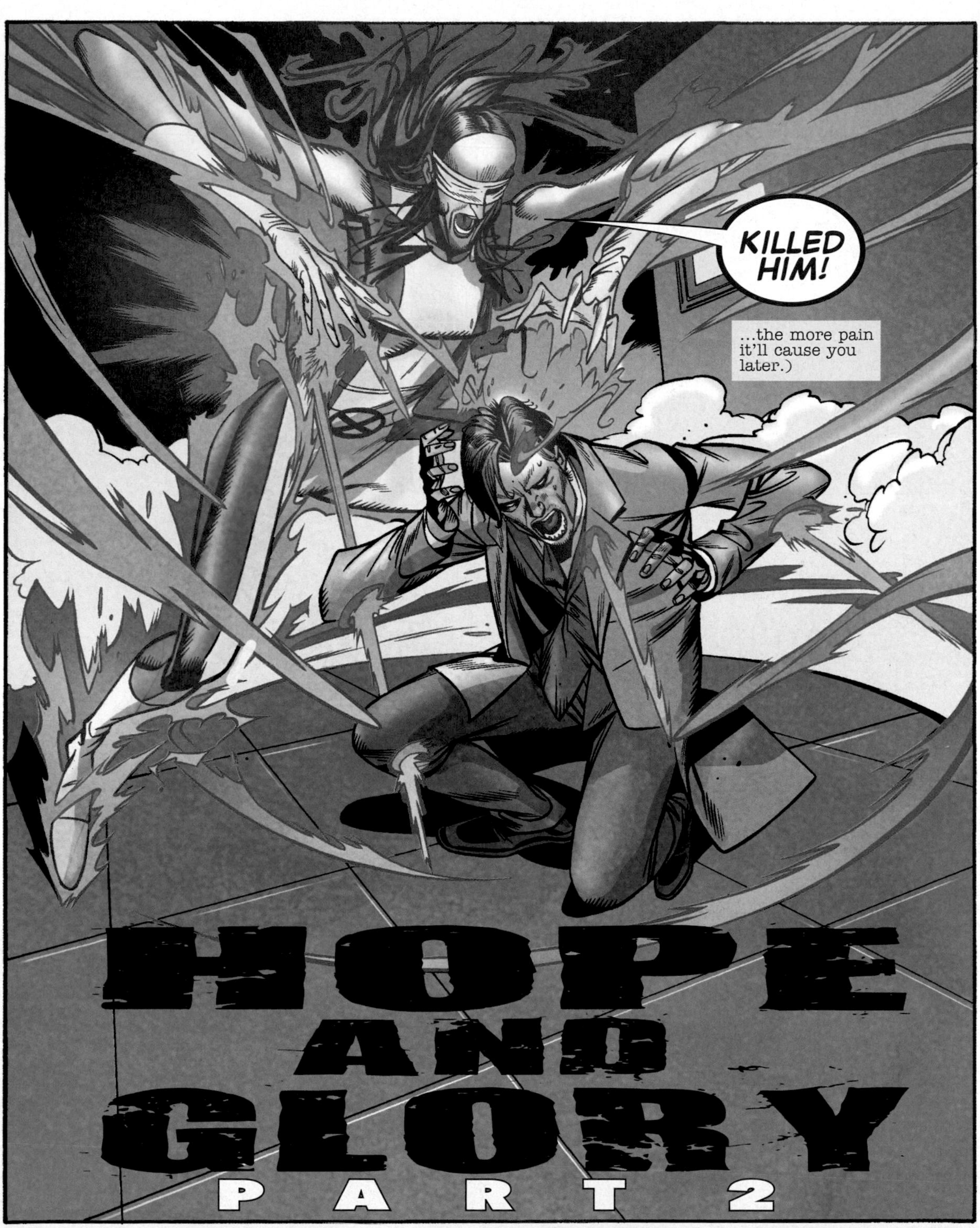
KILLED HIM!
...the more pain it'll cause you later.)
HOPE AND GLORY
PART 2

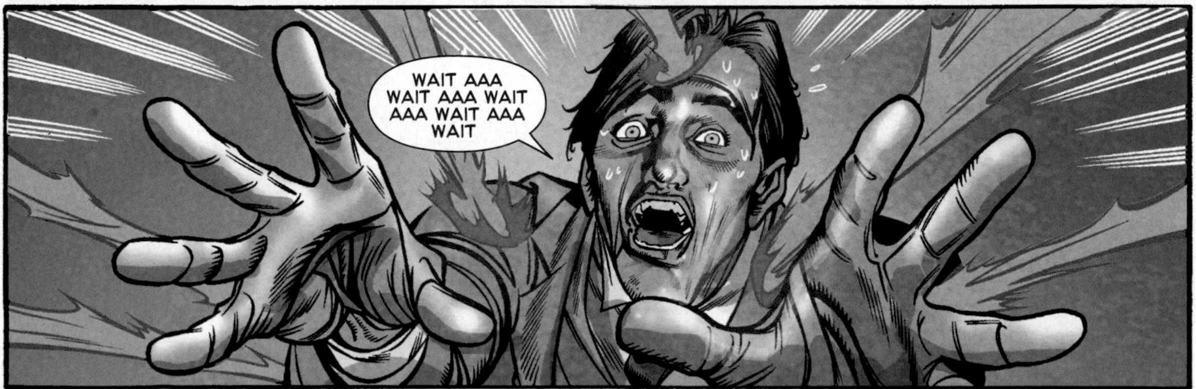
WAIT AAA WAIT AAA WAIT AAA WAIT AAA WAIT

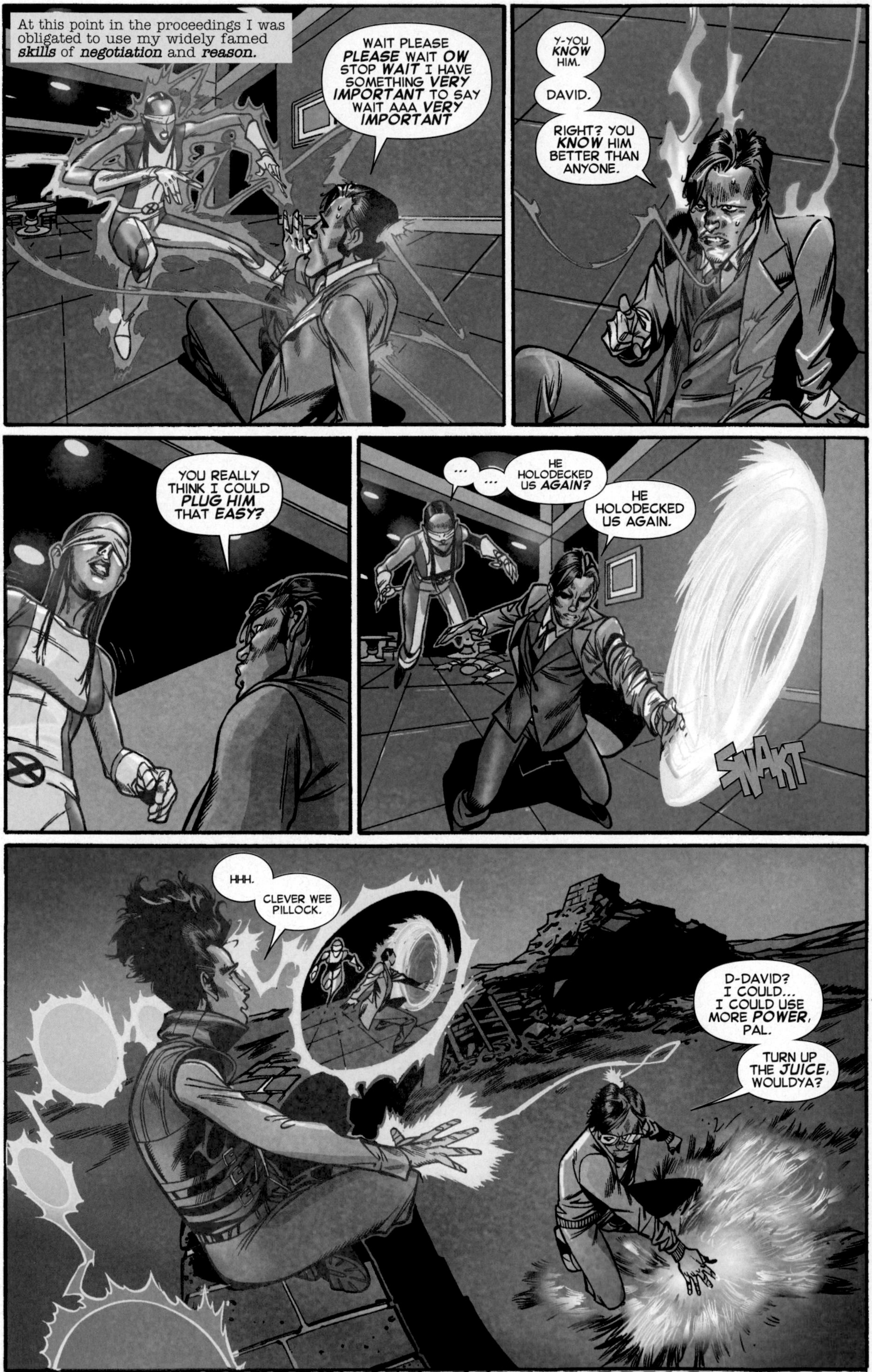
At this point in the proceedings I was obligated to use my widely famed *skills* of *negotiation* and *reason.*
WAIT PLEASE **PLEASE** WAIT **OW** STOP **WAIT** I HAVE SOMETHING **VERY IMPORTANT** TO SAY WAIT AAA **VERY IMPORTANT**
Y-YOU **KNOW** HIM.
DAVID.
RIGHT? YOU **KNOW** HIM BETTER THAN ANYONE.
YOU REALLY THINK I COULD **PLUG HIM** THAT **EASY?**
...
...
HE HOLODECKED US **AGAIN?**
HE HOLODECKED US AGAIN.
SNAKT
HHH.
CLEVER WEE PILLOCK.
D-DAVID? I COULD... I COULD USE MORE **POWER**, PAL.
TURN UP THE **JUICE**, WOULDYA?

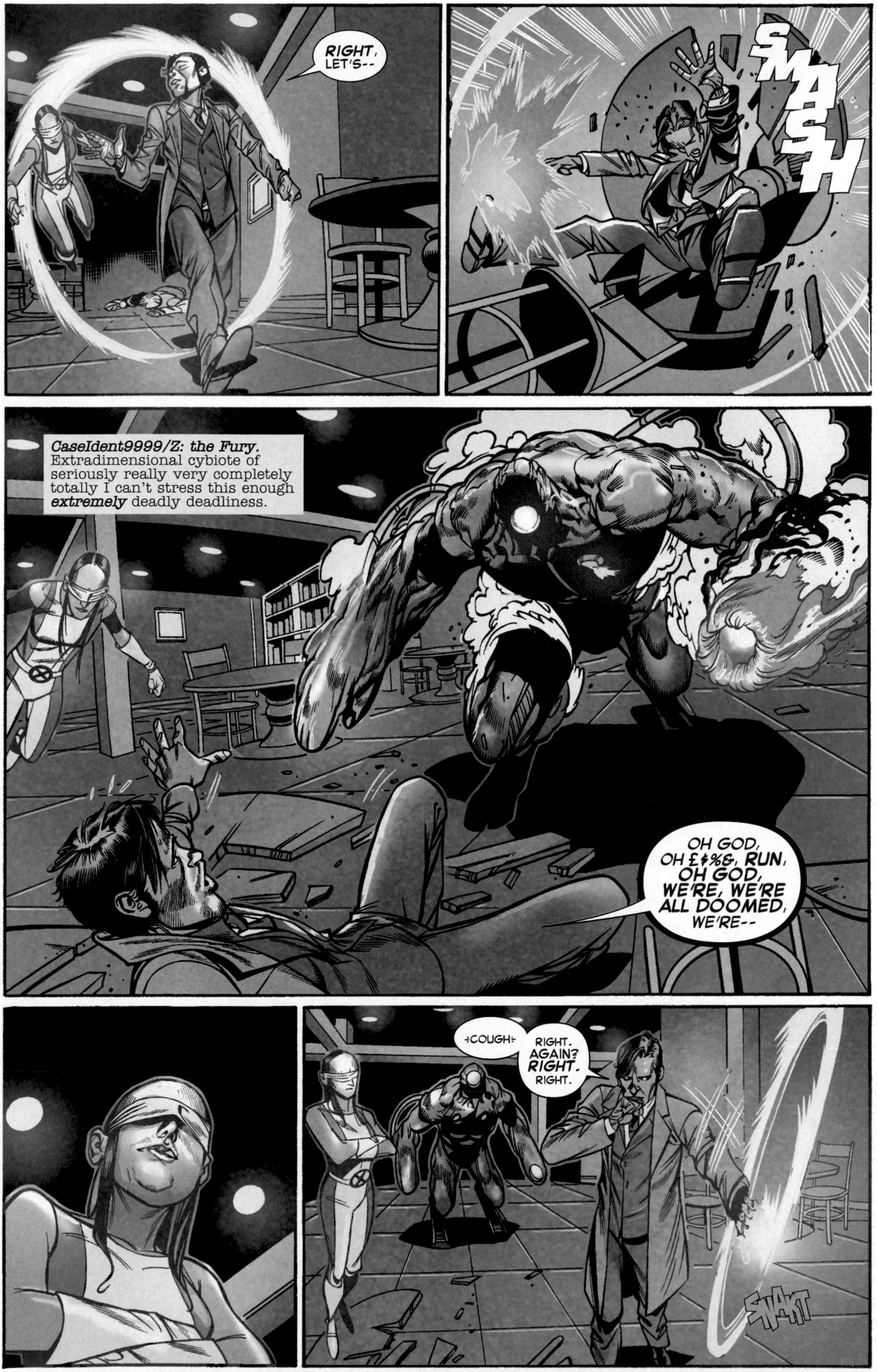
RIGHT, LET'S--
SMASH
CaseIdent9999/Z: the Fury. Extradimensional cybiote of seriously really very completely totally I can't stress this enough extremely deadly deadliness.
OH GOD, OH £$%&, RUN, OH GOD, WE'RE, WE'RE ALL DOOMED, WE'RE--
COUGH
RIGHT. AGAIN? RIGHT. RIGHT.
SNAKT

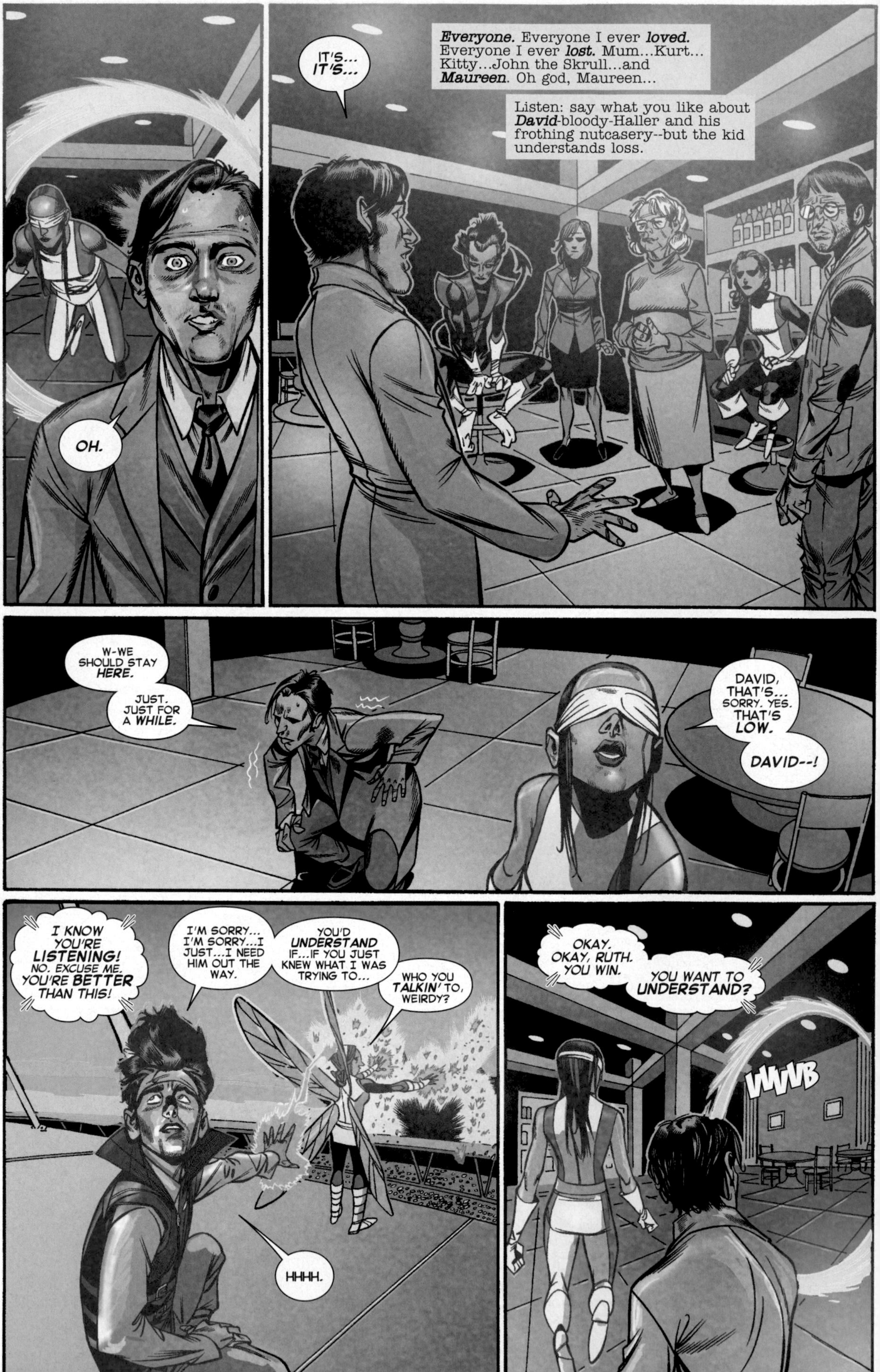
OH.
IT'S... IT'S...
Everyone. Everyone I ever loved. Everyone I ever lost. Mum...Kurt... Kitty...John the Skrull...and Maureen. Oh god, Maureen...
Listen: say what you like about David-bloody-Haller and his frothing nutcasery--but the kid understands loss.
W-WE SHOULD STAY HERE.
JUST. JUST FOR A WHILE.
DAVID, THAT'S... SORRY. YES. THAT'S LOW.
DAVID--!
I KNOW YOU'RE LISTENING! NO. EXCUSE ME. YOU'RE BETTER THAN THIS!
I'M SORRY... I'M SORRY...I JUST...I NEED HIM OUT THE WAY.
YOU'D UNDERSTAND IF...IF YOU JUST KNEW WHAT I WAS TRYING TO...
WHO YOU TALKIN' TO, WEIRDY?
HHHH.
OKAY. OKAY, RUTH. YOU WIN.
YOU WANT TO UNDERSTAND?
VVVVB

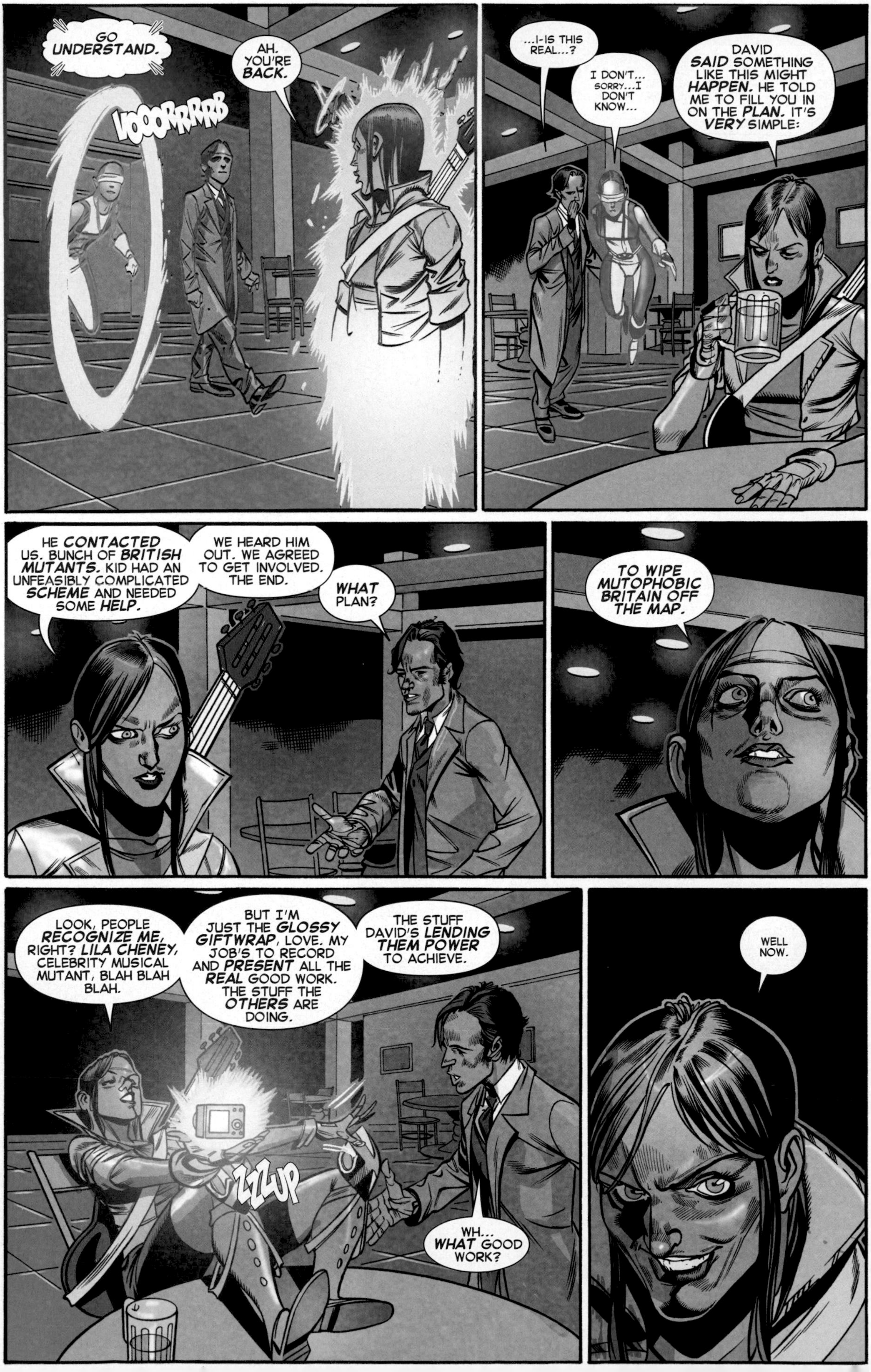
GO UNDERSTAND.
VOOORRRRB
AH. YOU'RE BACK.
...I-IS THIS REAL...?
I DON'T... SORRY...I DON'T KNOW...
DAVID SAID SOMETHING LIKE THIS MIGHT HAPPEN. HE TOLD ME TO FILL YOU IN ON THE PLAN. IT'S VERY SIMPLE:
HE CONTACTED US. BUNCH OF BRITISH MUTANTS. KID HAD AN UNFEASIBLY COMPLICATED SCHEME AND NEEDED SOME HELP.
WE HEARD HIM OUT. WE AGREED TO GET INVOLVED. THE END.
WHAT PLAN?
TO WIPE MUTOPHOBIC BRITAIN OFF THE MAP.
LOOK, PEOPLE RECOGNIZE ME, RIGHT? LILA CHENEY, CELEBRITY MUSICAL MUTANT, BLAH BLAH BLAH.
BUT I'M JUST THE GLOSSY GIFTWRAP, LOVE. MY JOB'S TO RECORD AND PRESENT ALL THE REAL GOOD WORK. THE STUFF THE OTHERS ARE DOING.
THE STUFF DAVID'S LENDING THEM POWER TO ACHIEVE.
ZZZUP
WH... WHAT GOOD WORK?
WELL NOW.

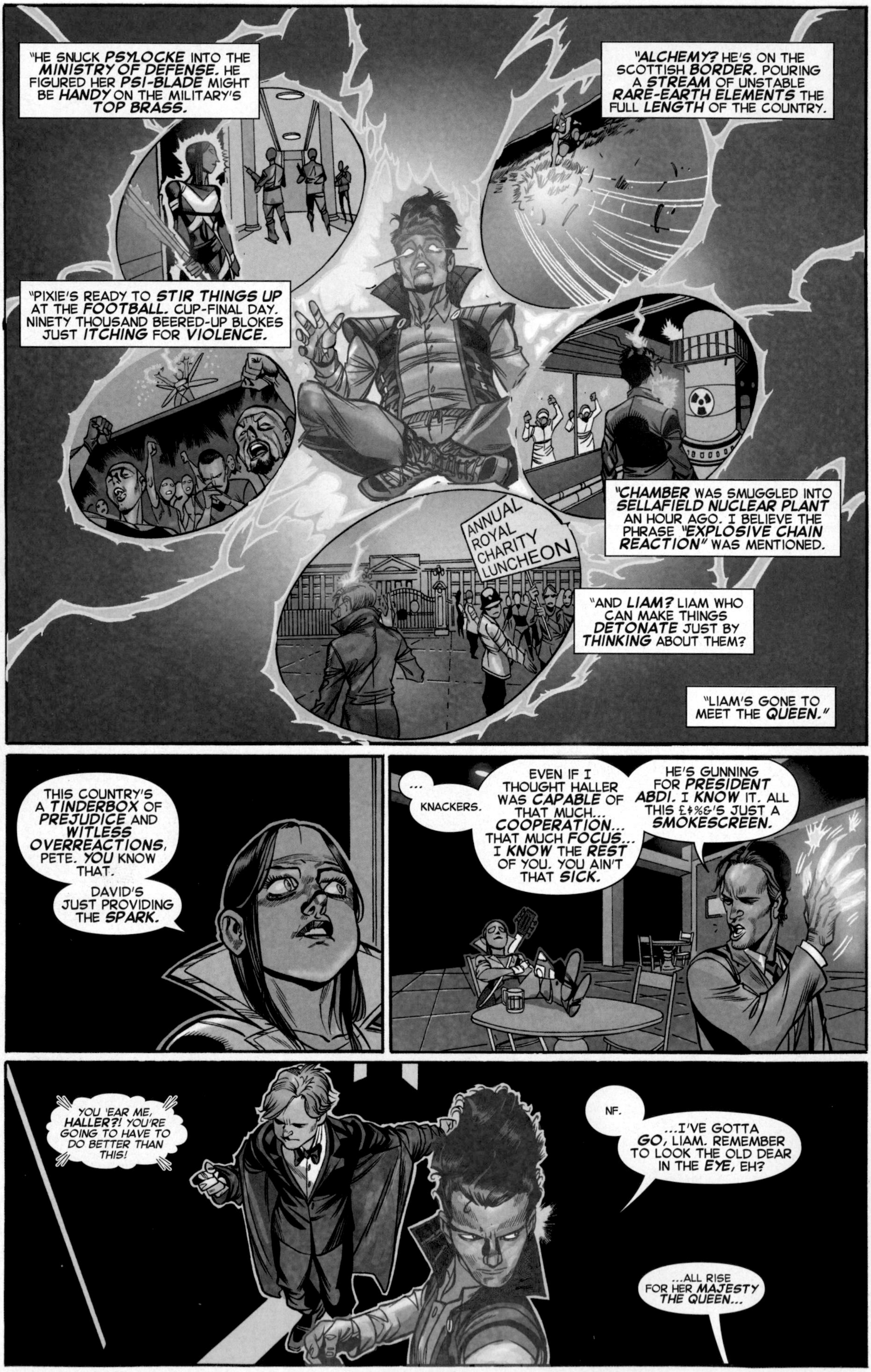
"HE SNUCK PSYLOCKE INTO THE MINISTRY OF DEFENSE. HE FIGURED HER PSI-BLADE MIGHT BE HANDY ON THE MILITARY'S TOP BRASS.
"ALCHEMY? HE'S ON THE SCOTTISH BORDER. POURING A STREAM OF UNSTABLE RARE-EARTH ELEMENTS THE FULL LENGTH OF THE COUNTRY.
"PIXIE'S READY TO STIR THINGS UP AT THE FOOTBALL. CUP-FINAL DAY. NINETY THOUSAND BEERED-UP BLOKES JUST ITCHING FOR VIOLENCE.
"CHAMBER WAS SMUGGLED INTO SELLAFIELD NUCLEAR PLANT AN HOUR AGO. I BELIEVE THE PHRASE "EXPLOSIVE CHAIN REACTION" WAS MENTIONED.
ANNUAL ROYAL CHARITY LUNCHEON
"AND LIAM? LIAM WHO CAN MAKE THINGS DETONATE JUST BY THINKING ABOUT THEM?
"LIAM'S GONE TO MEET THE QUEEN."
THIS COUNTRY'S A TINDERBOX OF PREJUDICE AND WITLESS OVERREACTIONS, PETE. YOU KNOW THAT.
DAVID'S JUST PROVIDING THE SPARK.
...
KNACKERS.
EVEN IF I THOUGHT HALLER WAS CAPABLE OF THAT MUCH... COOPERATION... THAT MUCH FOCUS... I KNOW THE REST OF YOU. YOU AIN'T THAT SICK.
HE'S GUNNING FOR PRESIDENT ABDI. I KNOW IT. ALL THIS £$%&'S JUST A SMOKESCREEN.
YOU 'EAR ME, HALLER?! YOU'RE GOING TO HAVE TO DO BETTER THAN THIS!
NF.
...I'VE GOTTA GO, LIAM. REMEMBER TO LOOK THE OLD DEAR IN THE EYE, EH?
...ALL RISE FOR HER MAJESTY THE QUEEN...

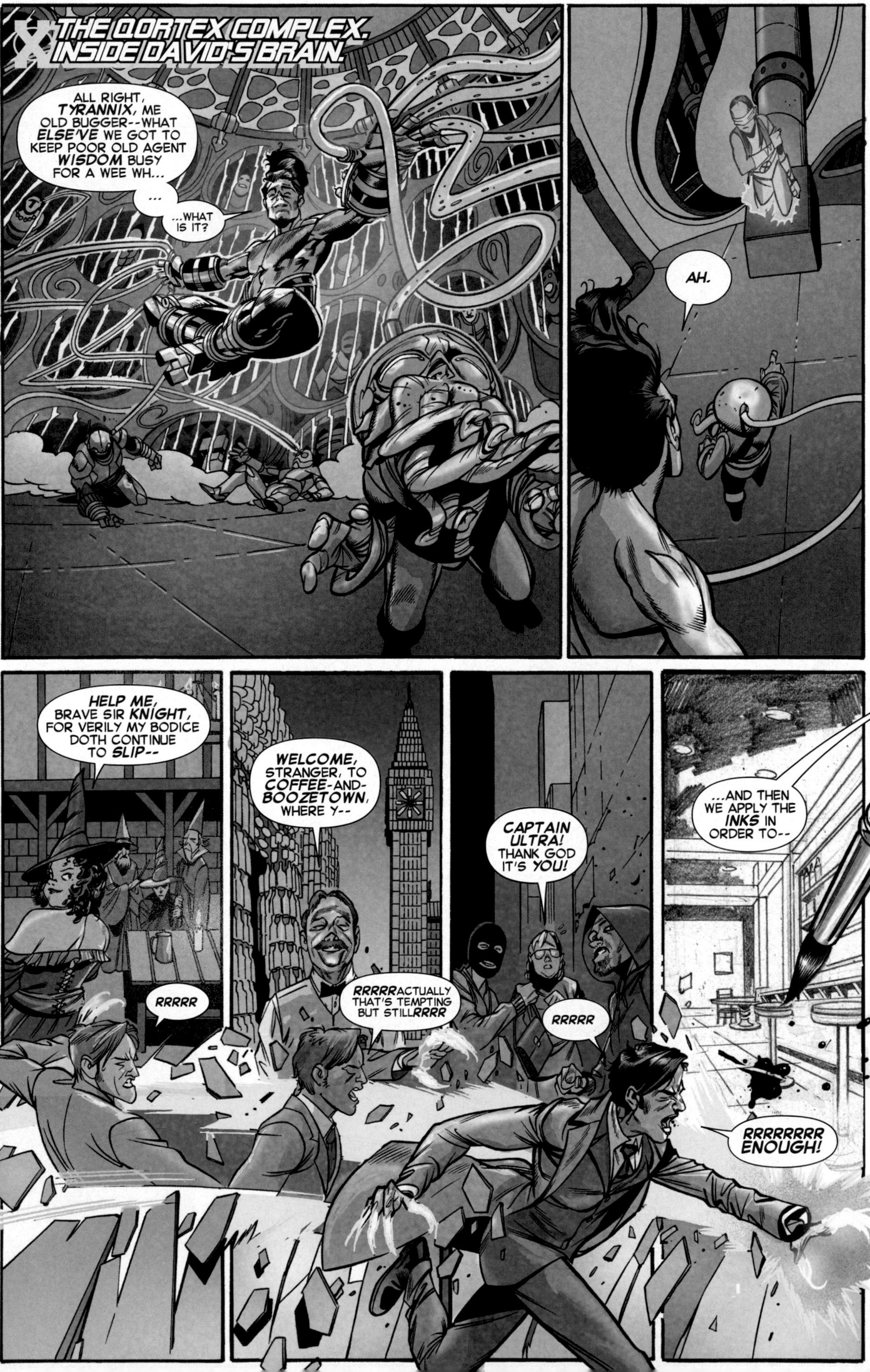
THE QORTEX COMPLEX. INSIDE DAVID'S BRAIN.
ALL RIGHT, TYRANNIX, ME OLD BUGGER--WHAT ELSE'VE WE GOT TO KEEP POOR OLD AGENT WISDOM BUSY FOR A WEE WH...
...
...WHAT IS IT?
AH.
HELP ME, BRAVE SIR KNIGHT, FOR VERILY MY BODICE DOTH CONTINUE TO SLIP--
RRRRR
WELCOME, STRANGER, TO COFFEE-AND-BOOZETOWN, WHERE Y--
RRRRRACTUALLY THAT'S TEMPTING BUT STILLRRRR
CAPTAIN ULTRA! THANK GOD IT'S YOU!
RRRRR
...AND THEN WE APPLY THE INKS IN ORDER TO--
RRRRRRRR ENOUGH!

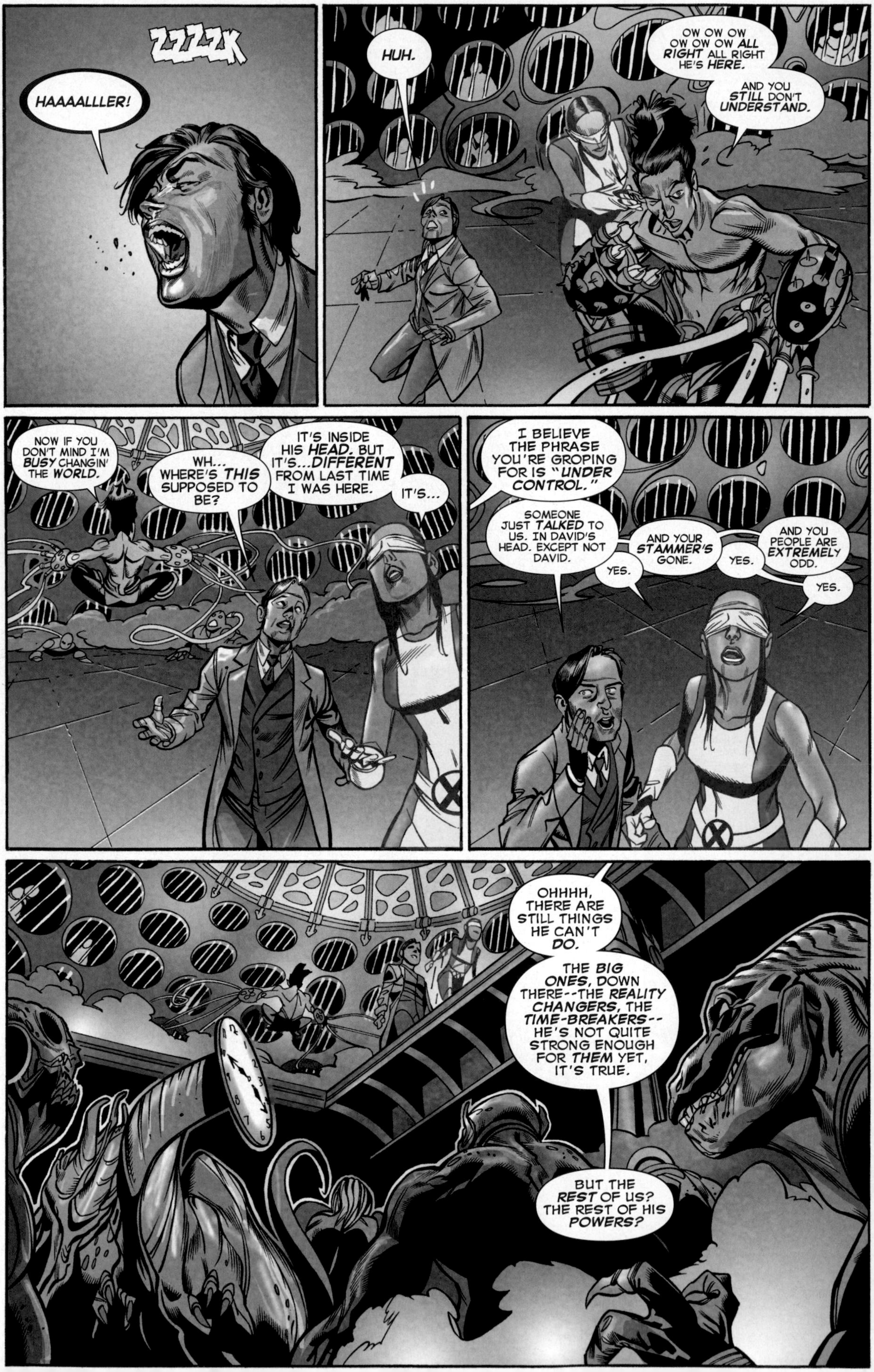
ZZZZK
HAAAALLLER!
HUH.
OW OW OW OW OW OW ALL RIGHT ALL RIGHT HE'S HERE.
AND YOU STILL DON'T UNDERSTAND.
NOW IF YOU DON'T MIND I'M BUSY CHANGIN' THE WORLD.
WH... WHERE'S THIS SUPPOSED TO BE?
IT'S INSIDE HIS HEAD. BUT IT'S...DIFFERENT FROM LAST TIME I WAS HERE.
IT'S...
I BELIEVE THE PHRASE YOU'RE GROPING FOR IS "UNDER CONTROL."
SOMEONE JUST TALKED TO US. IN DAVID'S HEAD. EXCEPT NOT DAVID.
YES.
AND YOUR STAMMER'S GONE.
YES.
AND YOU PEOPLE ARE EXTREMELY ODD.
YES.
OHHHH, THERE ARE STILL THINGS HE CAN'T DO.
THE BIG ONES, DOWN THERE--THE REALITY CHANGERS, THE TIME-BREAKERS-- HE'S NOT QUITE STRONG ENOUGH FOR THEM YET, IT'S TRUE.
BUT THE REST OF US? THE REST OF HIS POWERS?

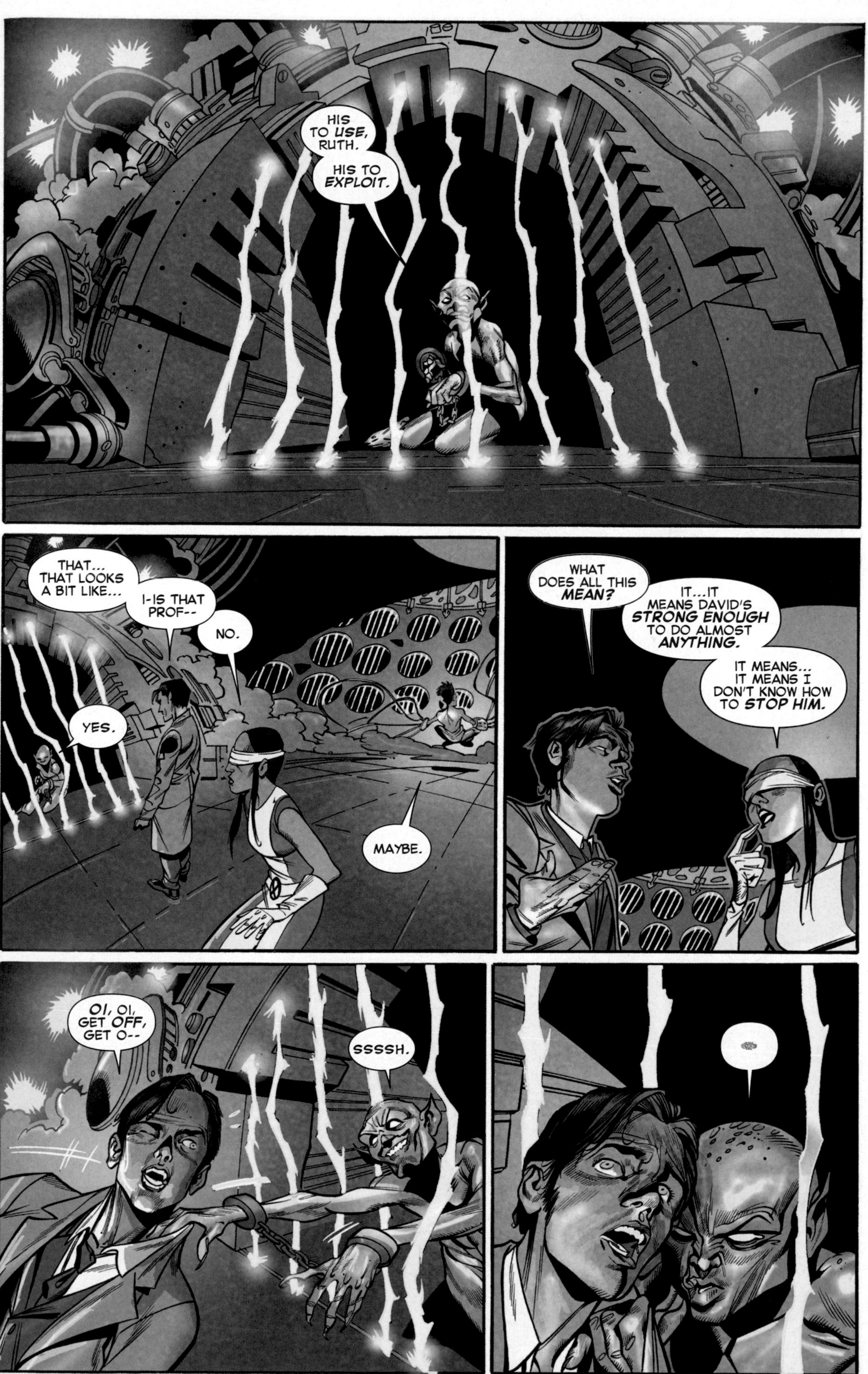
HIS TO USE, RUTH.
HIS TO EXPLOIT.
THAT... THAT LOOKS A BIT LIKE...
I-IS THAT PROF--
NO.
YES.
MAYBE.
WHAT DOES ALL THIS MEAN?
IT...IT MEANS DAVID'S STRONG ENOUGH TO DO ALMOST ANYTHING.
IT MEANS... IT MEANS I DON'T KNOW HOW TO STOP HIM.
OI, OI, GET OFF, GET O--
SSSSH.

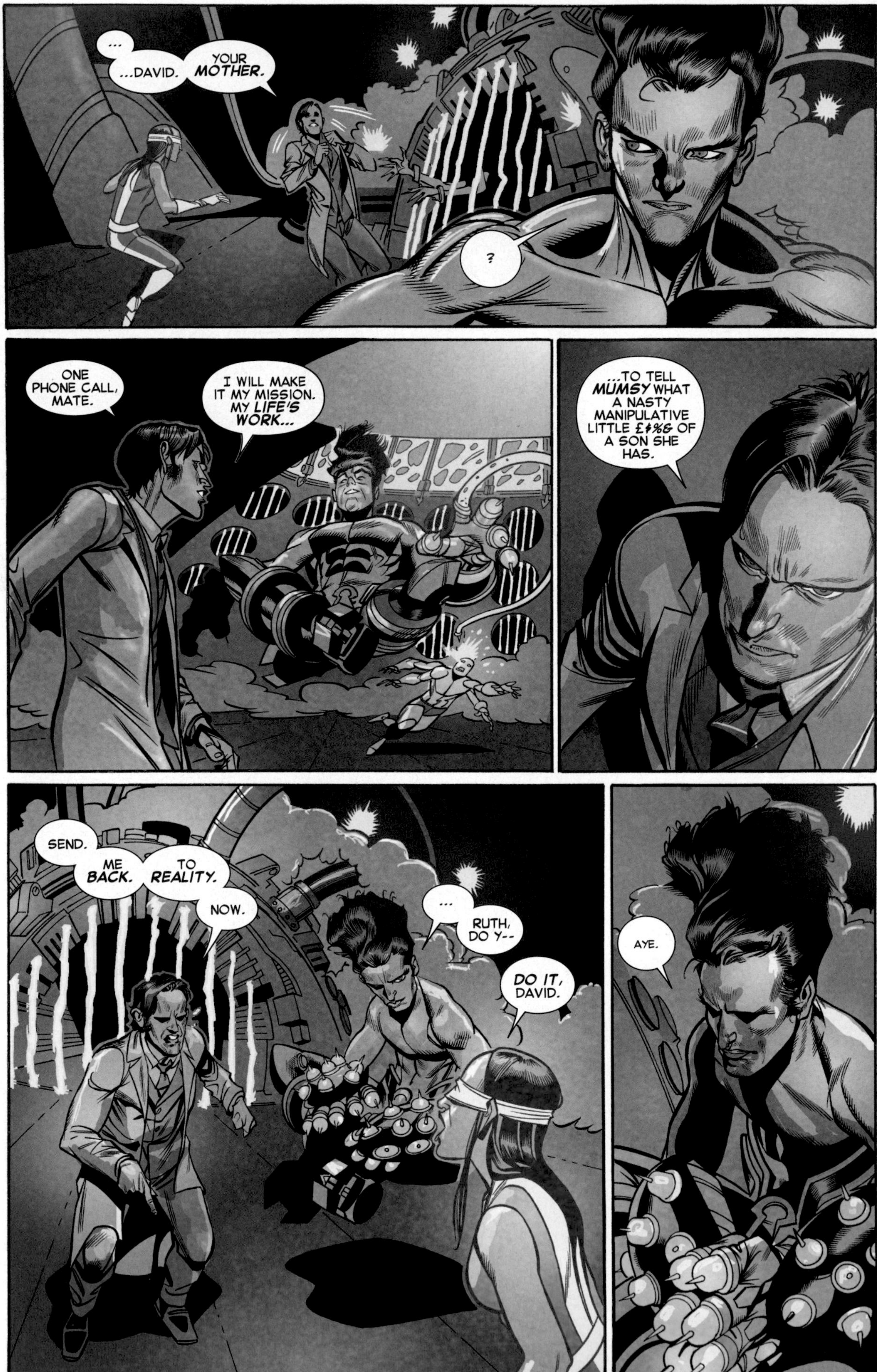
...
...DAVID.
YOUR MOTHER.
?
ONE PHONE CALL, MATE.
I WILL MAKE IT MY MISSION. MY LIFE'S WORK...
...TO TELL MUMSY WHAT A NASTY MANIPULATIVE LITTLE £$%& OF A SON SHE HAS.
SEND.
ME BACK.
TO REALITY.
NOW.
...
RUTH, DO Y--
DO IT, DAVID.
AYE.

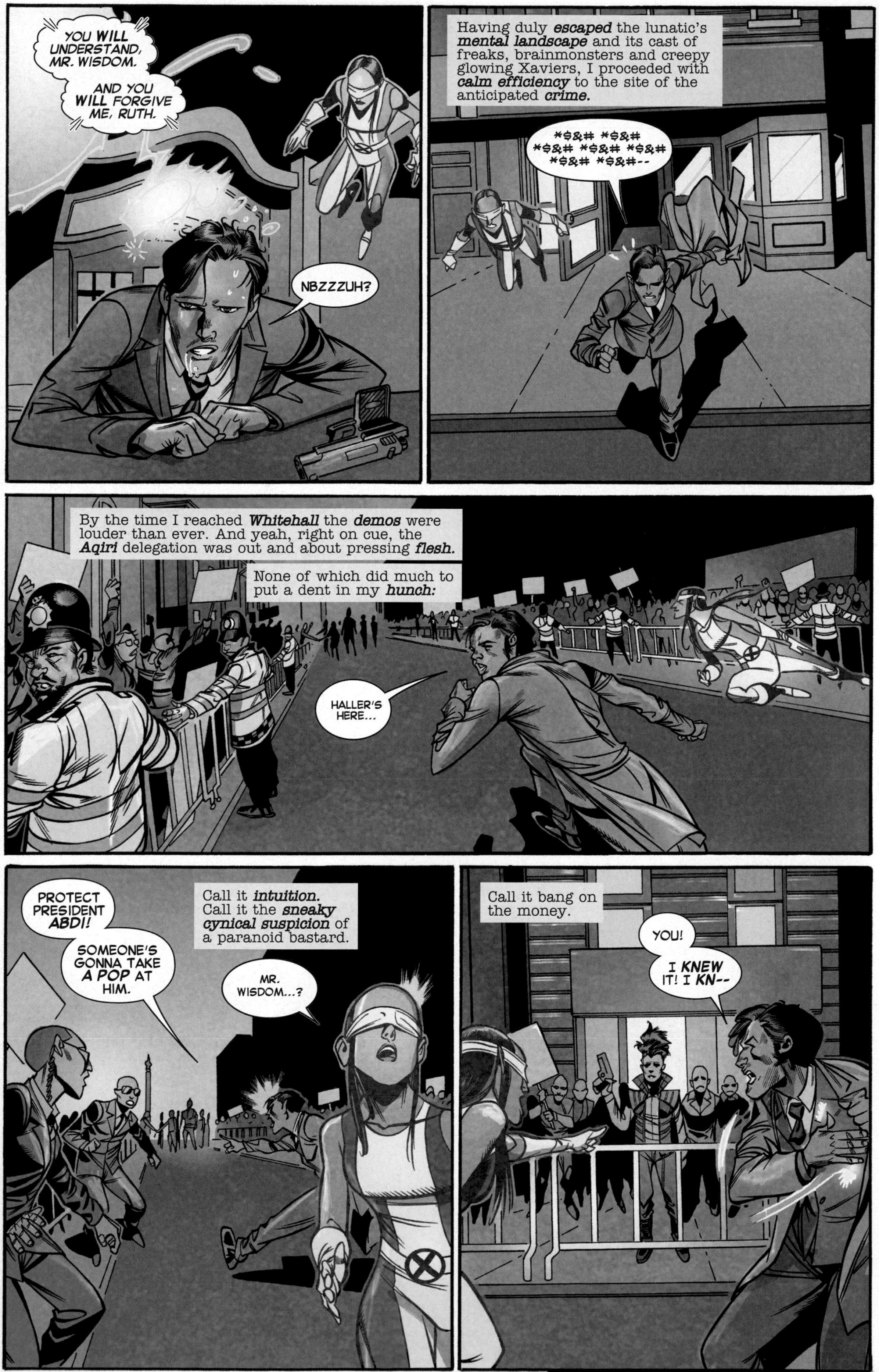
YOU WILL UNDERSTAND, MR. WISDOM.
AND YOU WILL FORGIVE ME, RUTH.
NBZZZUH?
Having duly escaped the lunatic's mental landscape and its cast of freaks, brainmonsters and creepy glowing Xaviers, I proceeded with calm efficiency to the site of the anticipated crime.
*$&# *$&# *$&# *$&# *$&# *$&# *$&#--
By the time I reached Whitehall the demos were louder than ever. And yeah, right on cue, the Aqiri delegation was out and about pressing flesh.
None of which did much to put a dent in my hunch:
HALLER'S HERE...
PROTECT PRESIDENT ABDI!
SOMEONE'S GONNA TAKE A POP AT HIM.
Call it intuition. Call it the sneaky cynical suspicion of a paranoid bastard.
MR. WISDOM...?
Call it bang on the money.
YOU!
I KNEW IT! I KN--

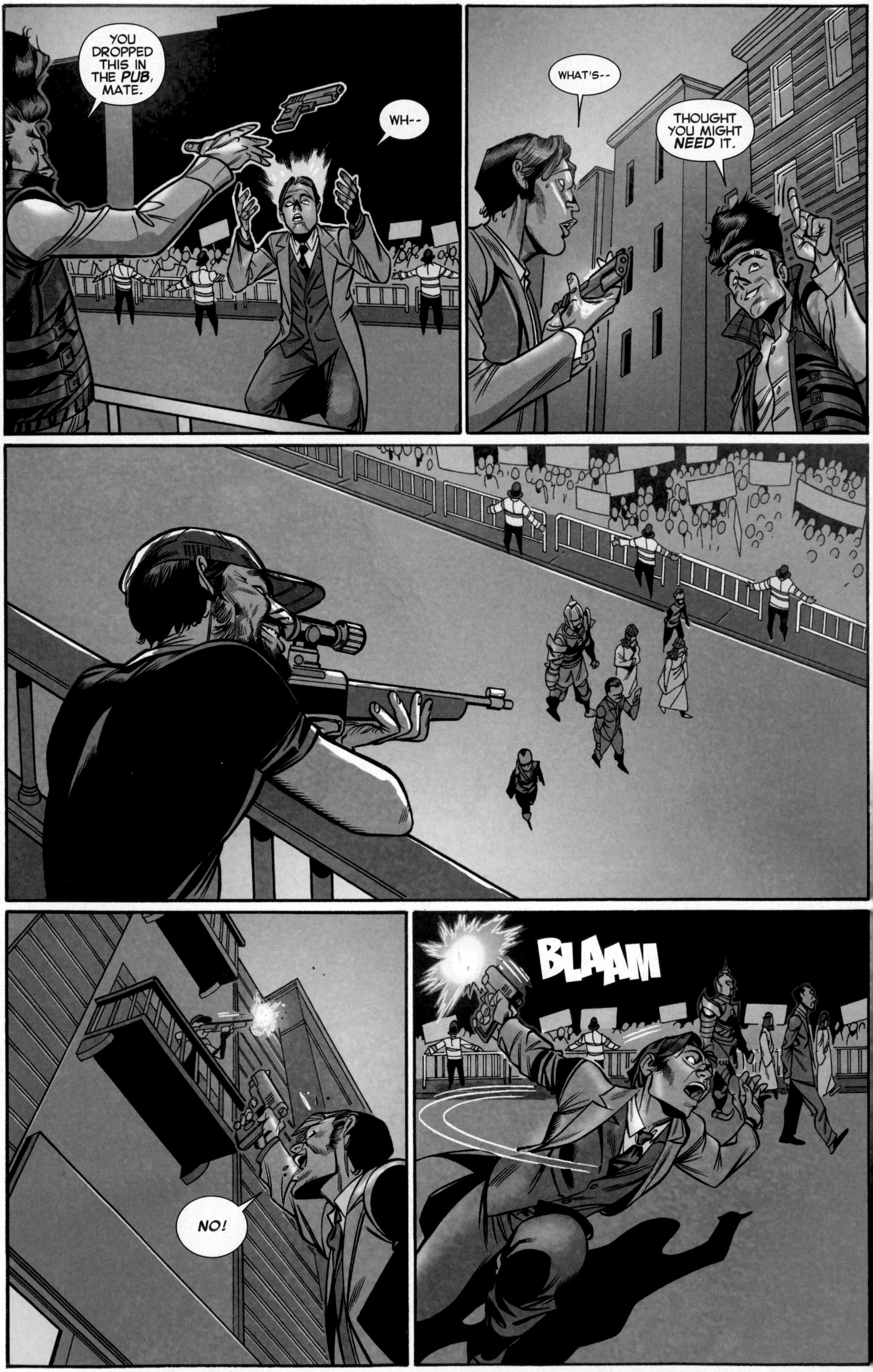
YOU DROPPED THIS IN THE PUB, MATE.
WH--
WHAT'S--
THOUGHT YOU MIGHT NEED IT.
NO!
BLAAM

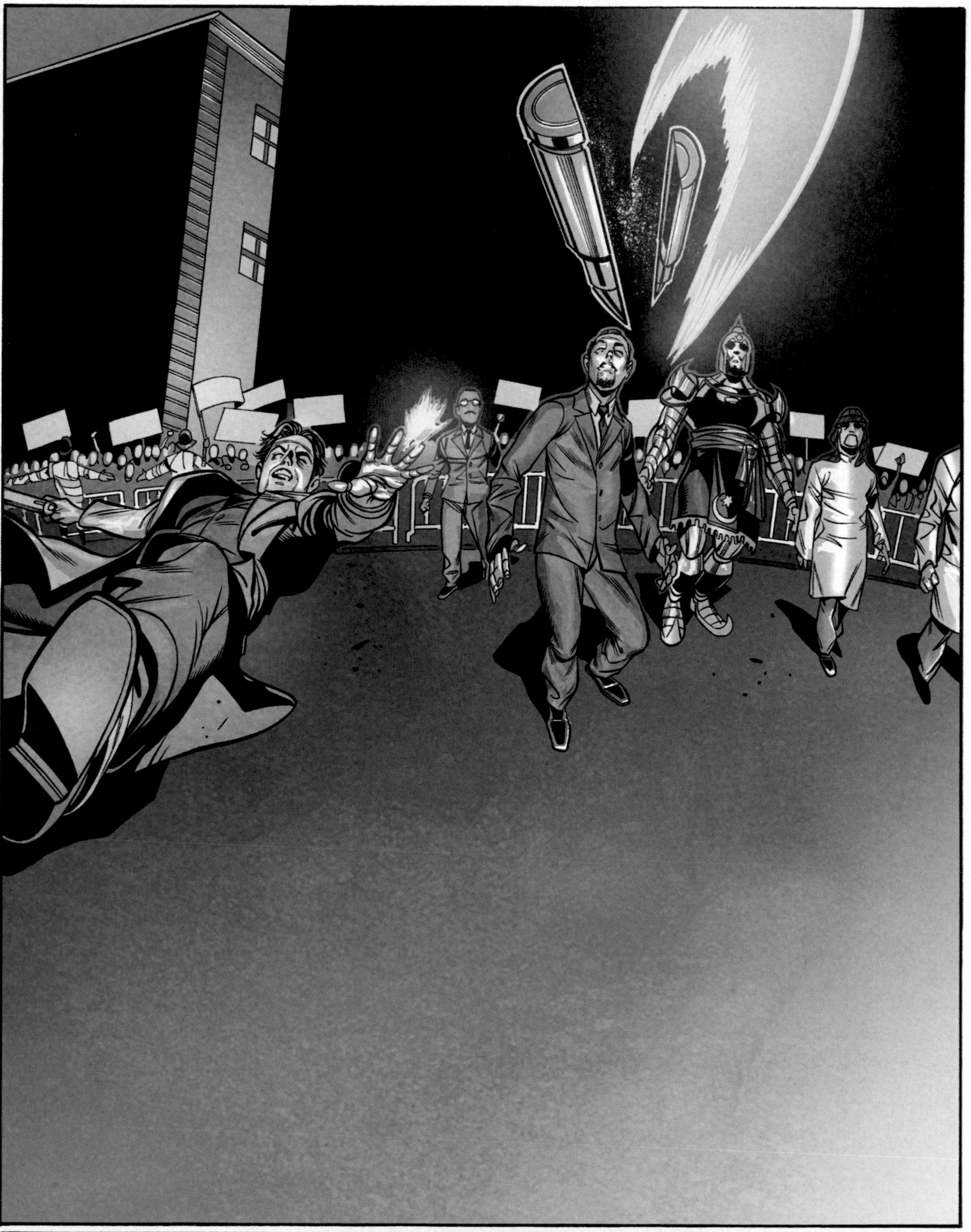
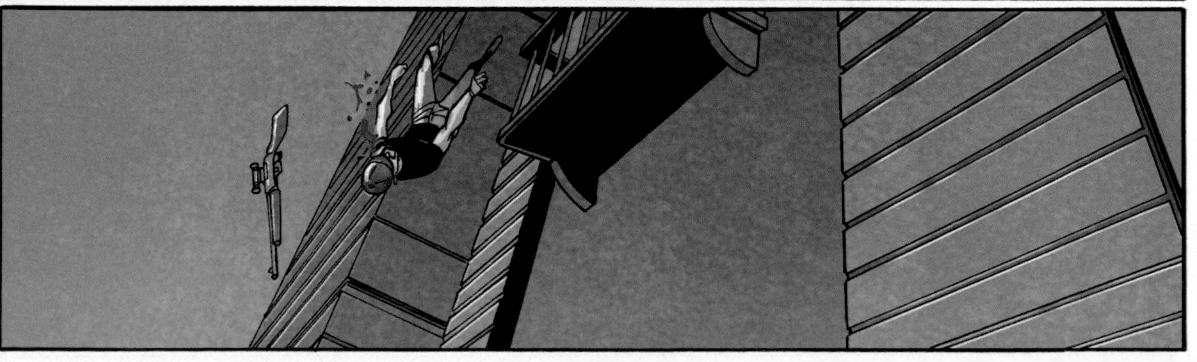

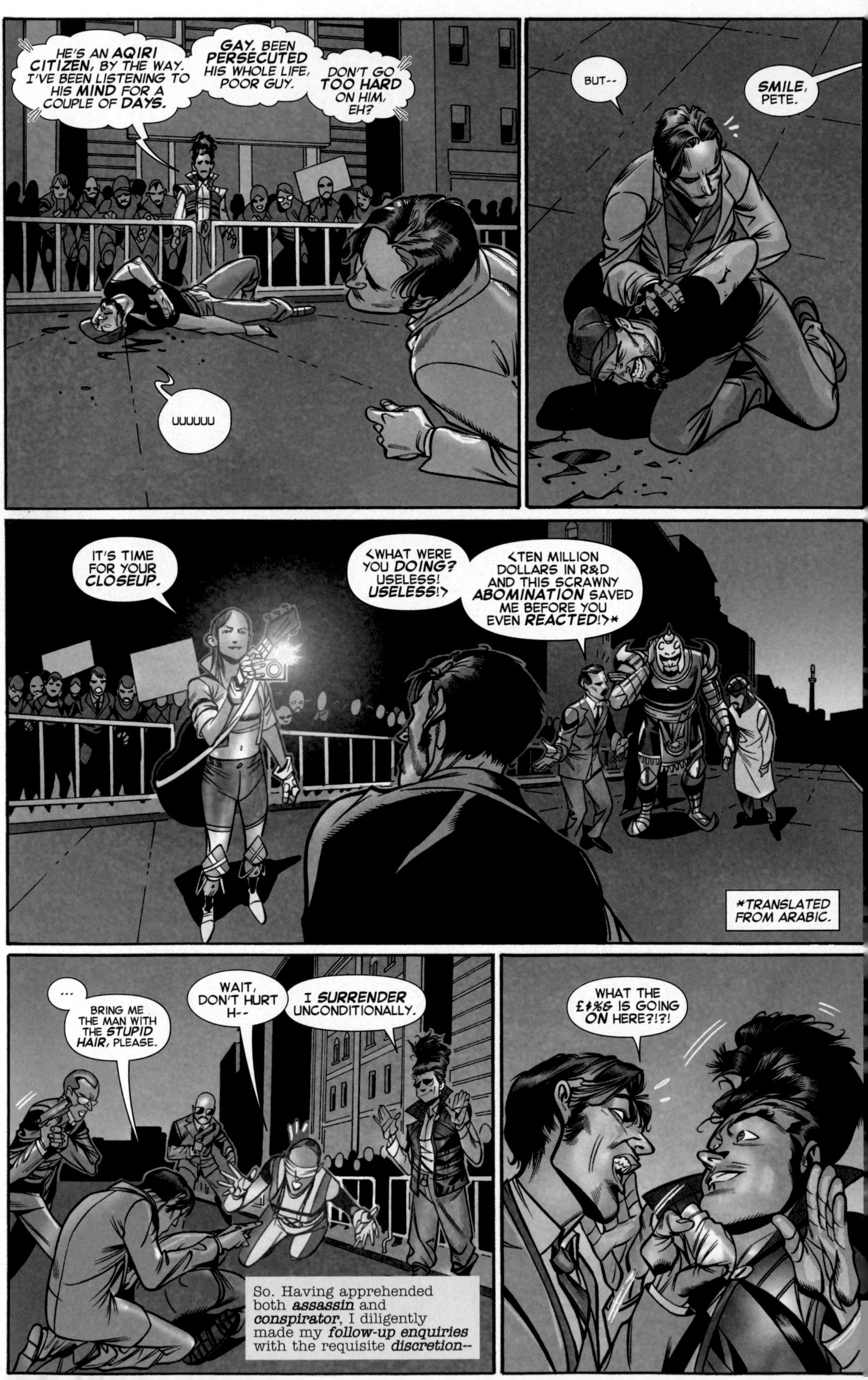
HE'S AN AQIRI CITIZEN, BY THE WAY. I'VE BEEN LISTENING TO HIS MIND FOR A COUPLE OF DAYS.
GAY. BEEN PERSECUTED HIS WHOLE LIFE, POOR GUY.
DON'T GO TOO HARD ON HIM, EH?
UUUUUU
BUT--
SMILE, PETE.
IT'S TIME FOR YOUR CLOSEUP.
<WHAT WERE YOU DOING? USELESS! USELESS!>
<TEN MILLION DOLLARS IN R&D AND THIS SCRAWNY ABOMINATION SAVED ME BEFORE YOU EVEN REACTED!>*
*TRANSLATED FROM ARABIC.
...
BRING ME THE MAN WITH THE STUPID HAIR, PLEASE.
WAIT, DON'T HURT H--
I SURRENDER UNCONDITIONALLY.
So. Having apprehended both assassin and conspirator, I diligently made my follow-up enquiries with the requisite discretion--
WHAT THE £¢%& IS GOING ON HERE?!?!

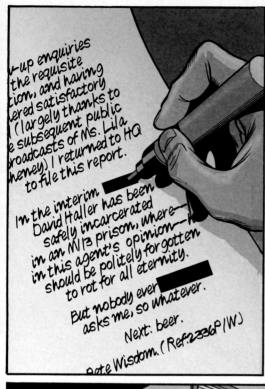

-up enquiries
the requisite
tion, and having
ered satisfactory
(largely thanks to
e subsequent public
roadcasts of Ms. Lila
heney) I returned to HQ
to file this report.
In the interim [redacted]
David Haller has been
safely incarcerated
in an MI13 prison, where--
in this agent's opinion--
should be politely forgotten
to rot for all eternity.
[redacted]
But nobody ever
asks me, so whatever.
Next: beer.
Pete Wisdom. (Ref:2336P/W.)
GOOD REPORT.
AAA!
FOR £$%& SAKE!
IF YOU TELEPORT OUT OF YOUR CELL ONE MORE BLEEDIN' TIME--
THERE'S JUST ONE WEE THING I TAKE ISSUE AT.
SPECIFICALLY THE WHOLE "HAVING DONE SOMETHING WRONG" PART.
I MEAN, WHAT PRECISELY IS MY CRIME?
YOU...
YOU MISLED AN OFFICER OF THE CROWN, COMPROMISED NATIONAL SECURITY 'N CONSPIRED TO DAMAGE THE REPUTATION OF THE UK.
HUH. RUTH?
YOU... SORRY, SORRY.
YOU KNOW THAT'S NOT TRUE, MR. WISDOM. PARDON ME. NO. YOU'VE SEEN THE BROADCAST.

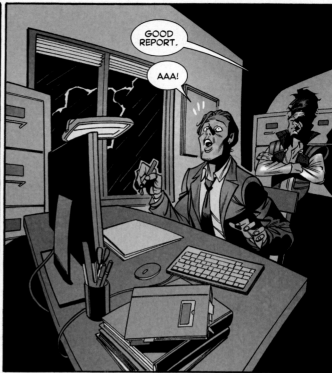

HI, FOLKS. YOU MIGHT *RECOGNIZE* ME--I'M LILA CHENEY.

SORRY ABOUT THE INTERRUPTION TO YOUR *REGULAR PROGRAMMING*--WE'LL GET BACK TO IT *RIGHT AWAY.* I'M ON TVS ALL 'ROUND THE WORLD RIGHT NOW THANKS TO SOME *UNCONVENTIONAL EQUIPMENT*--

--TO TELL YOU ABOUT *GREAT BRITAIN.*

AT SELLAFIELD WE FIND MR. JONOTHON STARSMORE--A *LONDON LAD*--SETTING OFF A *CONTROLLED NUCLEAR REACTION* USING HIS OWN FACE.

IF WE'VE DONE OUR *NUMBERS RIGHT* IT'LL KEEP *THE GRID* FED FOR A *FORTNIGHT* AND NOT COST A PENNY.

'SBEEN SORT OF *FUN,* SPENDIN' A DAY *NOT* BEATING PEOPLE UP.

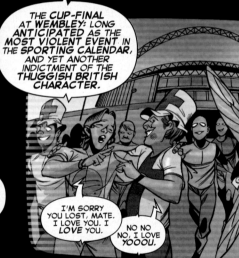

THE CUP-FINAL AT WEMBLEY: LONG ANTICIPATED AS THE *MOST VIOLENT EVENT* IN THE *SPORTING CALENDAR,* AND YET ANOTHER INDICTMENT OF THE *THUGGISH BRITISH CHARACTER.*

I'M SORRY YOU LOST, MATE. I LOVE YOU. I *LOVE* YOU.

NO NO NO, I LOVE *YOOOU.*

AND THAT'S LIAM CONNAUGHTON: NORTHERN IRISH, VAGUELY REPUBLICAN, FORMERLY CAUGHT UP IN THE *STRUGGLE FOR INDEPENDENCE,* ABLE TO GENERATE *EXPLOSIONS* AT WHIM--

HOW'RE YEH?

--WHO, LIKE MOST *NORMAL* PEOPLE, HAS MIRACULOUSLY CHOSEN *NOT* TO ATOMIZE HIS IDEOLOGICAL ENEMIES.

AND THE *CREAM* ON THE *CRUMPET,* LADIES AND GENTLEMEN: MI13'S OWN *MR. PETE WISDOM*--

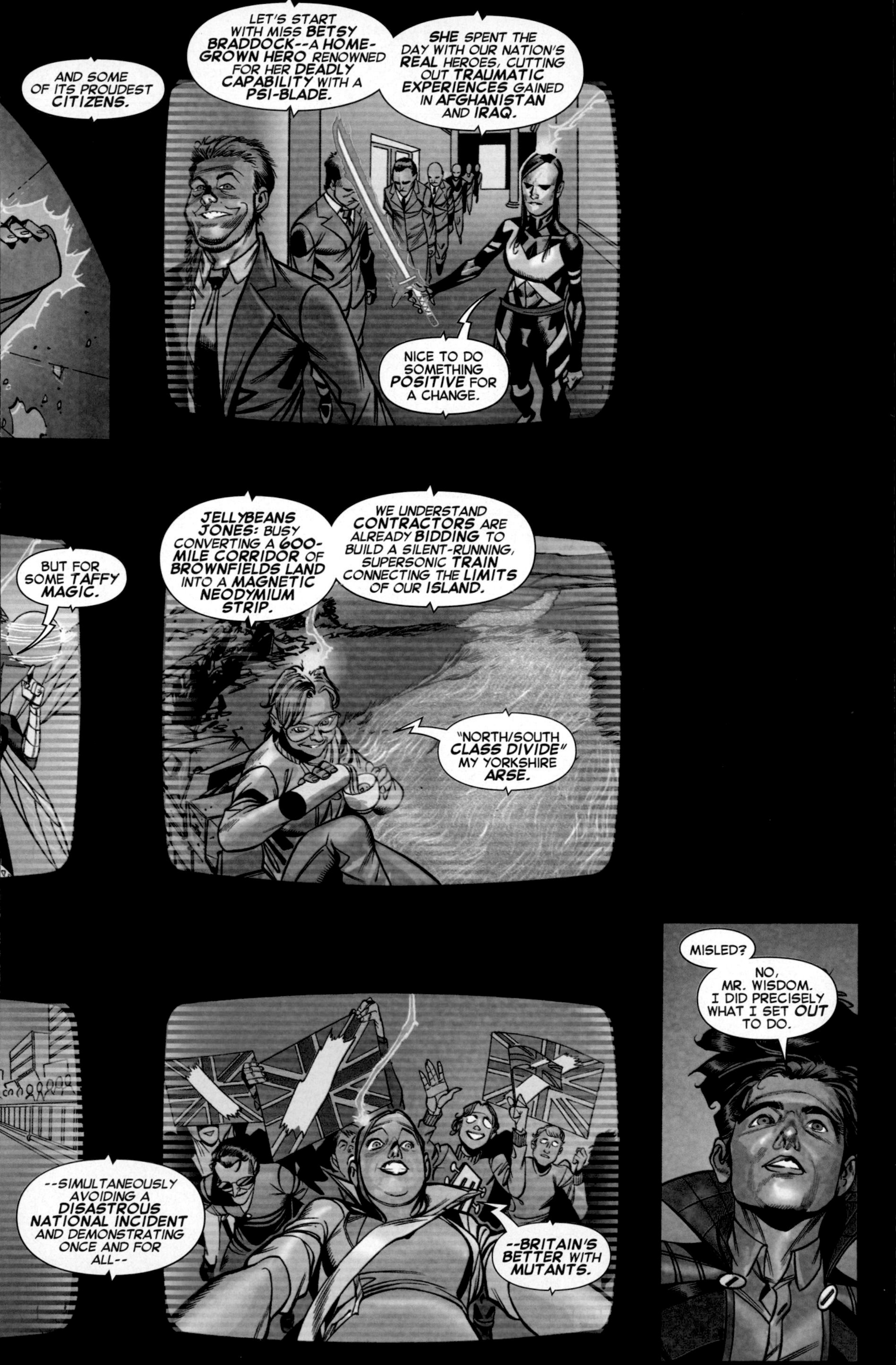
AND SOME OF ITS PROUDEST CITIZENS.
LET'S START WITH MISS BETSY BRADDOCK--A HOME-GROWN HERO RENOWNED FOR HER DEADLY CAPABILITY WITH A PSI-BLADE.
SHE SPENT THE DAY WITH OUR NATION'S REAL HEROES, CUTTING OUT TRAUMATIC EXPERIENCES GAINED IN AFGHANISTAN AND IRAQ.
NICE TO DO SOMETHING POSITIVE FOR A CHANGE.
BUT FOR SOME TAFFY MAGIC.
JELLYBEANS JONES: BUSY CONVERTING A 600-MILE CORRIDOR OF BROWNFIELDS LAND INTO A MAGNETIC NEODYMIUM STRIP.
WE UNDERSTAND CONTRACTORS ARE ALREADY BIDDING TO BUILD A SILENT-RUNNING, SUPERSONIC TRAIN CONNECTING THE LIMITS OF OUR ISLAND.
"NORTH/SOUTH CLASS DIVIDE" MY YORKSHIRE ARSE.
--SIMULTANEOUSLY AVOIDING A DISASTROUS NATIONAL INCIDENT AND DEMONSTRATING ONCE AND FOR ALL--
--BRITAIN'S BETTER WITH MUTANTS.
MISLED?
NO, MR. WISDOM. I DID PRECISELY WHAT I SET OUT TO DO.

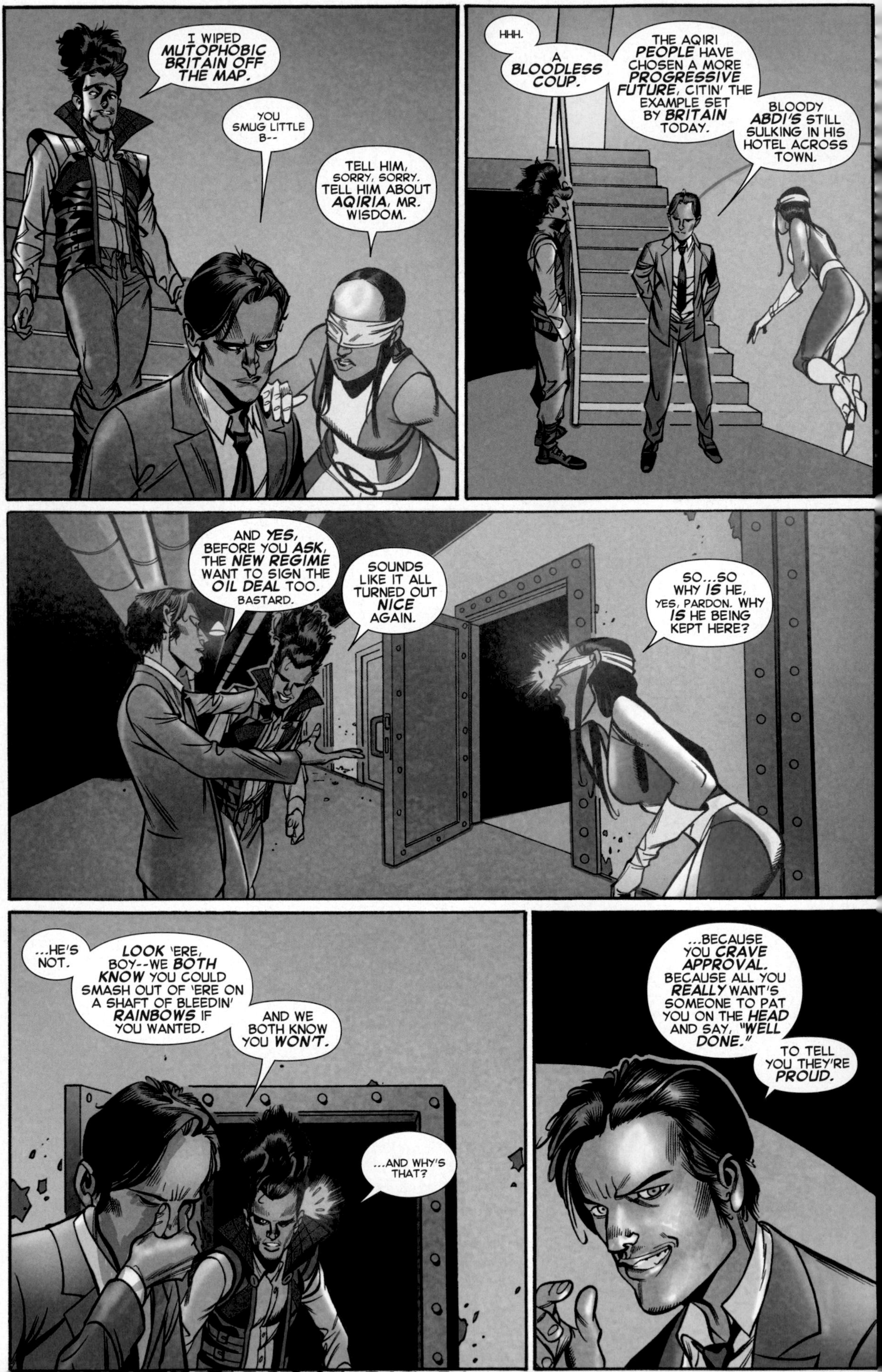
I WIPED MUTOPHOBIC BRITAIN OFF THE MAP.
YOU SMUG LITTLE B--
TELL HIM, SORRY, SORRY. TELL HIM ABOUT AQIRIA, MR. WISDOM.
HHH.
A BLOODLESS COUP.
THE AQIRI PEOPLE HAVE CHOSEN A MORE PROGRESSIVE FUTURE, CITIN' THE EXAMPLE SET BY BRITAIN TODAY.
BLOODY ABDI'S STILL SULKING IN HIS HOTEL ACROSS TOWN.
AND YES, BEFORE YOU ASK, THE NEW REGIME WANT TO SIGN THE OIL DEAL TOO. BASTARD.
SOUNDS LIKE IT ALL TURNED OUT NICE AGAIN.
SO...SO WHY IS HE, YES, PARDON. WHY IS HE BEING KEPT HERE?
...HE'S NOT.
LOOK 'ERE, BOY--WE BOTH KNOW YOU COULD SMASH OUT OF 'ERE ON A SHAFT OF BLEEDIN' RAINBOWS IF YOU WANTED.
AND WE BOTH KNOW YOU WON'T.
...AND WHY'S THAT?
...BECAUSE YOU CRAVE APPROVAL. BECAUSE ALL YOU REALLY WANT'S SOMEONE TO PAT YOU ON THE HEAD AND SAY, "WELL DONE."
TO TELL YOU THEY'RE PROUD.

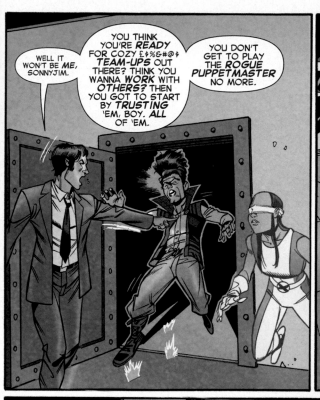

WELL IT WON'T BE *ME*, SONNYJIM.

YOU THINK YOU'RE *READY* FOR COZY £$%&#@$ *TEAM-UPS* OUT THERE? THINK YOU WANNA *WORK* WITH *OTHERS?* THEN YOU GOT TO START BY *TRUSTING* 'EM, BOY. *ALL* OF 'EM.

YOU DON'T GET TO PLAY THE *ROGUE PUPPETMASTER* NO MORE.

THIS BECAME AN *INTERNATIONAL INCIDENT* THE SECOND YOU FORGOT TO *RESPECT ME* BY SHARIN' YOUR *PLANS.*

I'VE BEEN *OBLIGATED* TO INFORM THE *AUTHORITIES* OF YOUR *HOMELAND. REGULATIONS.* YOU KNOW HOW IT *IS.*

Y... Y...YOU CALLED HER...?

TELEGRAM FROM THE *ISRAELI EMBASSY.*

THEY'RE SENDING A CAR. AND AN *ARMED GUARD,* I SHOULDN'T WONDER.

LET'S SEE HOW BLEEDIN' PROUD *MUMMY HALLER'S* FEELING TOWARDS HER LITTLE *INTERNATIONAL TERRORIST,* SHALL WE?

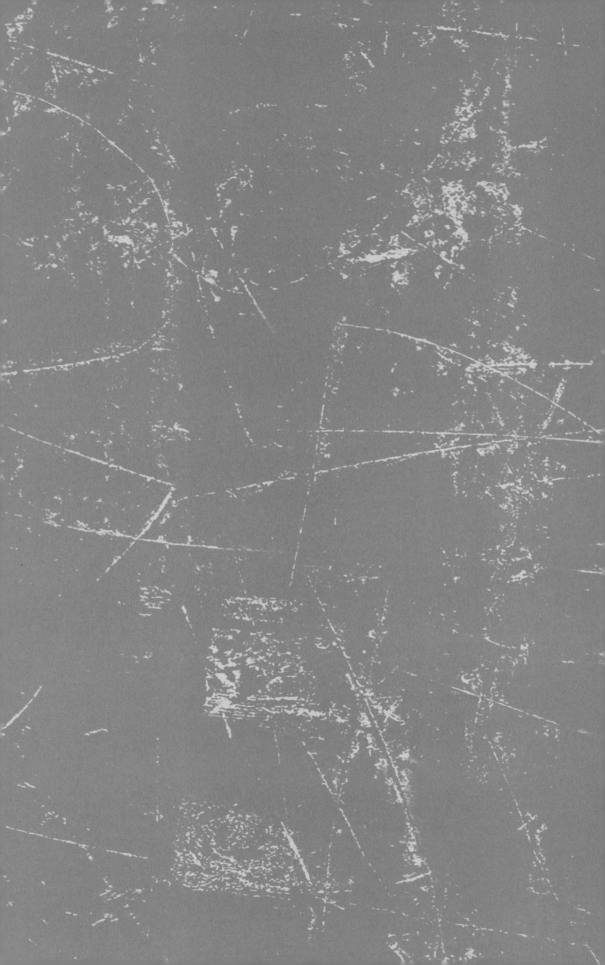

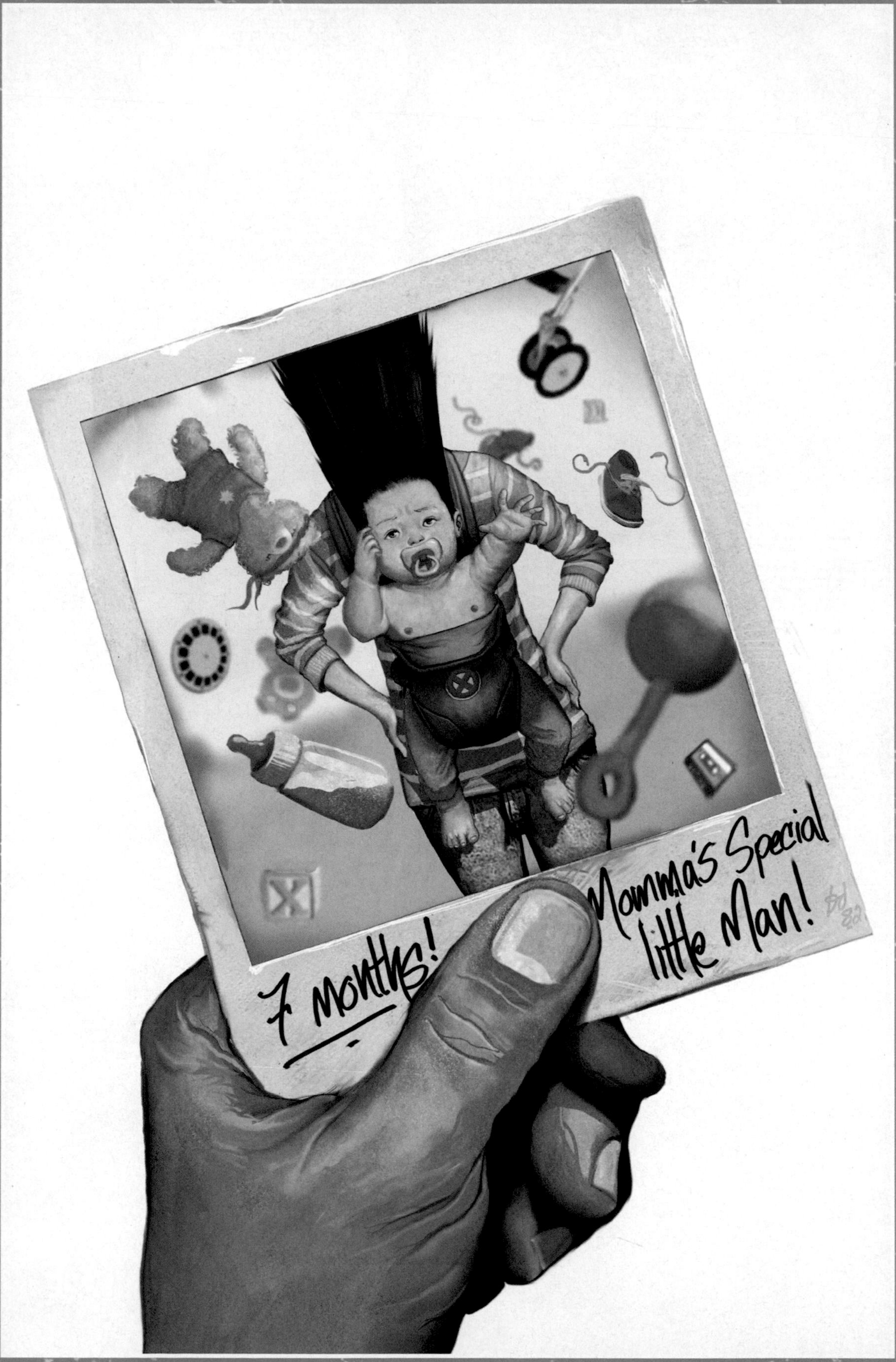
7 months!
Momma's Special little Man!

FIFTEEN

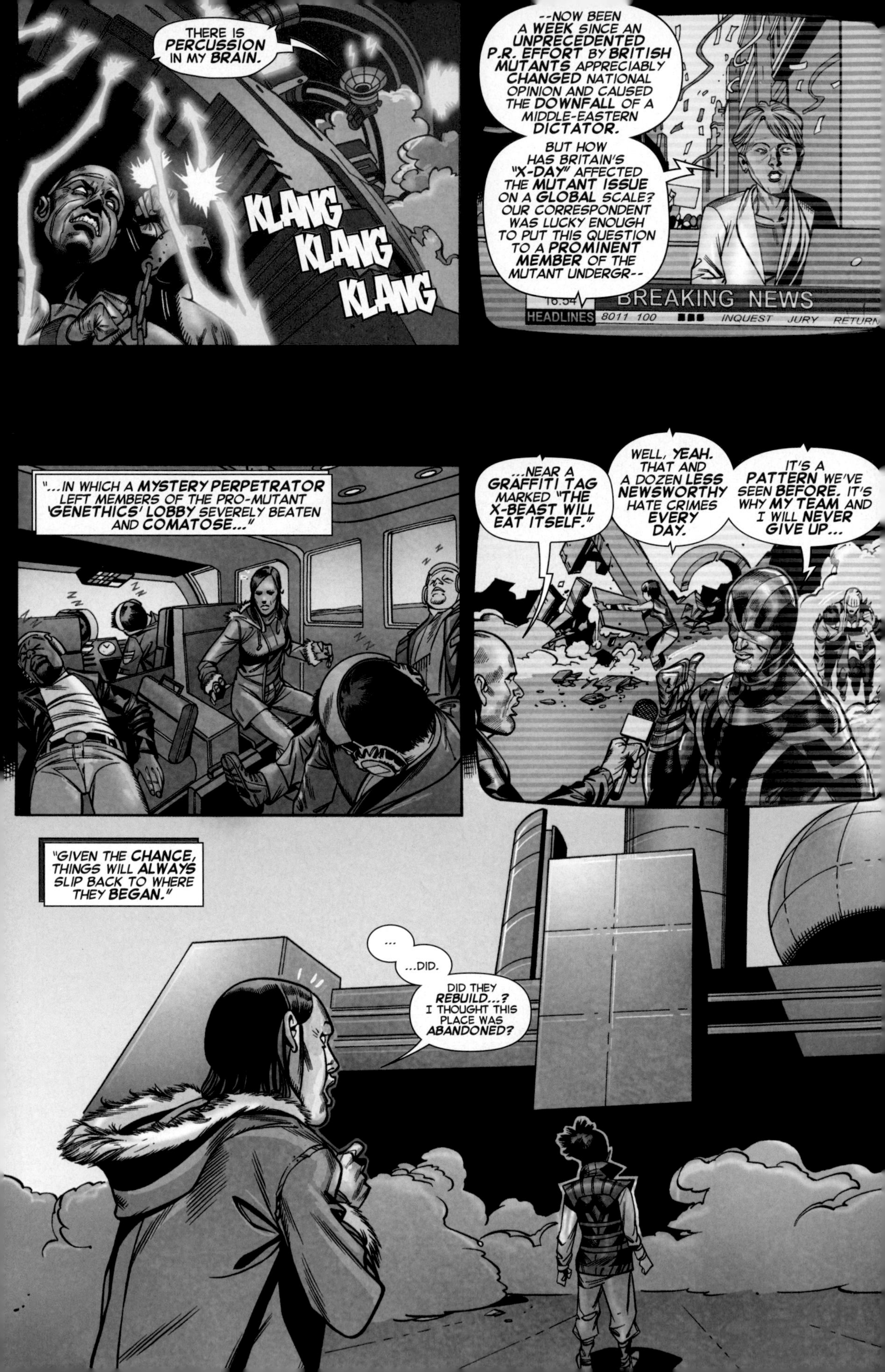
THERE IS PERCUSSION IN MY BRAIN.
KLANG KLANG KLANG
--NOW BEEN A WEEK SINCE AN UNPRECEDENTED P.R. EFFORT BY BRITISH MUTANTS APPRECIABLY CHANGED NATIONAL OPINION AND CAUSED THE DOWNFALL OF A MIDDLE-EASTERN DICTATOR.
BUT HOW HAS BRITAIN'S "X-DAY" AFFECTED THE MUTANT ISSUE ON A GLOBAL SCALE? OUR CORRESPONDENT WAS LUCKY ENOUGH TO PUT THIS QUESTION TO A PROMINENT MEMBER OF THE MUTANT UNDERGR--
BREAKING NEWS
HEADLINES
8011 100
INQUEST JURY RETURN
"...IN WHICH A MYSTERY PERPETRATOR LEFT MEMBERS OF THE PRO-MUTANT 'GENETHICS' LOBBY SEVERELY BEATEN AND COMATOSE..."
...NEAR A GRAFFITI TAG MARKED "THE X-BEAST WILL EAT ITSELF."
WELL, YEAH. THAT AND A DOZEN LESS NEWSWORTHY HATE CRIMES EVERY DAY.
IT'S A PATTERN WE'VE SEEN BEFORE. IT'S WHY MY TEAM AND I WILL NEVER GIVE UP...
"GIVEN THE CHANCE, THINGS WILL ALWAYS SLIP BACK TO WHERE THEY BEGAN."
...
...DID.
DID THEY REBUILD...? I THOUGHT THIS PLACE WAS ABANDONED?

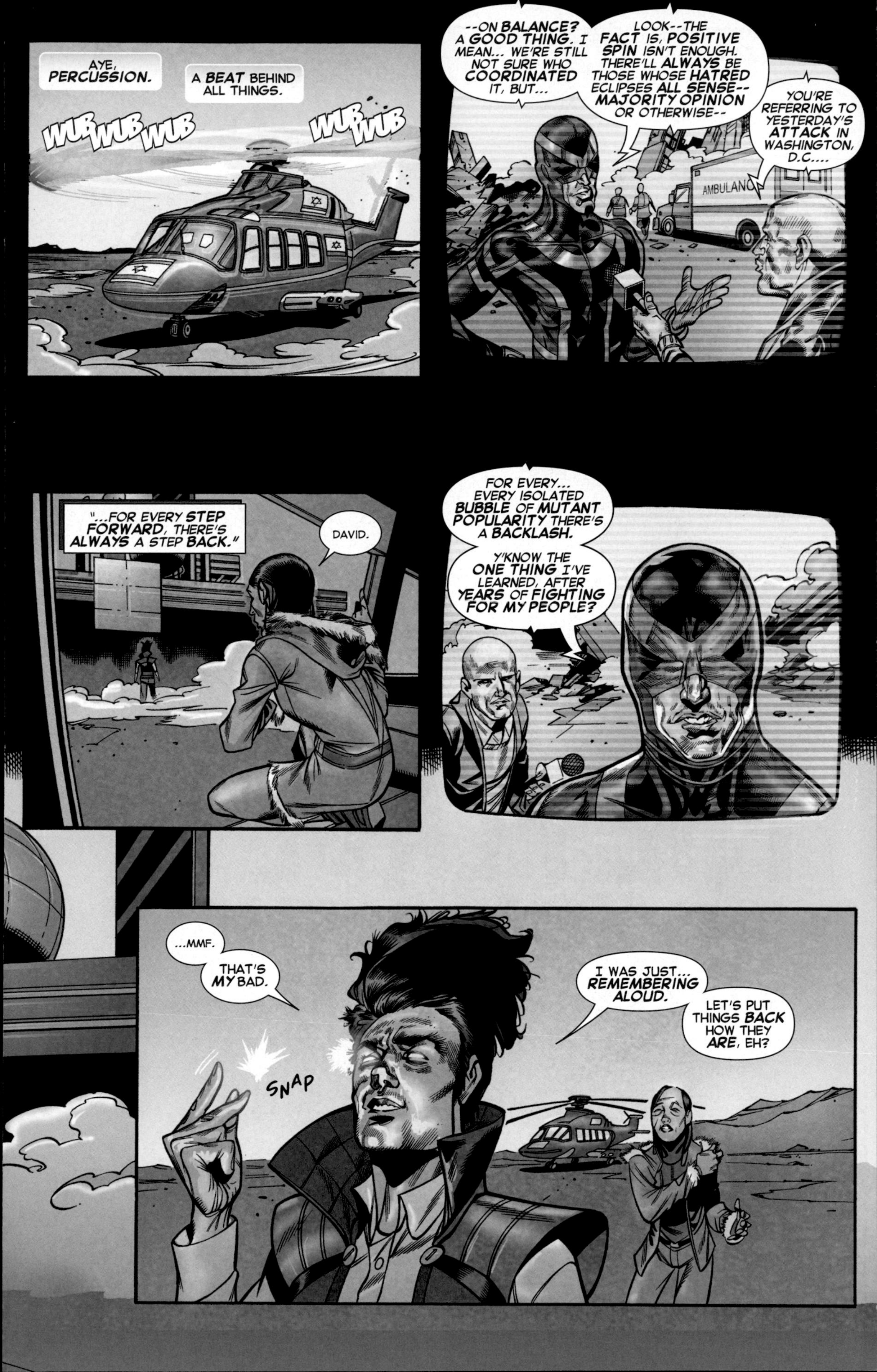
AYE, PERCUSSION.
A BEAT BEHIND ALL THINGS.
WUB WUB WUB
WUB WUB
--ON BALANCE? A GOOD THING. I MEAN... WE'RE STILL NOT SURE WHO COORDINATED IT, BUT...
LOOK--THE FACT IS, POSITIVE SPIN ISN'T ENOUGH. THERE'LL ALWAYS BE THOSE WHOSE HATRED ECLIPSES ALL SENSE--MAJORITY OPINION OR OTHERWISE--
YOU'RE REFERRING TO YESTERDAY'S ATTACK IN WASHINGTON, D.C....
"...FOR EVERY STEP FORWARD, THERE'S ALWAYS A STEP BACK."
DAVID.
FOR EVERY... EVERY ISOLATED BUBBLE OF MUTANT POPULARITY THERE'S A BACKLASH.
Y'KNOW THE ONE THING I'VE LEARNED, AFTER YEARS OF FIGHTING FOR MY PEOPLE?
...MMF.
THAT'S MY BAD.
SNAP
I WAS JUST... REMEMBERING ALOUD.
LET'S PUT THINGS BACK HOW THEY ARE, EH?

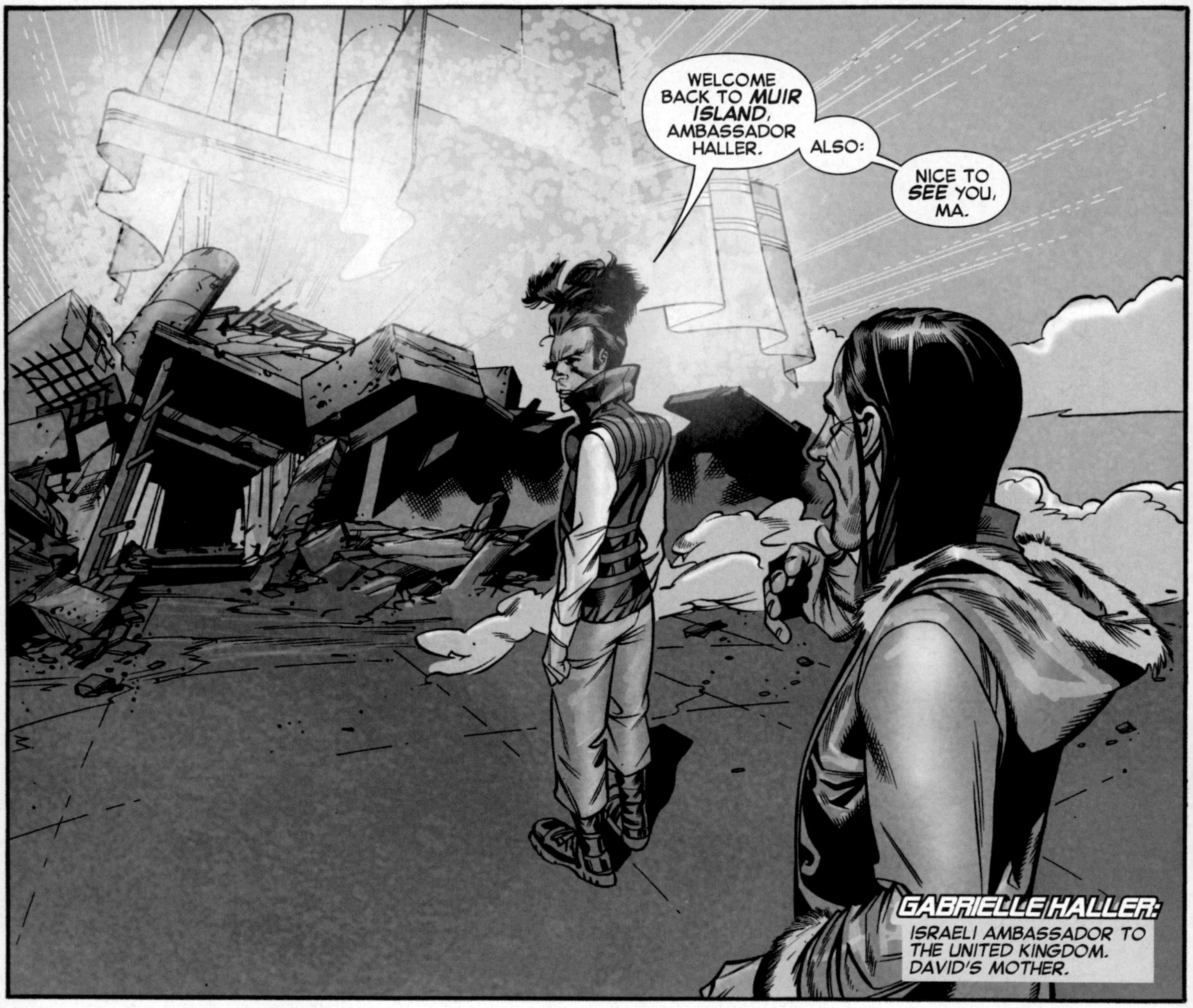
WELCOME BACK TO MUIR ISLAND, AMBASSADOR HALLER.
ALSO:
NICE TO SEE YOU, MA.
GABRIELLE HALLER:
ISRAELI AMBASSADOR TO THE UNITED KINGDOM. DAVID'S MOTHER.

THE PLACE OF BROKEN THINGS

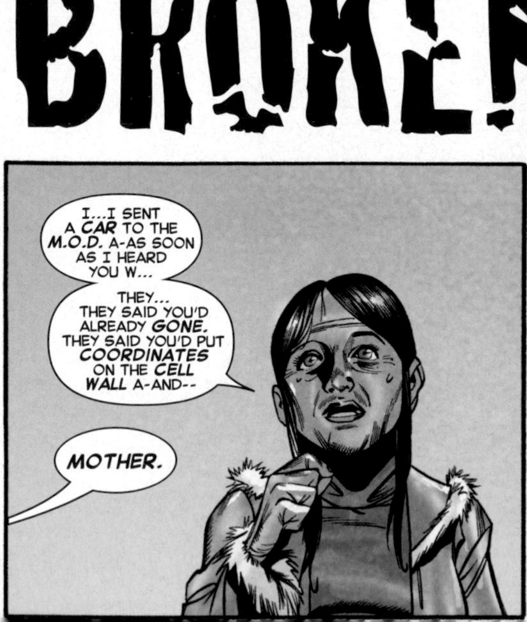
I...I SENT A CAR TO THE M.O.D. A-AS SOON AS I HEARD YOU W...
THEY... THEY SAID YOU'D ALREADY GONE. THEY SAID YOU'D PUT COORDINATES ON THE CELL WALL A-AND--
MOTHER.

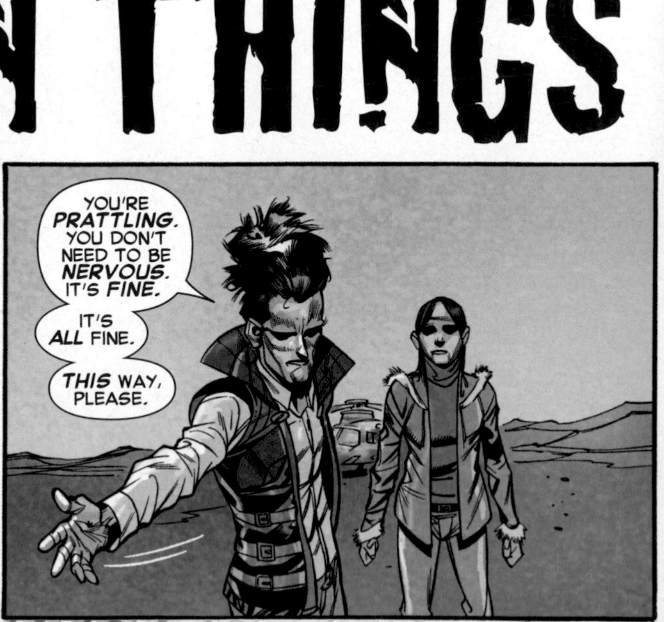
YOU'RE PRATTLING. YOU DON'T NEED TO BE NERVOUS. IT'S FINE.
IT'S ALL FINE.
THIS WAY, PLEASE.

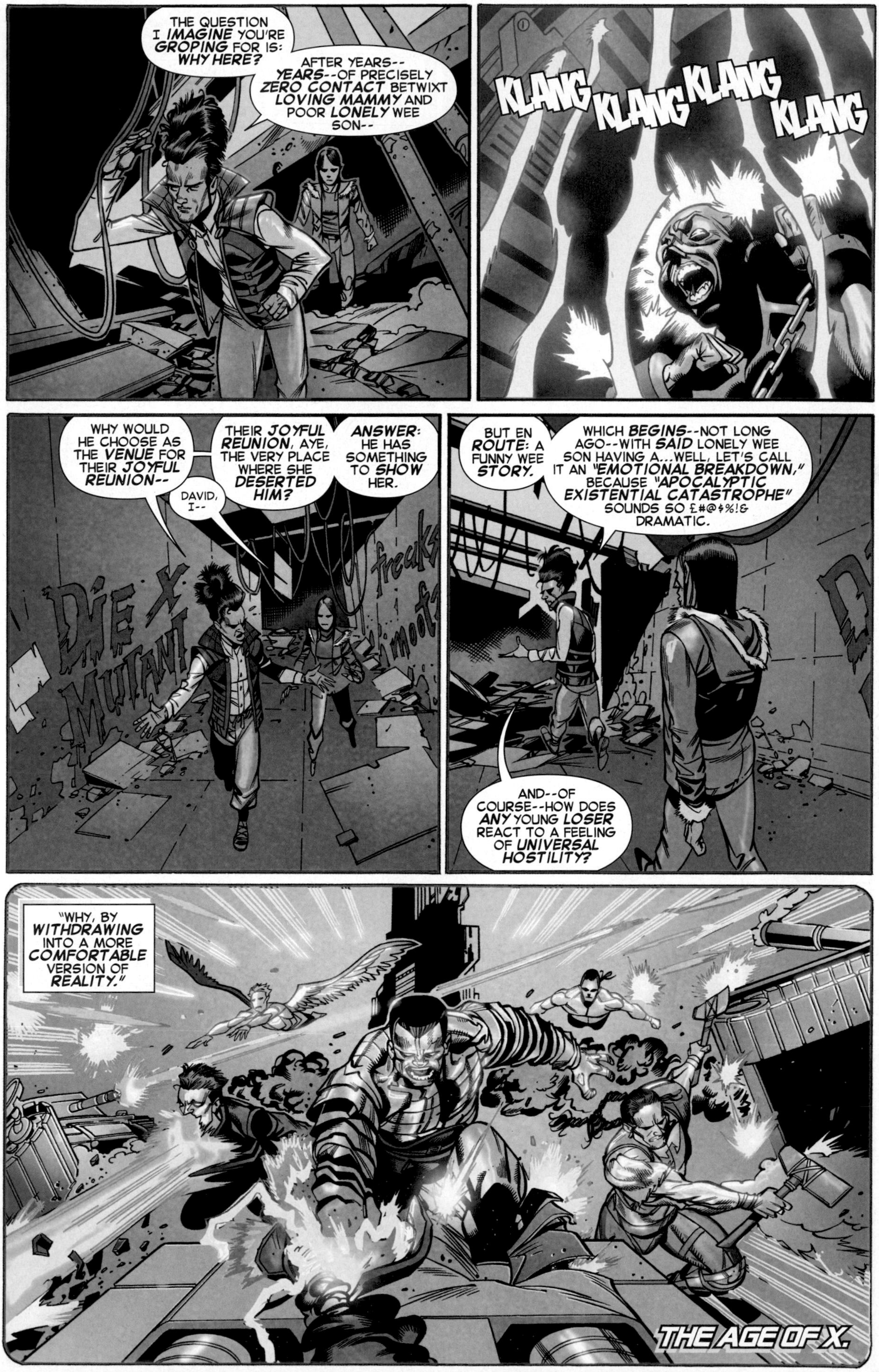
THE QUESTION I IMAGINE YOU'RE GROPING FOR IS: WHY HERE?
AFTER YEARS-- YEARS--OF PRECISELY ZERO CONTACT BETWIXT LOVING MAMMY AND POOR LONELY WEE SON--
KLANG KLANG KLANG KLANG
WHY WOULD HE CHOOSE AS THE VENUE FOR THEIR JOYFUL REUNION--
THEIR JOYFUL REUNION, AYE, THE VERY PLACE WHERE SHE DESERTED HIM?
DAVID, I--
ANSWER: HE HAS SOMETHING TO SHOW HER.
DIE X MUTANT
BUT EN ROUTE: A FUNNY WEE STORY.
WHICH BEGINS--NOT LONG AGO--WITH SAID LONELY WEE SON HAVING A...WELL, LET'S CALL IT AN "EMOTIONAL BREAKDOWN," BECAUSE "APOCALYPTIC EXISTENTIAL CATASTROPHE" SOUNDS SO £#@$%!& DRAMATIC.
AND--OF COURSE--HOW DOES ANY YOUNG LOSER REACT TO A FEELING OF UNIVERSAL HOSTILITY?
"WHY, BY WITHDRAWING INTO A MORE COMFORTABLE VERSION OF REALITY."
THE AGE OF X.

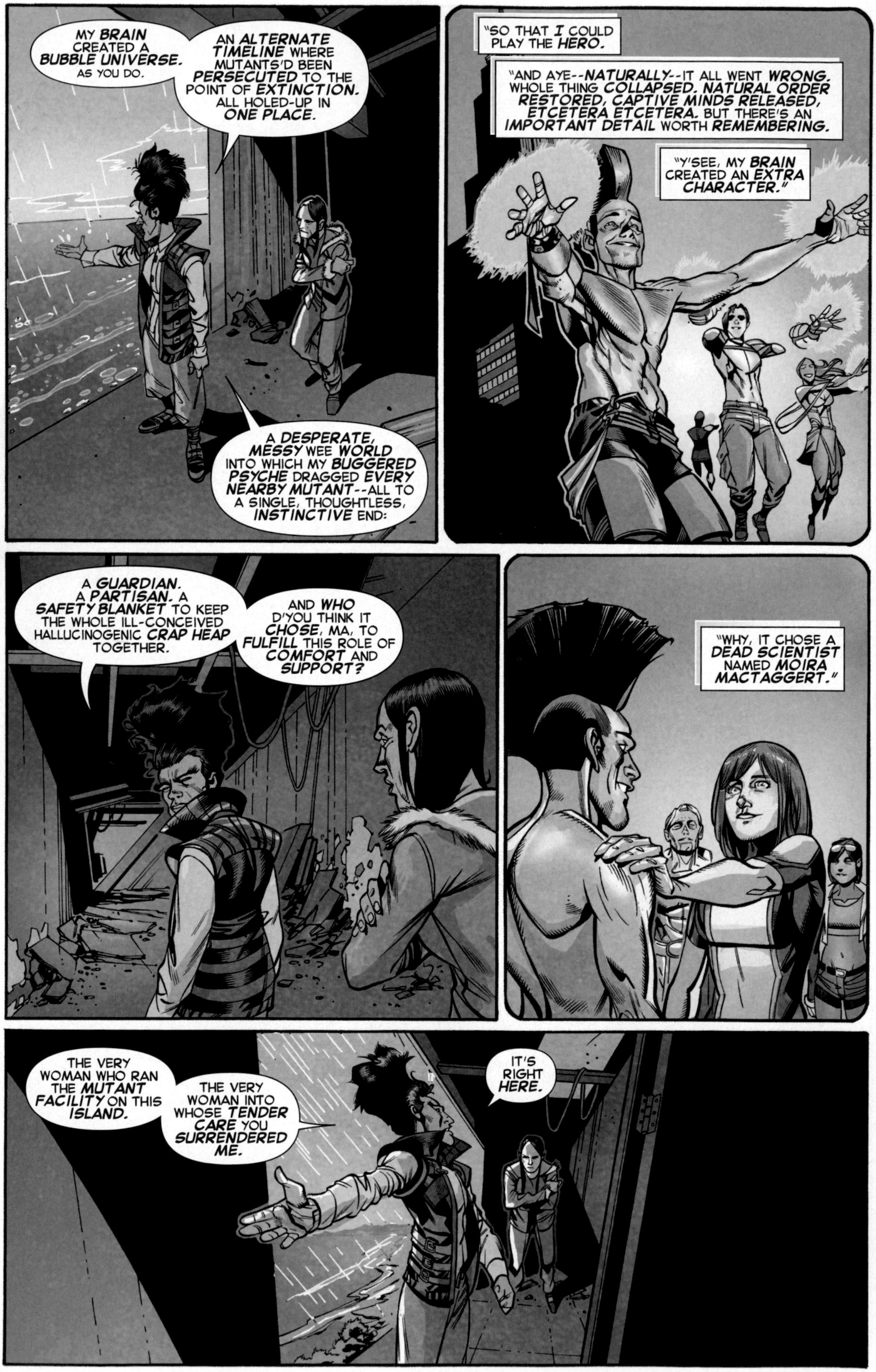
MY BRAIN CREATED A BUBBLE UNIVERSE. AS YOU DO.
AN ALTERNATE TIMELINE WHERE MUTANTS'D BEEN PERSECUTED TO THE POINT OF EXTINCTION. ALL HOLED-UP IN ONE PLACE.
A DESPERATE, MESSY WEE WORLD INTO WHICH MY BUGGERED PSYCHE DRAGGED EVERY NEARBY MUTANT--ALL TO A SINGLE, THOUGHTLESS, INSTINCTIVE END:
"SO THAT I COULD PLAY THE HERO.
"AND AYE--NATURALLY--IT ALL WENT WRONG. WHOLE THING COLLAPSED. NATURAL ORDER RESTORED, CAPTIVE MINDS RELEASED, ETCETERA ETCETERA. BUT THERE'S AN IMPORTANT DETAIL WORTH REMEMBERING.
"Y'SEE, MY BRAIN CREATED AN EXTRA CHARACTER."
A GUARDIAN. A PARTISAN. A SAFETY BLANKET TO KEEP THE WHOLE ILL-CONCEIVED HALLUCINOGENIC CRAP HEAP TOGETHER.
AND WHO D'YOU THINK IT CHOSE, MA, TO FULFILL THIS ROLE OF COMFORT AND SUPPORT?
"WHY, IT CHOSE A DEAD SCIENTIST NAMED MOIRA MACTAGGERT."
THE VERY WOMAN WHO RAN THE MUTANT FACILITY ON THIS ISLAND.
THE VERY WOMAN INTO WHOSE TENDER CARE YOU SURRENDERED ME.
IT'S RIGHT HERE.

I...I DON'T--

HERE. LET ME HELP.

OH.

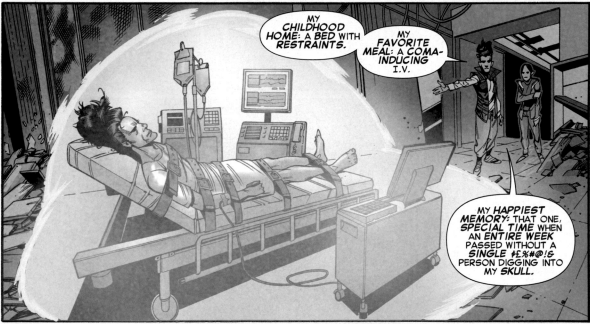

MY CHILDHOOD HOME: A BED WITH RESTRAINTS.

MY FAVORITE MEAL: A COMA-INDUCING I.V.

MY HAPPIEST MEMORY: THAT ONE, SPECIAL TIME WHEN AN ENTIRE WEEK PASSED WITHOUT A SINGLE #£%#@!§ PERSON DIGGING INTO MY SKULL.

AND YET WHEN IT CAME DOWN TO IT... WHEN LEFT TO ITS OWN DEVICES... WHEN IT NEEDED TO PLUCK A MOTHER FIGURE OUT OF THE ETHER...

...MY MIND STILL CHOSE THE WOMAN WHO'D CAUSED ME SUCH PAIN--

--INSTEAD OF YOU.

...

...

WHERE HAVE YOU BEEN, MA?

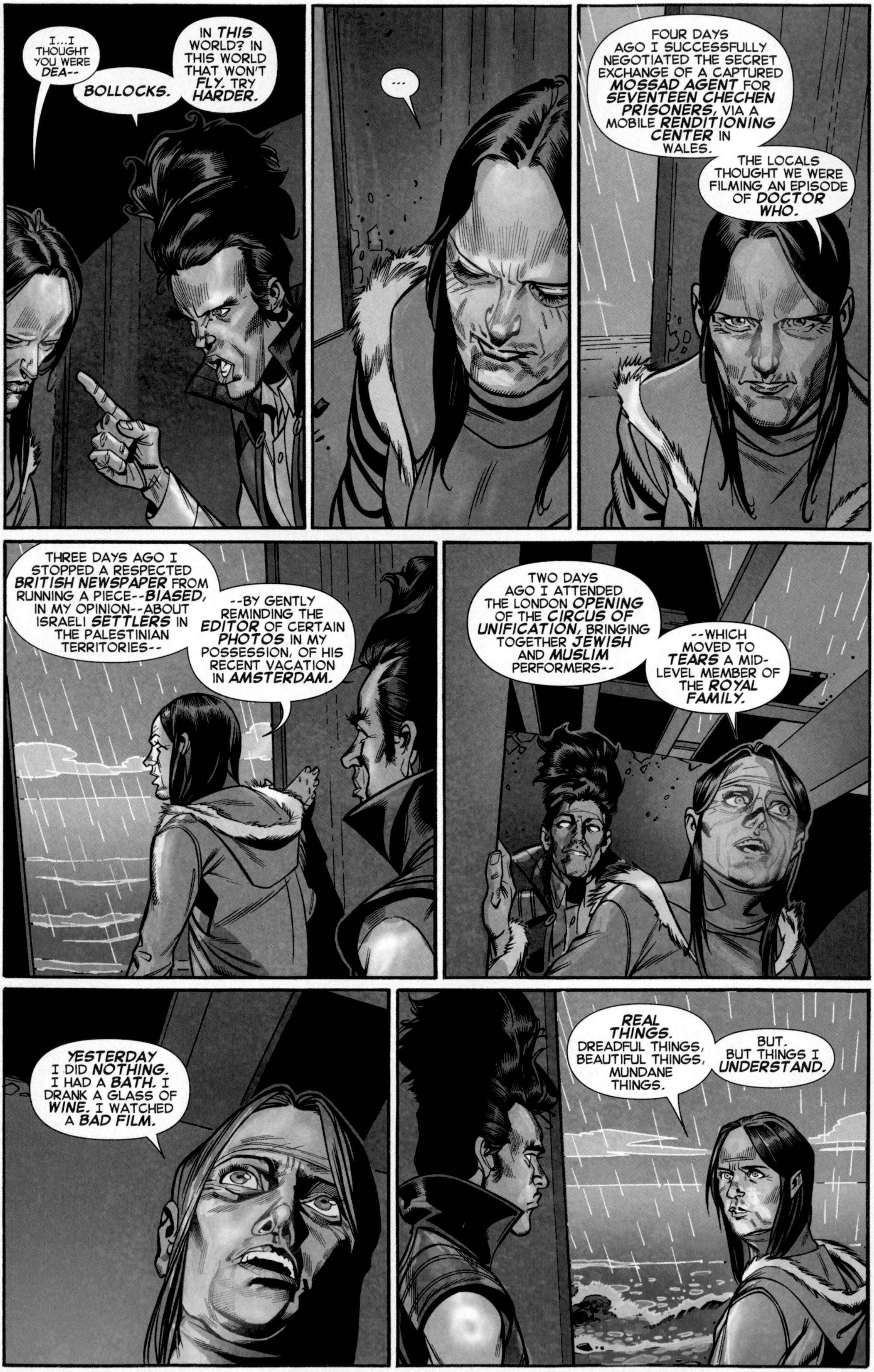
I...I THOUGHT YOU WERE DEA--
BOLLOCKS.
IN THIS WORLD? IN THIS WORLD THAT WON'T FLY. TRY HARDER.
...
FOUR DAYS AGO I SUCCESSFULLY NEGOTIATED THE SECRET EXCHANGE OF A CAPTURED MOSSAD AGENT FOR SEVENTEEN CHECHEN PRISONERS, VIA A MOBILE RENDITIONING CENTER IN WALES.
THE LOCALS THOUGHT WE WERE FILMING AN EPISODE OF DOCTOR WHO.
THREE DAYS AGO I STOPPED A RESPECTED BRITISH NEWSPAPER FROM RUNNING A PIECE--BIASED, IN MY OPINION--ABOUT ISRAELI SETTLERS IN THE PALESTINIAN TERRITORIES--
--BY GENTLY REMINDING THE EDITOR OF CERTAIN PHOTOS IN MY POSSESSION, OF HIS RECENT VACATION IN AMSTERDAM.
TWO DAYS AGO I ATTENDED THE LONDON OPENING OF THE CIRCUS OF UNIFICATION, BRINGING TOGETHER JEWISH AND MUSLIM PERFORMERS--
--WHICH MOVED TO TEARS A MID-LEVEL MEMBER OF THE ROYAL FAMILY.
YESTERDAY I DID NOTHING. I HAD A BATH. I DRANK A GLASS OF WINE. I WATCHED A BAD FILM.
REAL THINGS. DREADFUL THINGS, BEAUTIFUL THINGS, MUNDANE THINGS.
BUT. BUT THINGS I UNDERSTAND.

YOU...? M-MY SON... MY...MY POOR SON.

YOU COME FROM ANOTHER WORLD. A WORLD OF...OF COSTUMES. POWERS.

A WORLD WHERE YOU'RE A HERO OR A VILLAIN, OR NOTHING IN BETWEEN. A WORLD WHERE PEOPLE WON'T STAY DEAD.

KLANG KLANG KLANG

"YOUR FATHER'S WORLD."

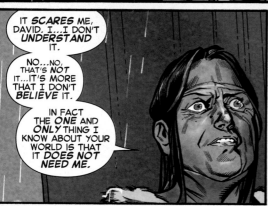

IT SCARES ME, DAVID. I...I DON'T UNDERSTAND IT.

NO...NO, THAT'S NOT IT...IT'S MORE THAT I DON'T BELIEVE IT.

IN FACT THE ONE AND ONLY THING I KNOW ABOUT YOUR WORLD IS THAT IT DOES NOT NEED ME.

HOW COULD I COMPETE? I LOST YOU THE MOMENT CHARLES...D-DEAR CHARLES... LEARNED YOU WERE HIS.

...

...

...

DIDN'T...

D-DIDN'T IT EVER OCCUR TO YOU I MIGHT PREFER YOUR WORLD TO HIS...?

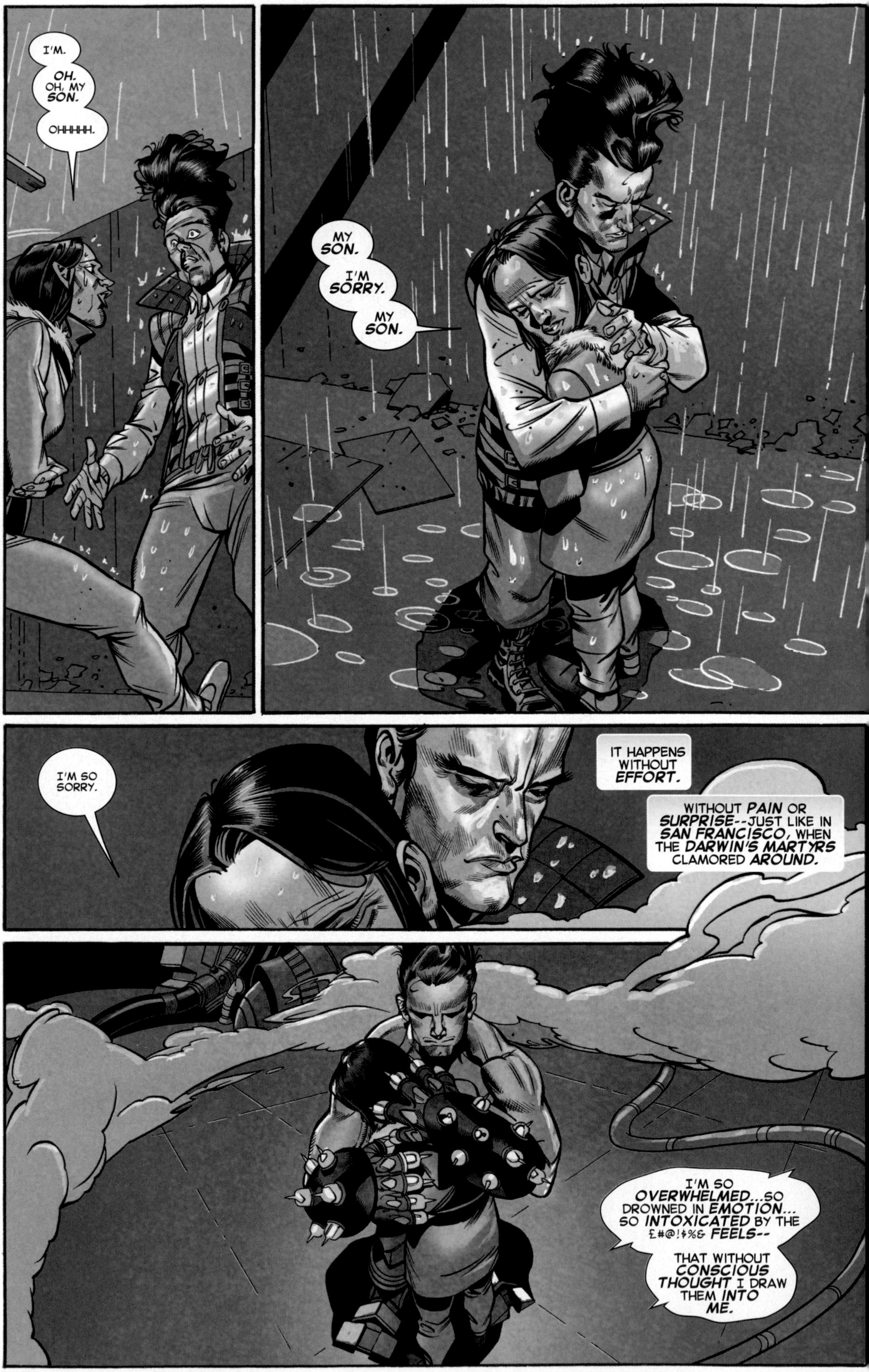
I'M.
OH. OH, MY SON.
OHHHHH.
MY SON.
I'M SORRY.
MY SON.
I'M SO SORRY.
IT HAPPENS WITHOUT EFFORT.
WITHOUT PAIN OR SURPRISE--JUST LIKE IN SAN FRANCISCO, WHEN THE DARWIN'S MARTYRS CLAMORED AROUND.
I'M SO OVERWHELMED...SO DROWNED IN EMOTION... SO INTOXICATED BY THE £#@!$%& FEELS--
THAT WITHOUT CONSCIOUS THOUGHT I DRAW THEM INTO ME.

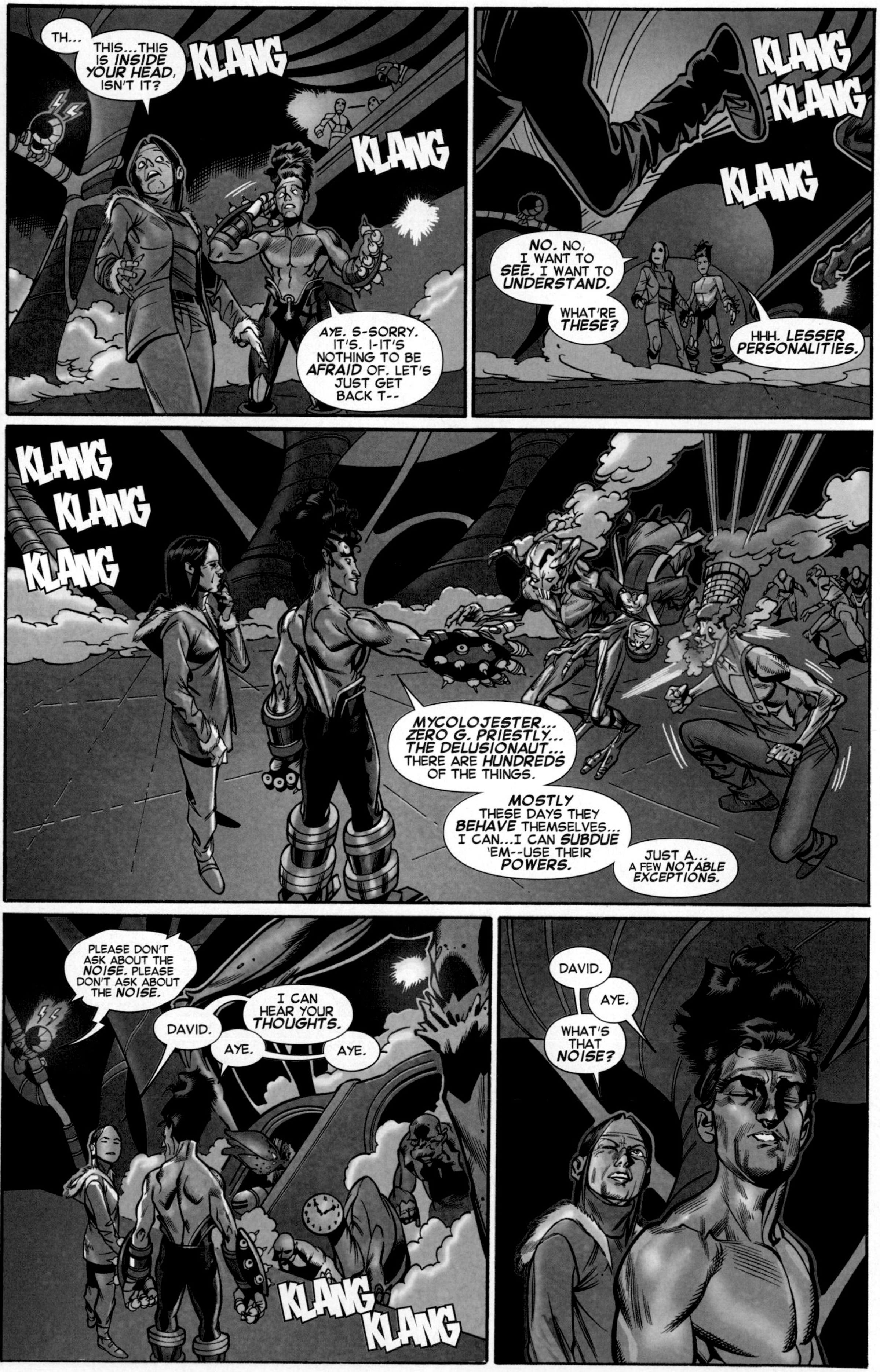
TH...
THIS...THIS IS INSIDE YOUR HEAD, ISN'T IT?
KLANG
KLANG
AYE. S-SORRY. IT'S. I-IT'S NOTHING TO BE AFRAID OF. LET'S JUST GET BACK T--
KLANG
KLANG
KLANG
NO. NO, I WANT TO SEE. I WANT TO UNDERSTAND.
WHAT'RE THESE?
HHH. LESSER PERSONALITIES.
KLANG
KLANG
KLANG
MYCOLOJESTER... ZERO G. PRIESTLY... THE DELUSIONAUT... THERE ARE HUNDREDS OF THE THINGS.
MOSTLY THESE DAYS THEY BEHAVE THEMSELVES... I CAN...I CAN SUBDUE 'EM--USE THEIR POWERS.
JUST A... A FEW NOTABLE EXCEPTIONS.
PLEASE DON'T ASK ABOUT THE NOISE. PLEASE DON'T ASK ABOUT THE NOISE.
I CAN HEAR YOUR THOUGHTS.
DAVID.
AYE.
AYE.
KLANG
KLANG
DAVID.
AYE.
WHAT'S THAT NOISE?

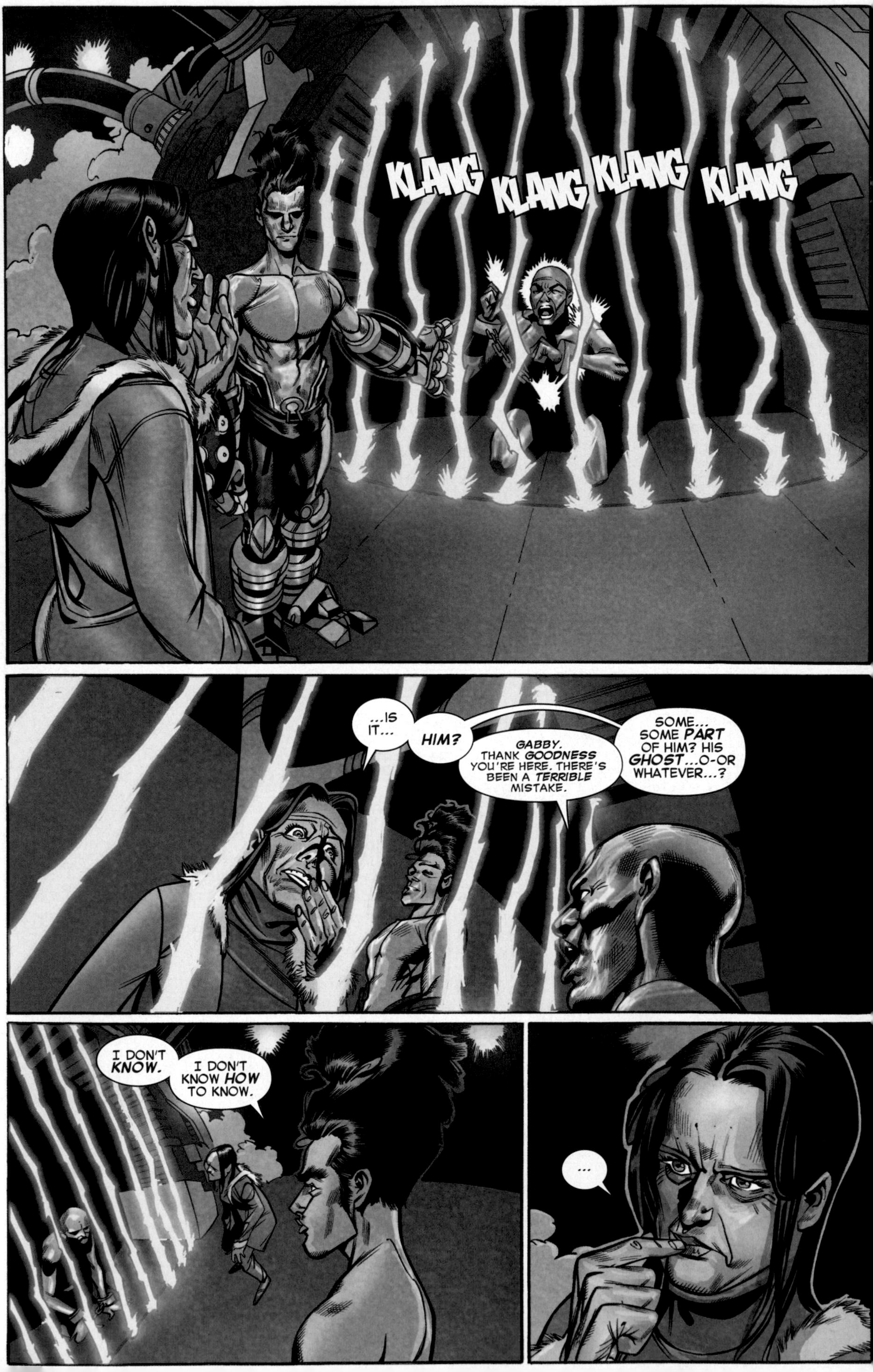
KLANG KLANG KLANG KLANG
...IS IT...
HIM?
GABBY. THANK GOODNESS YOU'RE HERE. THERE'S BEEN A TERRIBLE MISTAKE.
SOME... SOME PART OF HIM? HIS GHOST...O-OR WHATEVER...?
I DON'T KNOW.
I DON'T KNOW HOW TO KNOW.
...

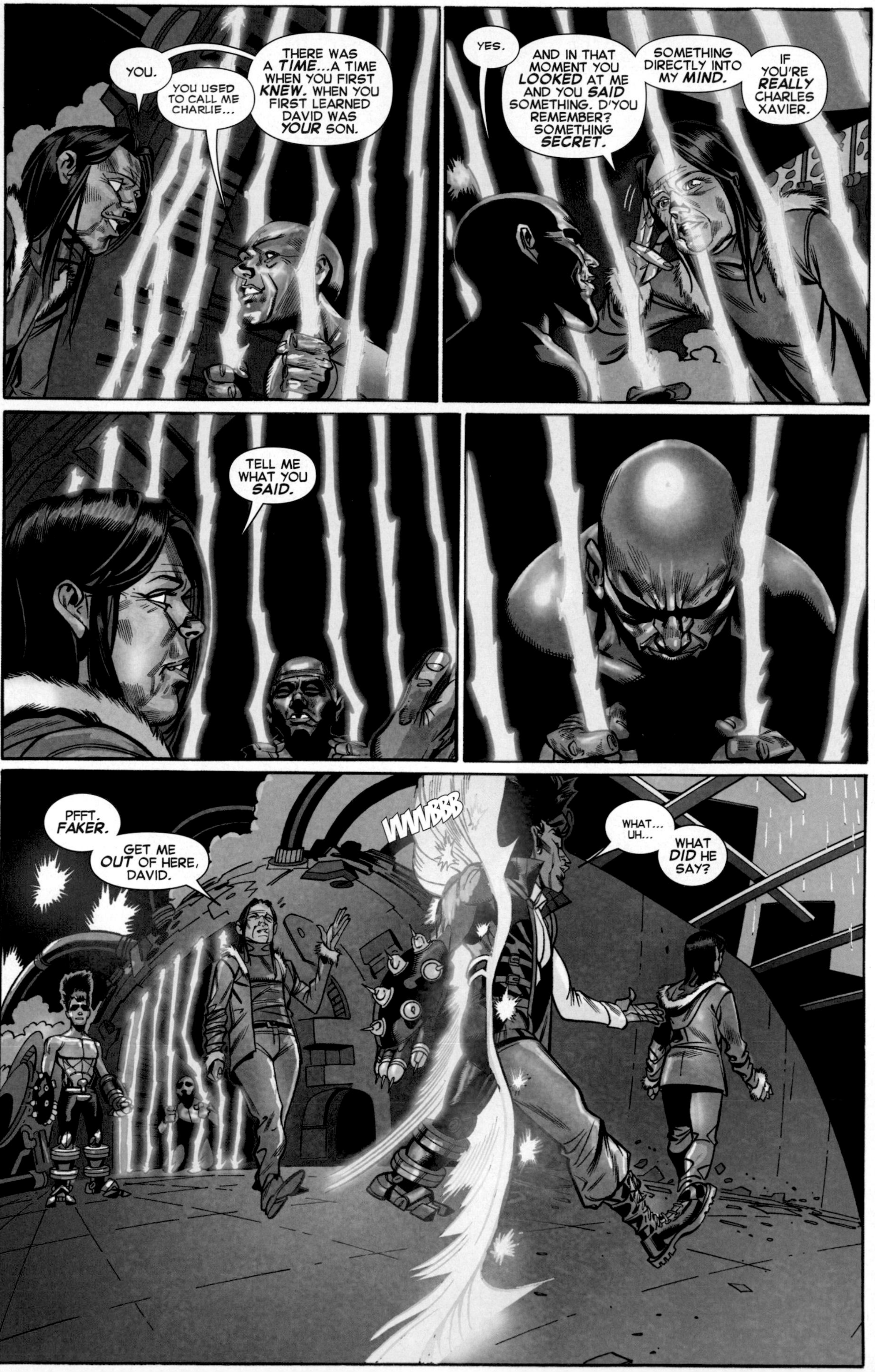
YOU.
YOU USED TO CALL ME CHARLIE...
THERE WAS A *TIME*...A TIME WHEN YOU FIRST *KNEW.* WHEN YOU FIRST LEARNED DAVID WAS *YOUR* SON.
YES.
AND IN THAT MOMENT YOU *LOOKED* AT ME AND YOU *SAID* SOMETHING. D'YOU REMEMBER? SOMETHING *SECRET.*
SOMETHING DIRECTLY INTO MY *MIND.*
IF YOU'RE *REALLY* CHARLES XAVIER.
TELL ME WHAT YOU *SAID.*
PFFT. *FAKER.*
GET ME *OUT* OF HERE, DAVID.
WWWBBB
WHAT... UH...
WHAT *DID* HE SAY?

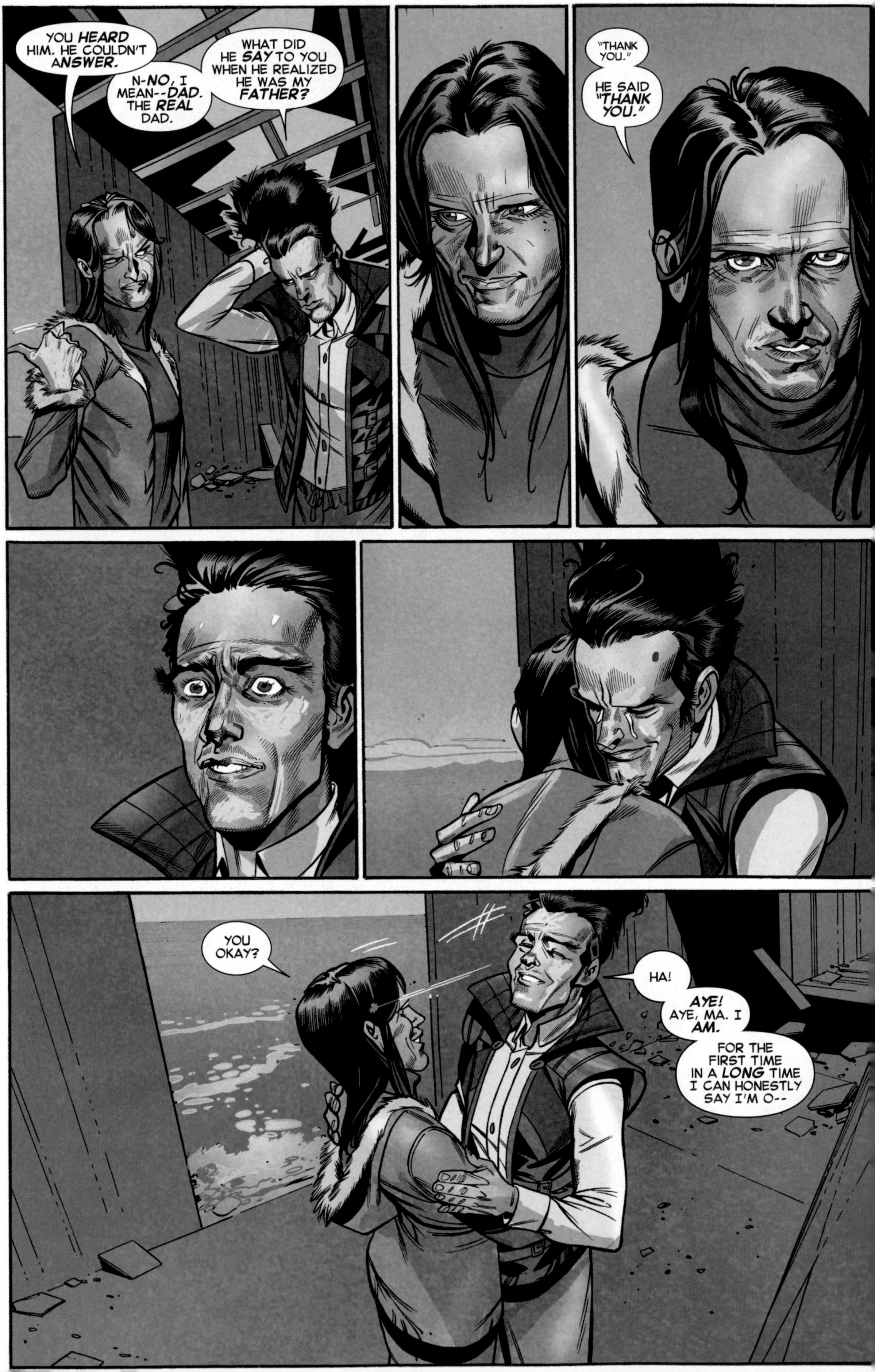
YOU HEARD HIM. HE COULDN'T ANSWER.
N-NO, I MEAN--DAD. THE REAL DAD.
WHAT DID HE SAY TO YOU WHEN HE REALIZED HE WAS MY FATHER?
"THANK YOU."
HE SAID "THANK YOU."
YOU OKAY?
HA!
AYE! AYE, MA. I AM.
FOR THE FIRST TIME IN A LONG TIME I CAN HONESTLY SAY I'M O--

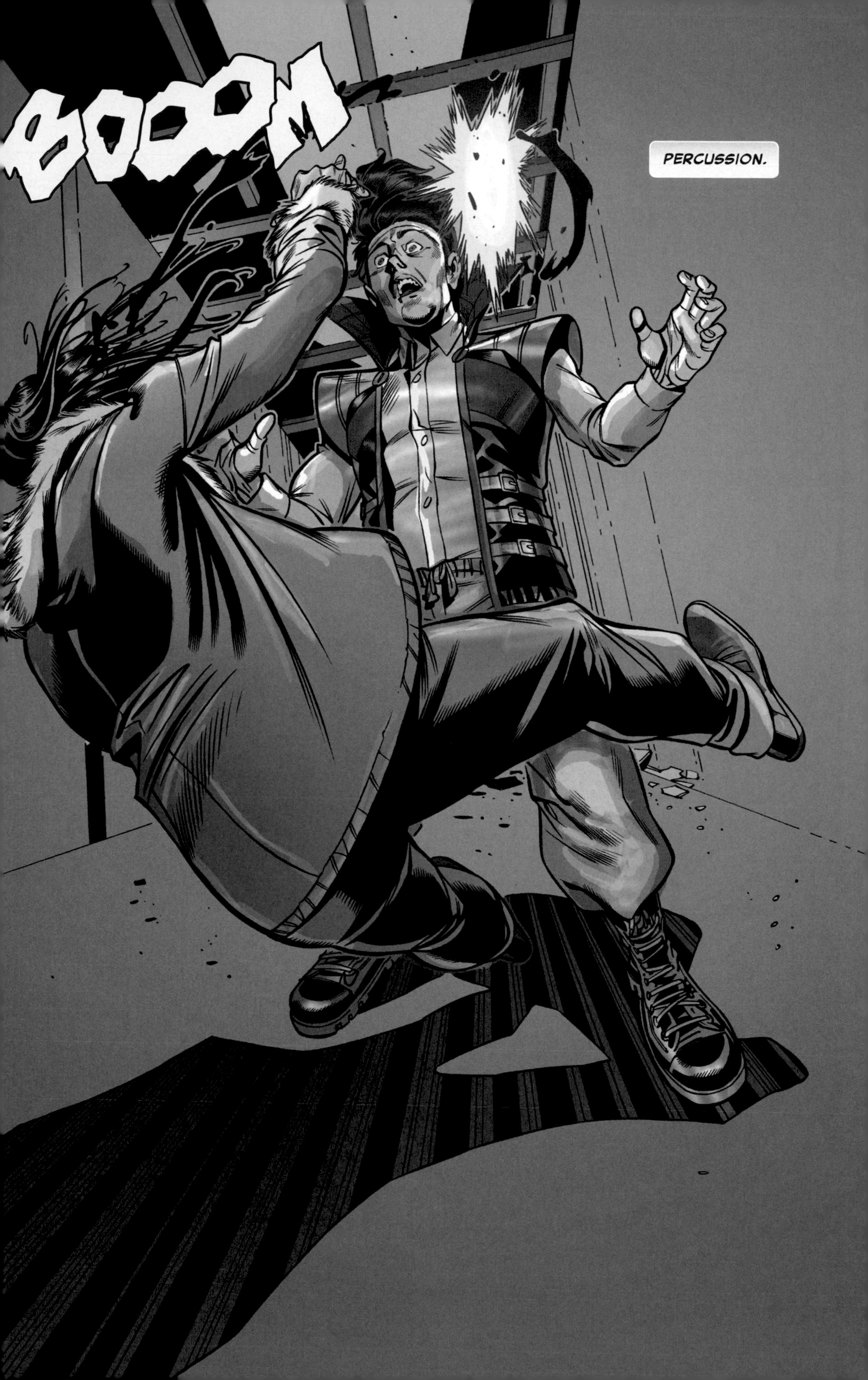
BOOOM
PERCUSSION.

AN ENDLESS BEAT.

<IMBECILE! THREE DAYS TRACKING THE ABOMINATION WHO UNSEATED ME AND YOU CAN'T EVEN H-->*

<HE MOVED!>

*TRANSLATED FROM ARABIC.

SMASH SMASH

POWERS.

NOW.

A BEAT IN MY BLOOD. IN MY HEAD.

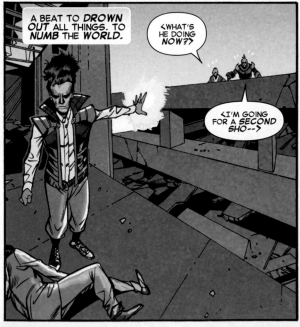

A BEAT TO DROWN OUT ALL THINGS. TO NUMB THE WORLD.

<WHAT'S HE DOING NOW?>

<I'M GOING FOR A SECOND SHO-->

A BEAT RINGING FROM EDGE TO EDGE OF MY CRUMPLED, SHRIVELLED, USELESS %¢£&#@ SOUL.

AAAA AAAA AAAA

SMASH

SMASH

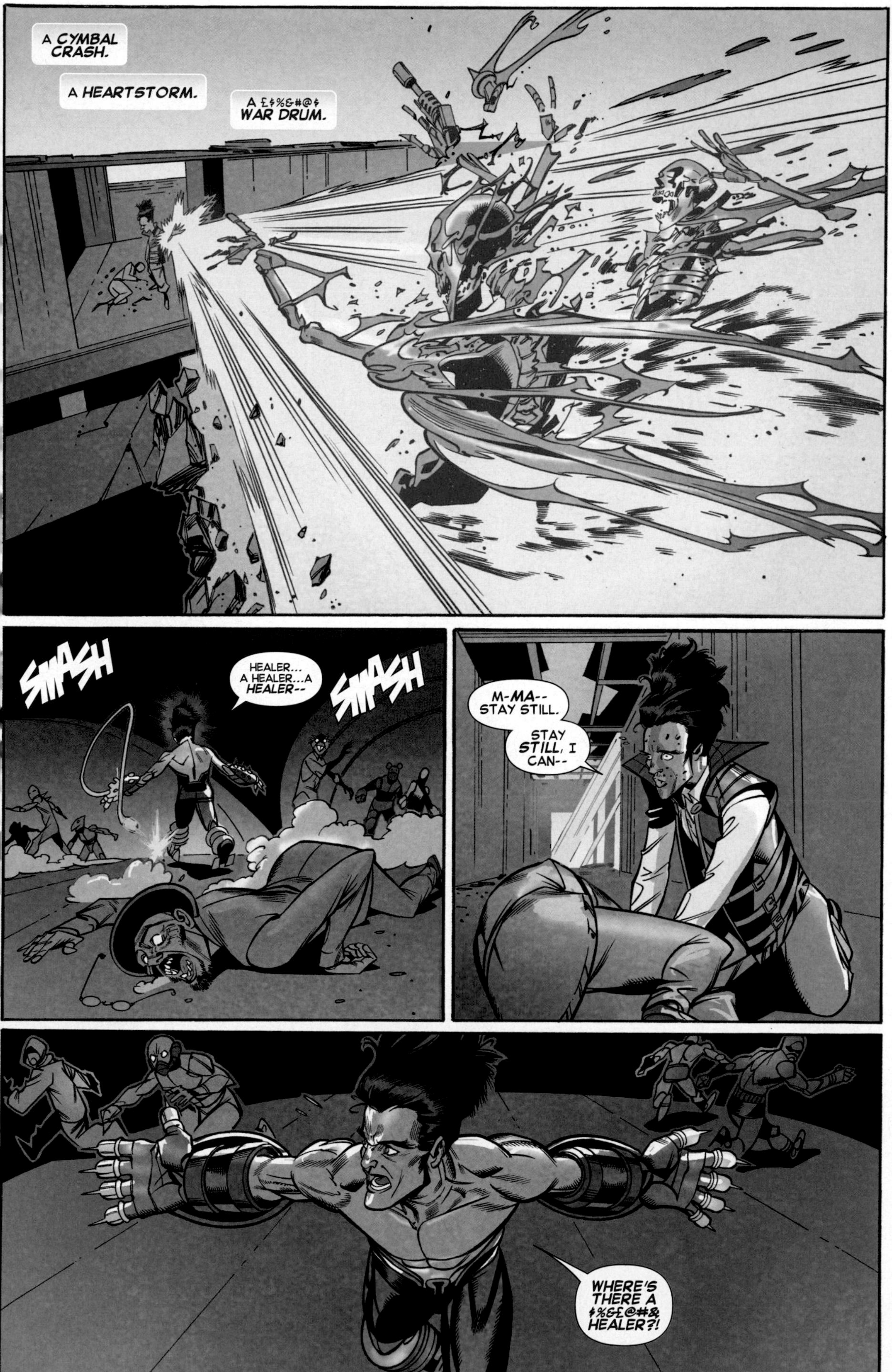
A CYMBAL CRASH.
A HEARTSTORM.
A £$%&#@$ WAR DRUM.
SMASH
HEALER... A HEALER...A HEALER--
SMASH
M-MA-- STAY STILL.
STAY STILL, I CAN--
WHERE'S THERE A $%&£@#& HEALER?!

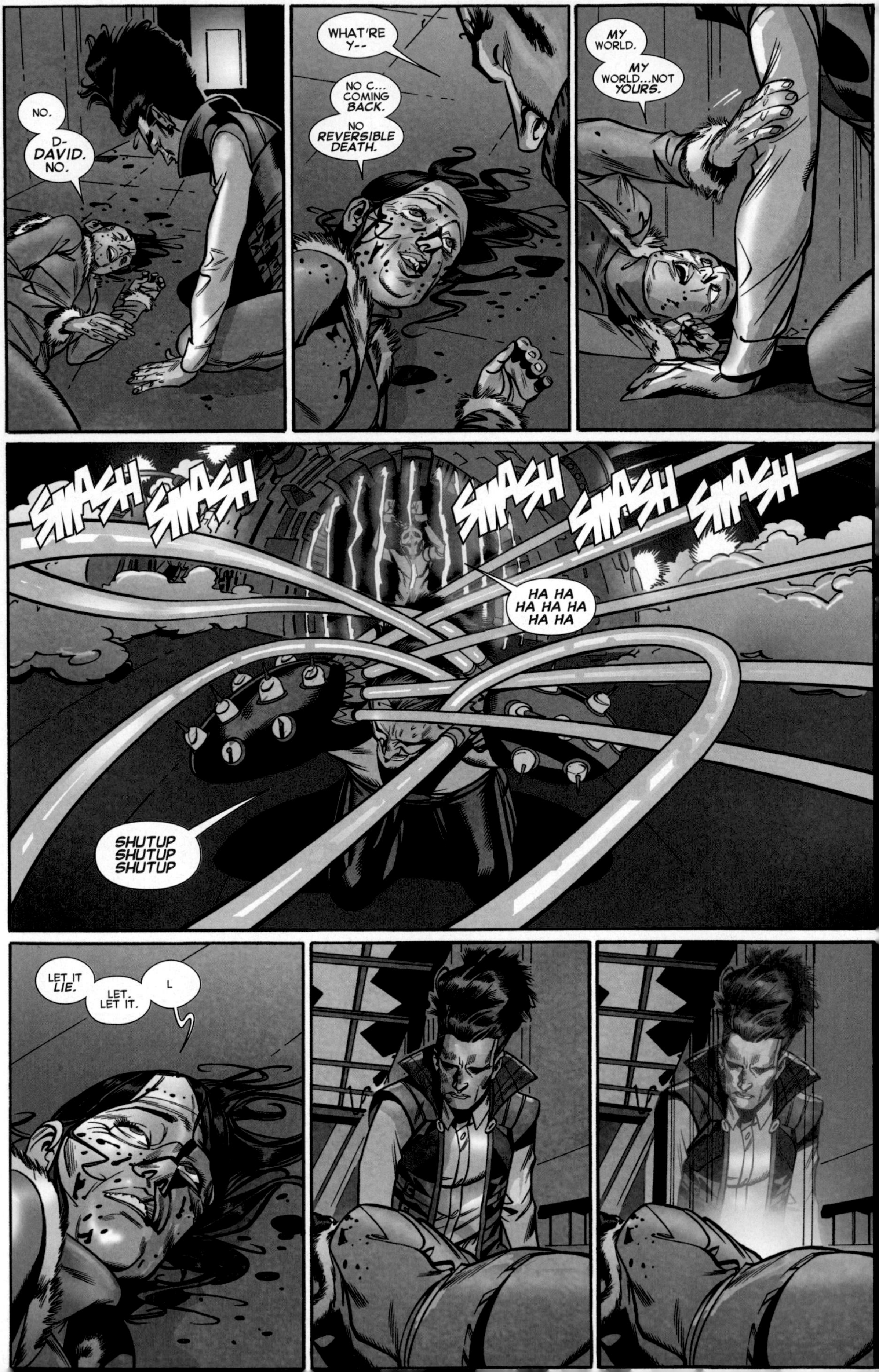
NO.
D-DAVID. NO.
WHAT'RE Y--
NO C... COMING BACK.
NO REVERSIBLE DEATH.
MY WORLD.
MY WORLD...NOT YOURS.
SMASH SMASH SMASH SMASH SMASH
HA HA HA HA HA HA HA
SHUTUP SHUTUP SHUTUP
LET IT LIE.
LET. LET IT.
L

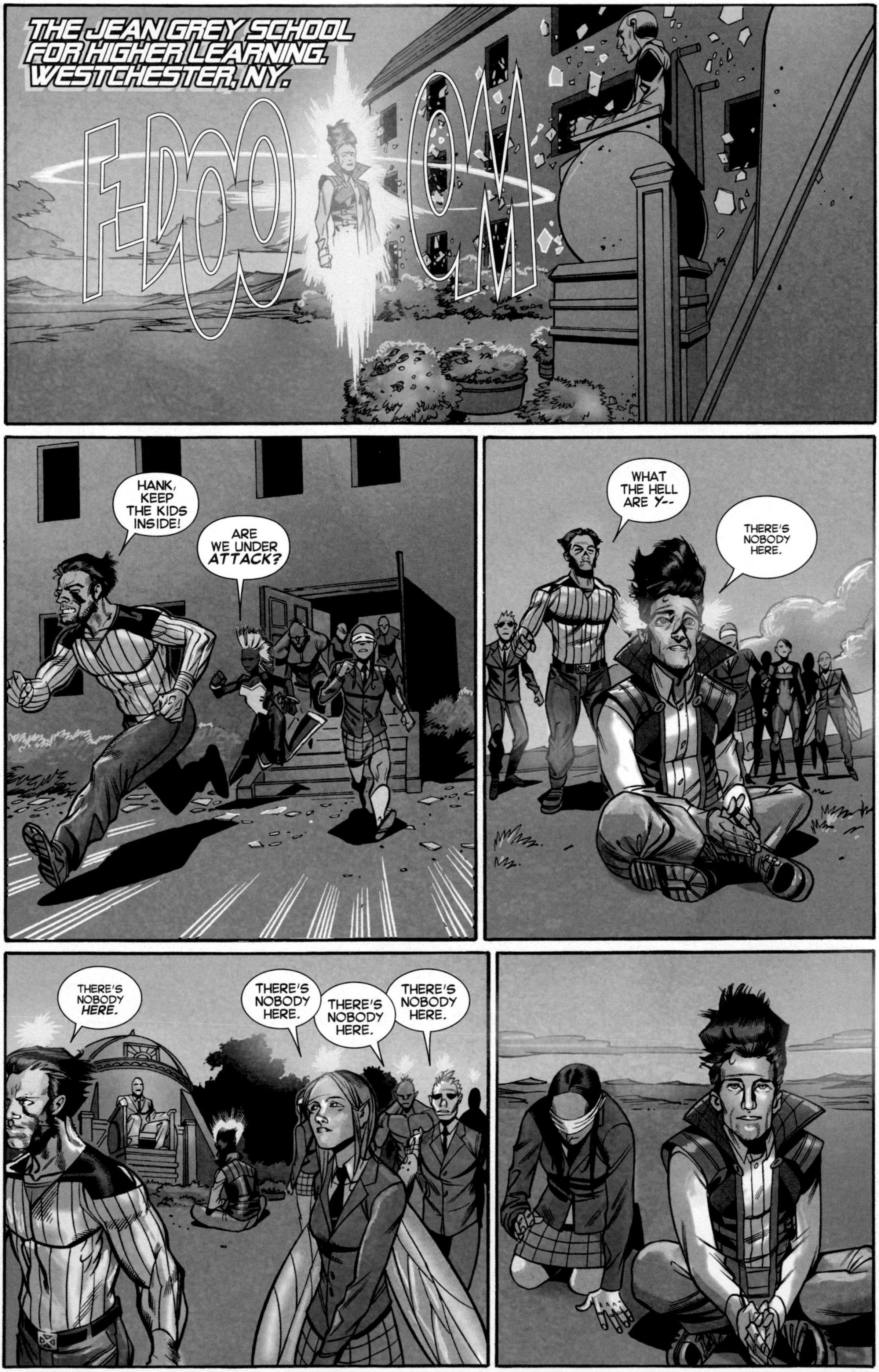
THE JEAN GREY SCHOOL FOR HIGHER LEARNING. WESTCHESTER, NY.
F-DOOOM
HANK, KEEP THE KIDS INSIDE!
ARE WE UNDER ATTACK?
WHAT THE HELL ARE Y--
THERE'S NOBODY HERE.
THERE'S NOBODY HERE.
THERE'S NOBODY HERE.
THERE'S NOBODY HERE.
THERE'S NOBODY HERE.

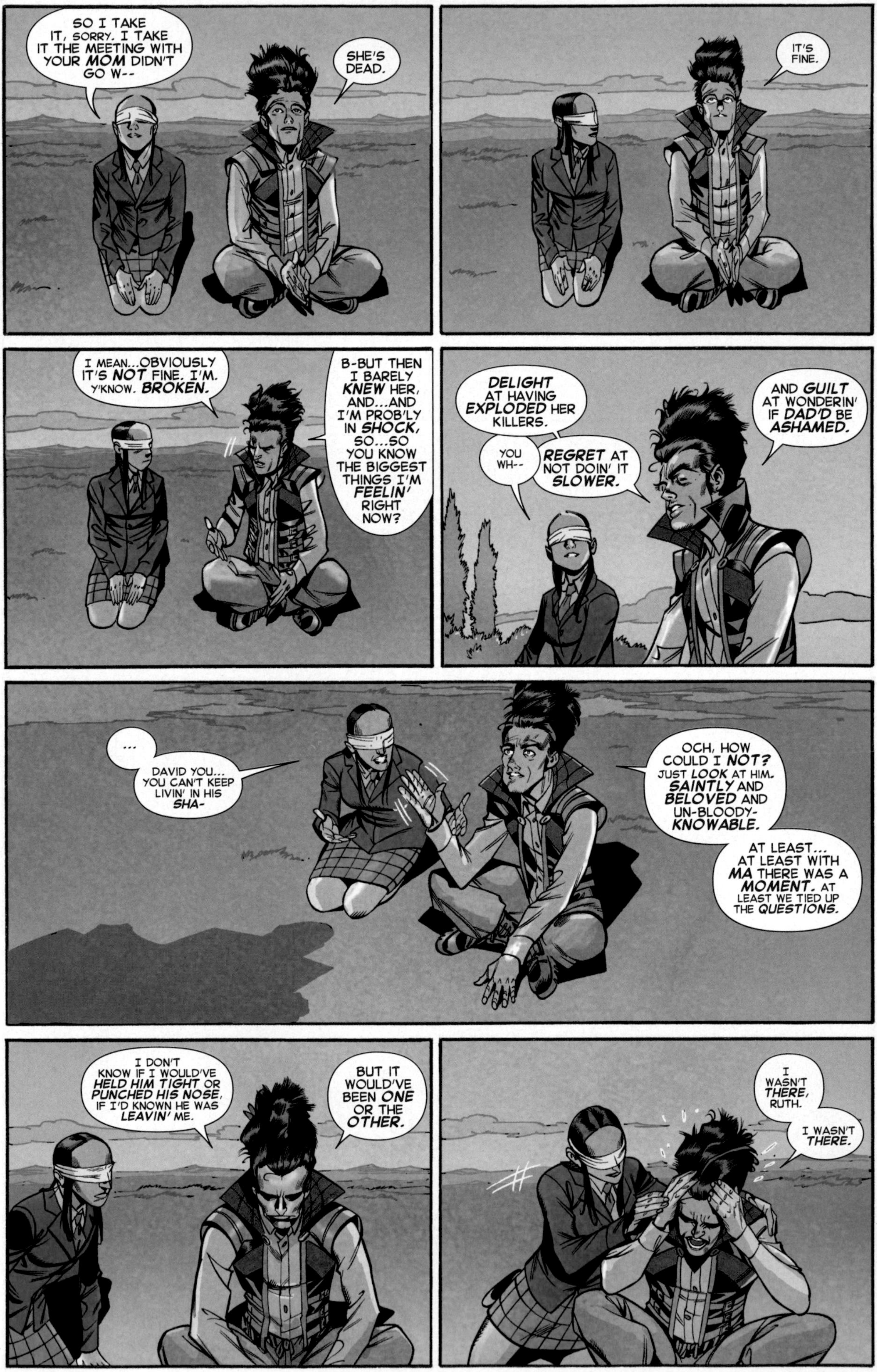
SO I TAKE IT, SORRY. I TAKE IT THE MEETING WITH YOUR MOM DIDN'T GO W--
SHE'S DEAD.
IT'S FINE.
I MEAN...OBVIOUSLY IT'S NOT FINE. I'M. Y'KNOW. BROKEN.
B-BUT THEN I BARELY KNEW HER, AND...AND I'M PROB'LY IN SHOCK, SO...SO YOU KNOW THE BIGGEST THINGS I'M FEELIN' RIGHT NOW?
DELIGHT AT HAVING EXPLODED HER KILLERS.
YOU WH--
REGRET AT NOT DOIN' IT SLOWER.
AND GUILT AT WONDERIN' IF DAD'D BE ASHAMED.
...
DAVID YOU... YOU CAN'T KEEP LIVIN' IN HIS SHA-
OCH, HOW COULD I NOT? JUST LOOK AT HIM. SAINTLY AND BELOVED AND UN-BLOODY-KNOWABLE.
AT LEAST... AT LEAST WITH MA THERE WAS A MOMENT. AT LEAST WE TIED UP THE QUESTIONS.
I DON'T KNOW IF I WOULD'VE HELD HIM TIGHT OR PUNCHED HIS NOSE, IF I'D KNOWN HE WAS LEAVIN' ME.
BUT IT WOULD'VE BEEN ONE OR THE OTHER.
I WASN'T THERE, RUTH.
I WASN'T THERE.

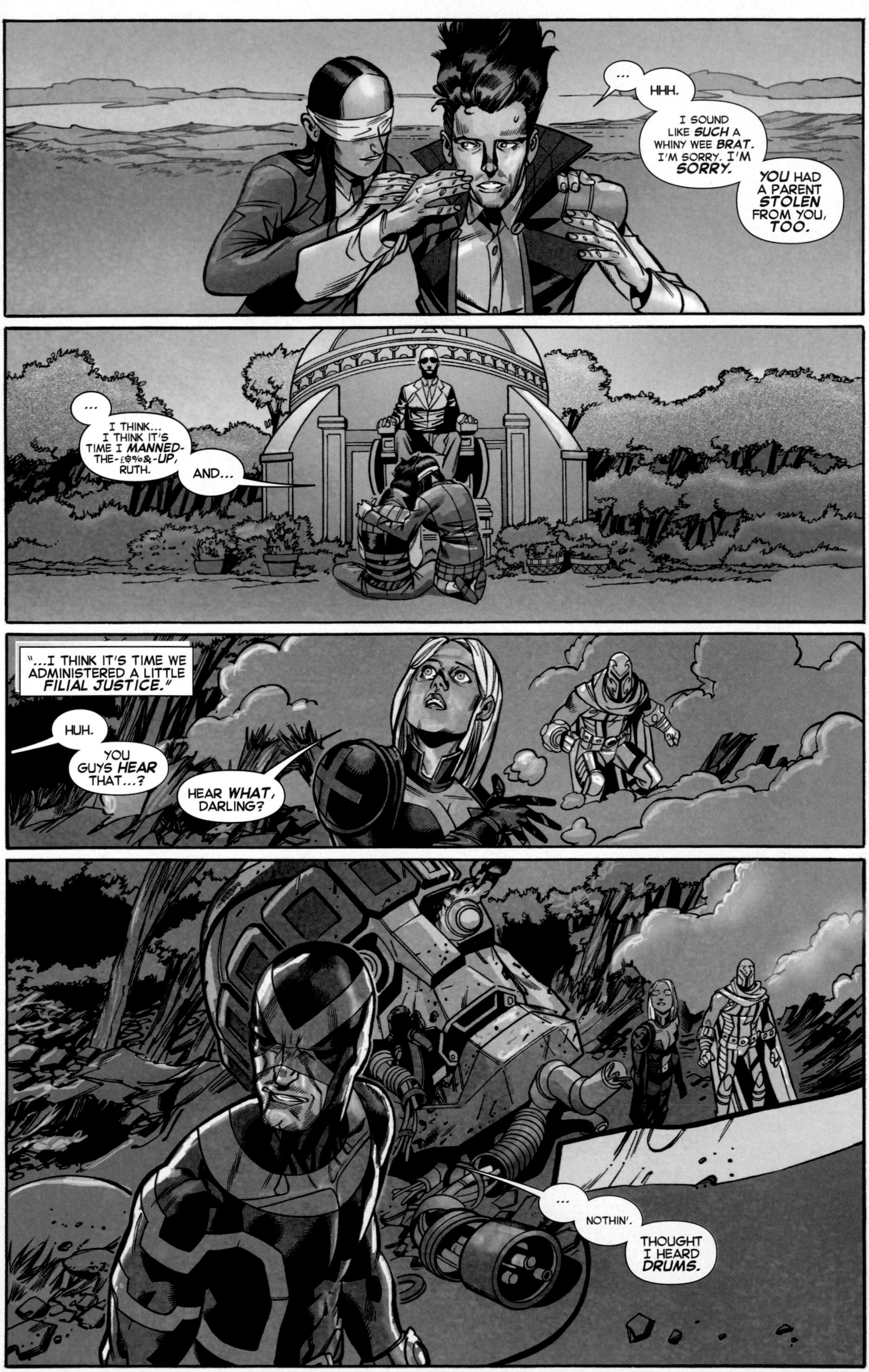
...
HHH.
I SOUND LIKE SUCH A WHINY WEE BRAT. I'M SORRY. I'M SORRY.
YOU HAD A PARENT STOLEN FROM YOU, TOO.
...
I THINK... I THINK IT'S TIME I MANNED-THE-£$%&-UP, RUTH.
AND...
"...I THINK IT'S TIME WE ADMINISTERED A LITTLE FILIAL JUSTICE."
HUH.
YOU GUYS HEAR THAT...?
HEAR WHAT, DARLING?
...
NOTHIN'.
THOUGHT I HEARD DRUMS.

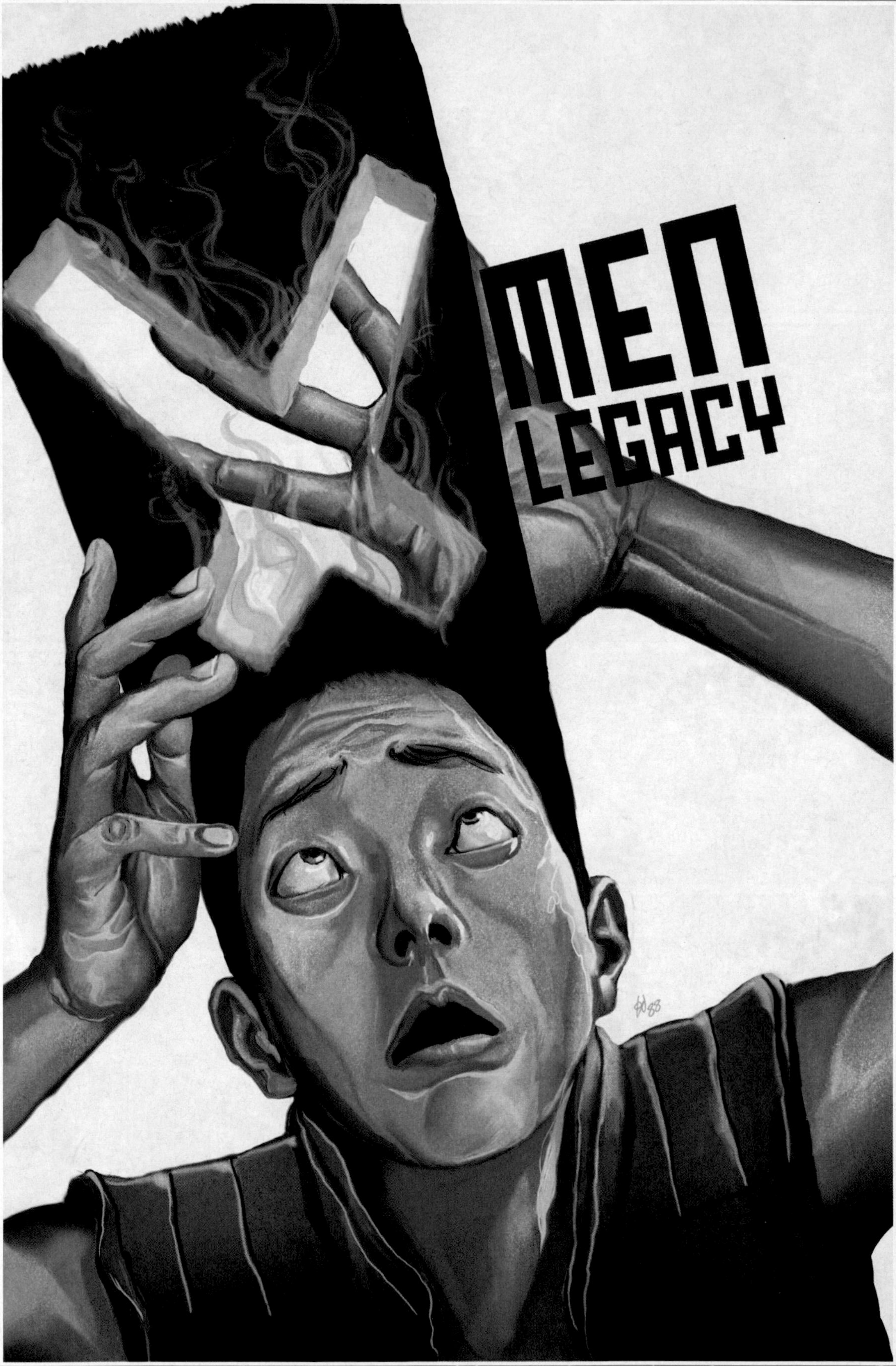
MEN
LEGACY

SIXTEEN

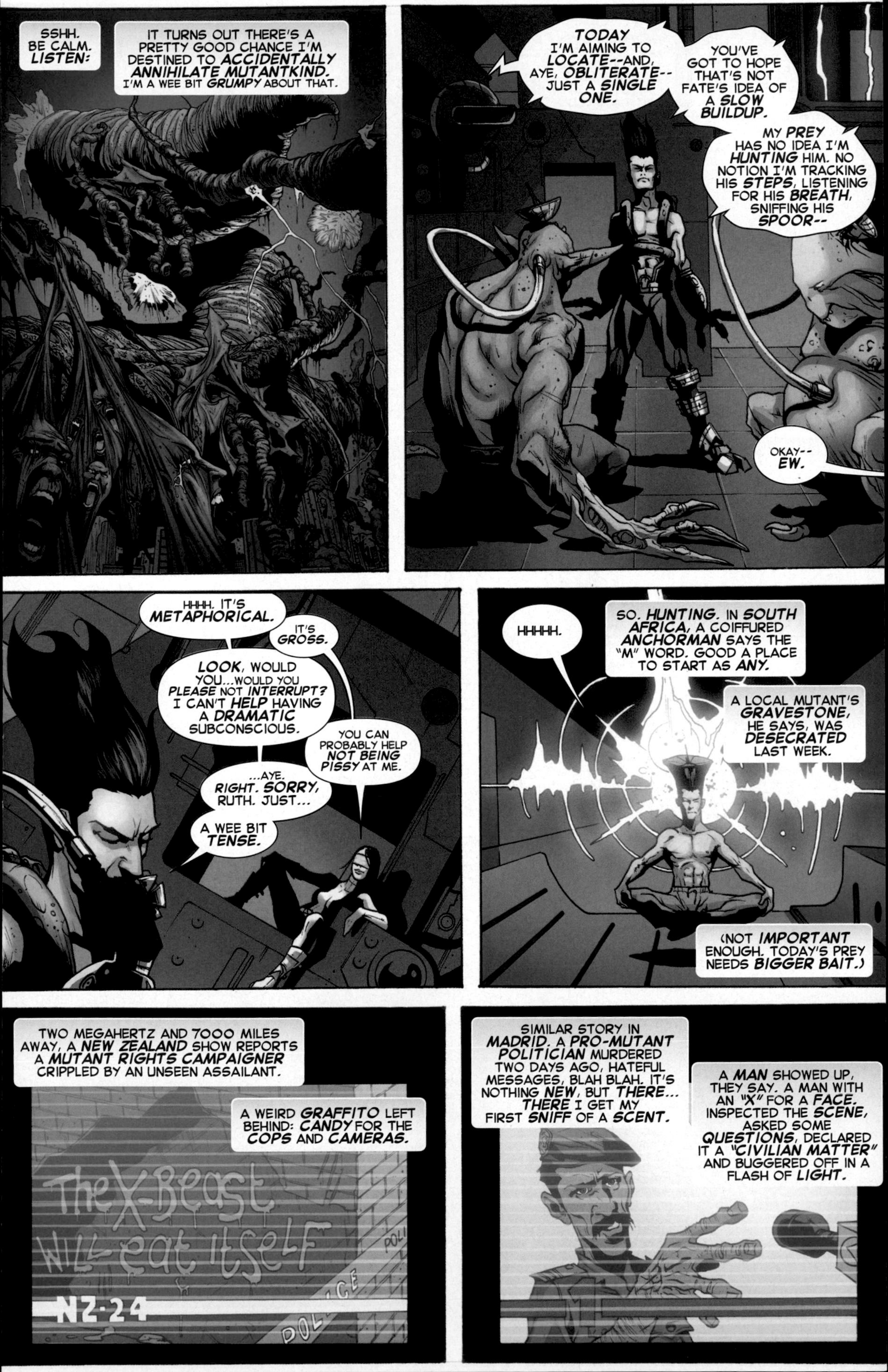
SSHH. BE CALM. LISTEN:
IT TURNS OUT THERE'S A PRETTY GOOD CHANCE I'M DESTINED TO ACCIDENTALLY ANNIHILATE MUTANTKIND. I'M A WEE BIT GRUMPY ABOUT THAT.
TODAY I'M AIMING TO LOCATE--AND, AYE, OBLITERATE--JUST A SINGLE ONE.
YOU'VE GOT TO HOPE THAT'S NOT FATE'S IDEA OF A SLOW BUILDUP.
MY PREY HAS NO IDEA I'M HUNTING HIM. NO NOTION I'M TRACKING HIS STEPS, LISTENING FOR HIS BREATH, SNIFFING HIS SPOOR--
OKAY-- EW.
HHHH. IT'S METAPHORICAL.
IT'S GROSS.
LOOK, WOULD YOU...WOULD YOU PLEASE NOT INTERRUPT? I CAN'T HELP HAVING A DRAMATIC SUBCONSCIOUS.
YOU CAN PROBABLY HELP NOT BEING PISSY AT ME.
...AYE. RIGHT. SORRY, RUTH. JUST...
A WEE BIT TENSE.
HHHHH.
SO. HUNTING. IN SOUTH AFRICA, A COIFFURED ANCHORMAN SAYS THE "M" WORD. GOOD A PLACE TO START AS ANY.
A LOCAL MUTANT'S GRAVESTONE, HE SAYS, WAS DESECRATED LAST WEEK.
(NOT IMPORTANT ENOUGH. TODAY'S PREY NEEDS BIGGER BAIT.)
TWO MEGAHERTZ AND 7000 MILES AWAY, A NEW ZEALAND SHOW REPORTS A MUTANT RIGHTS CAMPAIGNER CRIPPLED BY AN UNSEEN ASSAILANT.
A WEIRD GRAFFITO LEFT BEHIND: CANDY FOR THE COPS AND CAMERAS.
The X-Beast WILL eat itself
POLI
POLICE
NZ-24
SIMILAR STORY IN MADRID. A PRO-MUTANT POLITICIAN MURDERED TWO DAYS AGO, HATEFUL MESSAGES, BLAH BLAH. IT'S NOTHING NEW, BUT THERE... THERE I GET MY FIRST SNIFF OF A SCENT.
A MAN SHOWED UP, THEY SAY. A MAN WITH AN "X" FOR A FACE. INSPECTED THE SCENE, ASKED SOME QUESTIONS, DECLARED IT A "CIVILIAN MATTER" AND BUGGERED OFF IN A FLASH OF LIGHT.

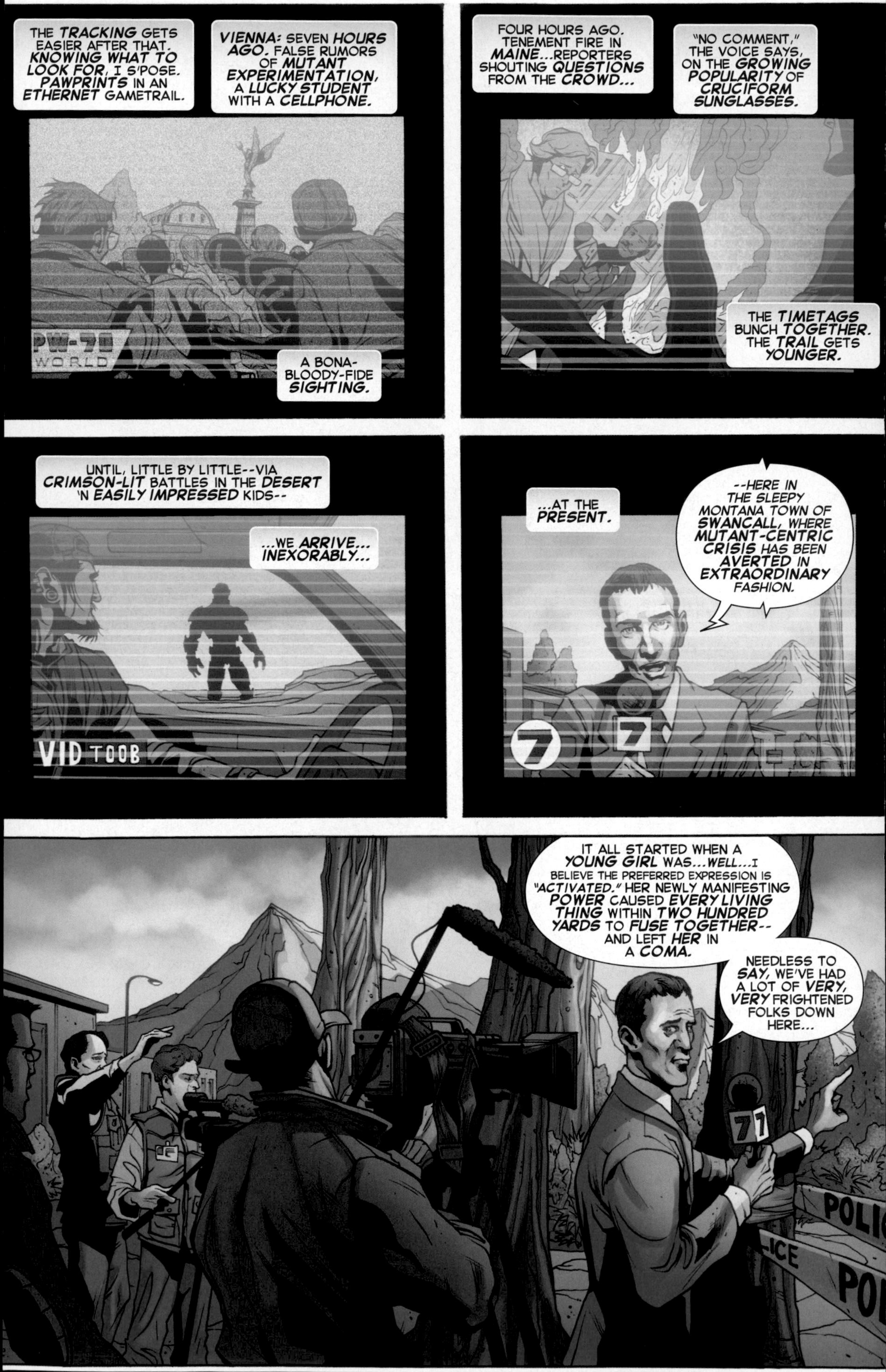
THE TRACKING GETS EASIER AFTER THAT. KNOWING WHAT TO LOOK FOR, I S'POSE. PAWPRINTS IN AN ETHERNET GAMETRAIL.
VIENNA: SEVEN HOURS AGO. FALSE RUMORS OF MUTANT EXPERIMENTATION, A LUCKY STUDENT WITH A CELLPHONE.
PW-7
WORLD
A BONA-BLOODY-FIDE SIGHTING.
FOUR HOURS AGO. TENEMENT FIRE IN MAINE...REPORTERS SHOUTING QUESTIONS FROM THE CROWD...
"NO COMMENT," THE VOICE SAYS, ON THE GROWING POPULARITY OF CRUCIFORM SUNGLASSES.
THE TIMETAGS BUNCH TOGETHER. THE TRAIL GETS YOUNGER.
UNTIL, LITTLE BY LITTLE--VIA CRIMSON-LIT BATTLES IN THE DESERT 'N EASILY IMPRESSED KIDS--
...WE ARRIVE... INEXORABLY...
VID TOOB
...AT THE PRESENT.
--HERE IN THE SLEEPY MONTANA TOWN OF SWANCALL, WHERE MUTANT-CENTRIC CRISIS HAS BEEN AVERTED IN EXTRAORDINARY FASHION.
7
IT ALL STARTED WHEN A YOUNG GIRL WAS...WELL...I BELIEVE THE PREFERRED EXPRESSION IS "ACTIVATED." HER NEWLY MANIFESTING POWER CAUSED EVERY LIVING THING WITHIN TWO HUNDRED YARDS TO FUSE TOGETHER--AND LEFT HER IN A COMA.
NEEDLESS TO SAY, WE'VE HAD A LOT OF VERY, VERY FRIGHTENED FOLKS DOWN HERE...
7
POLIC
ICE

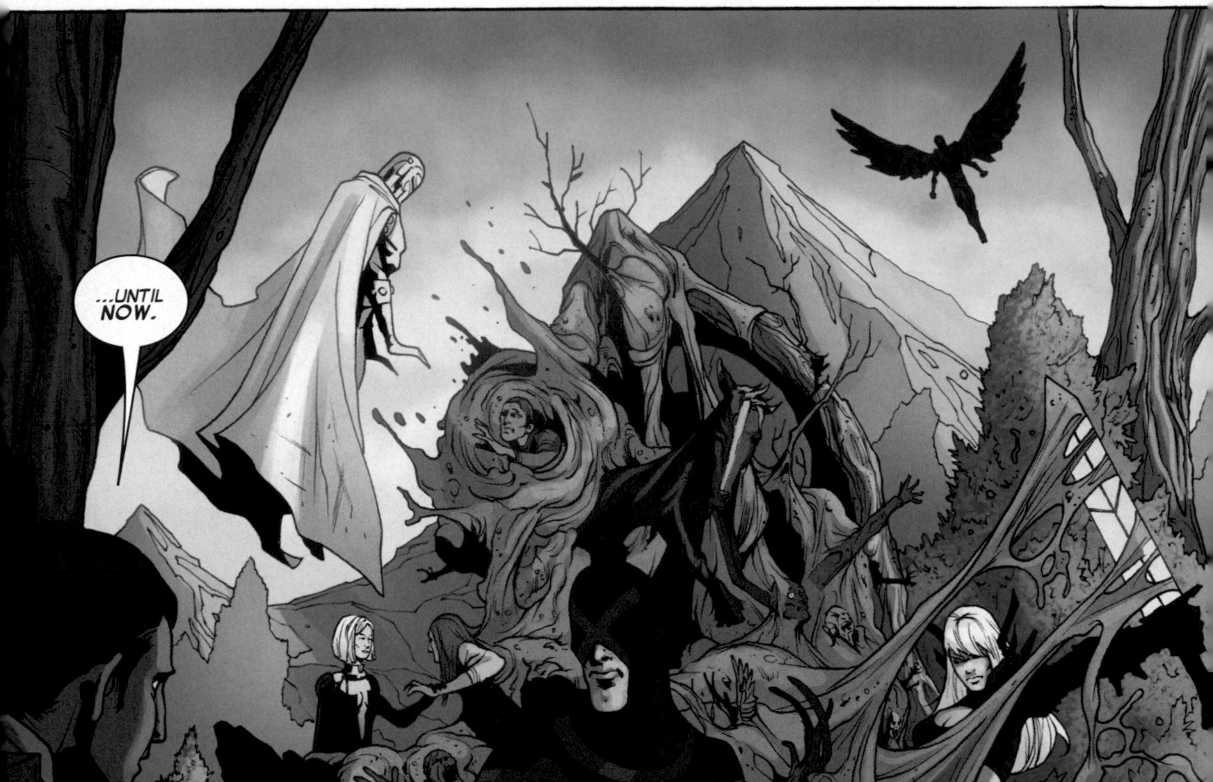
...UNTIL NOW.
NOTHING TO WORRY ABOUT, FOLKS. WE GOT THIS.
POLICE
POLICE

WEAR THE GRUDGE

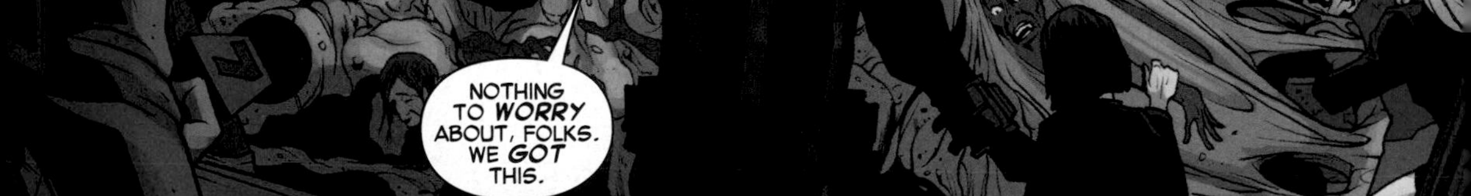
GOT YOU, YOU FATHER-MURDERING NUMPTY £$%&.

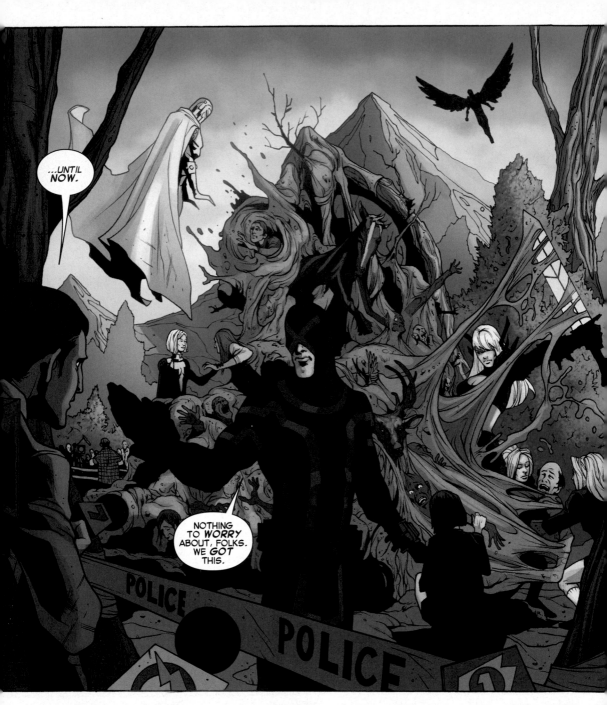

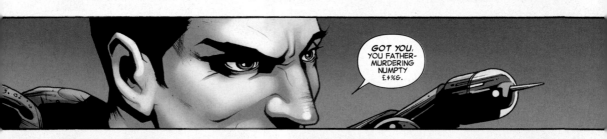

LIKE A CROWN

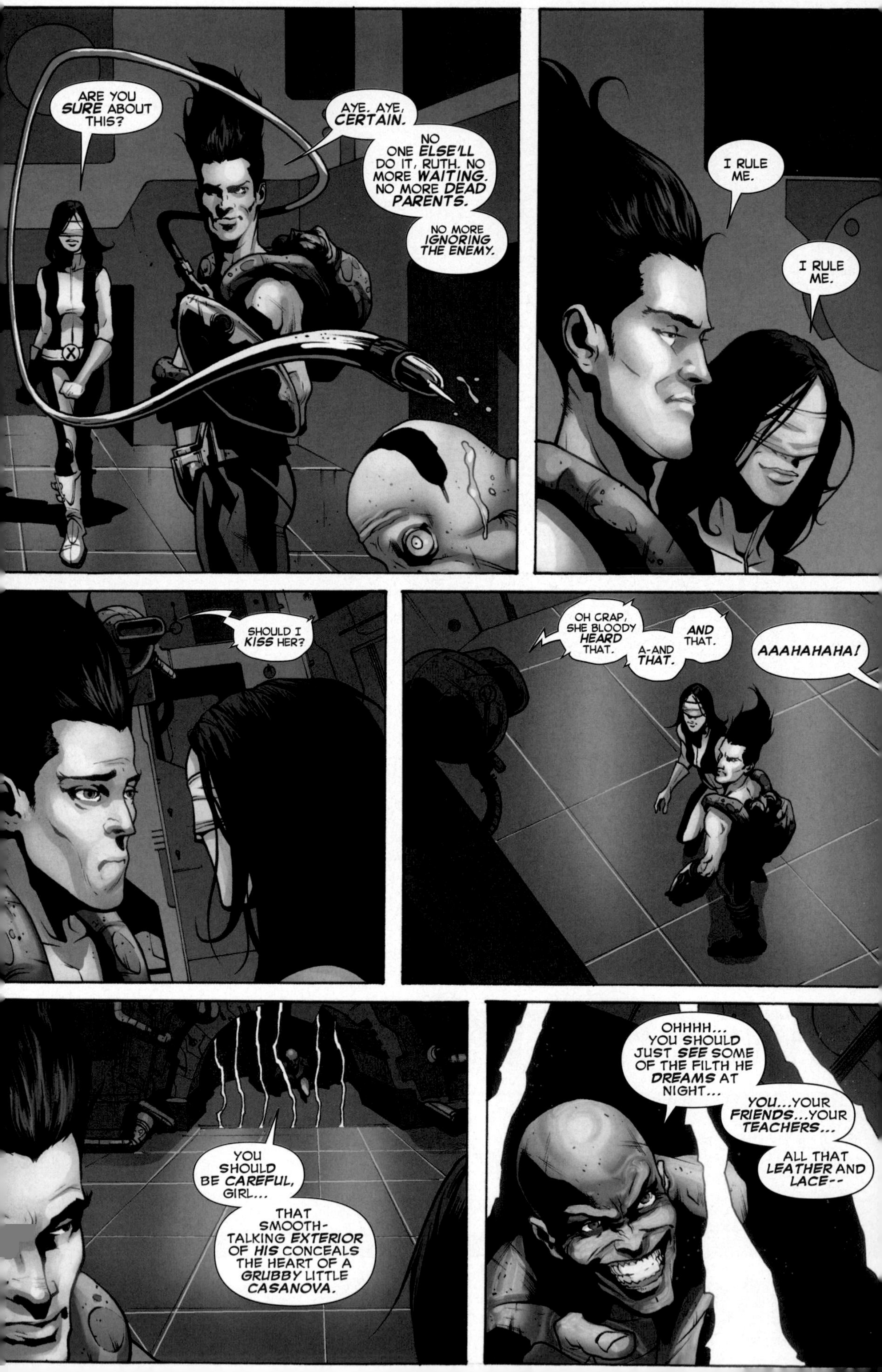
ARE YOU SURE ABOUT THIS?
AYE. AYE, CERTAIN.
NO ONE ELSE'LL DO IT, RUTH. NO MORE WAITING. NO MORE DEAD PARENTS.
NO MORE IGNORING THE ENEMY.
I RULE ME.
I RULE ME.
SHOULD I KISS HER?
OH CRAP, SHE BLOODY HEARD THAT.
AND THAT.
A-AND THAT.
AAAHAHAHA!
YOU SHOULD BE CAREFUL, GIRL...
THAT SMOOTH-TALKING EXTERIOR OF HIS CONCEALS THE HEART OF A GRUBBY LITTLE CASANOVA.
OHHHH... YOU SHOULD JUST SEE SOME OF THE FILTH HE DREAMS AT NIGHT...
YOU...YOUR FRIENDS...YOUR TEACHERS...
ALL THAT LEATHER AND LACE--

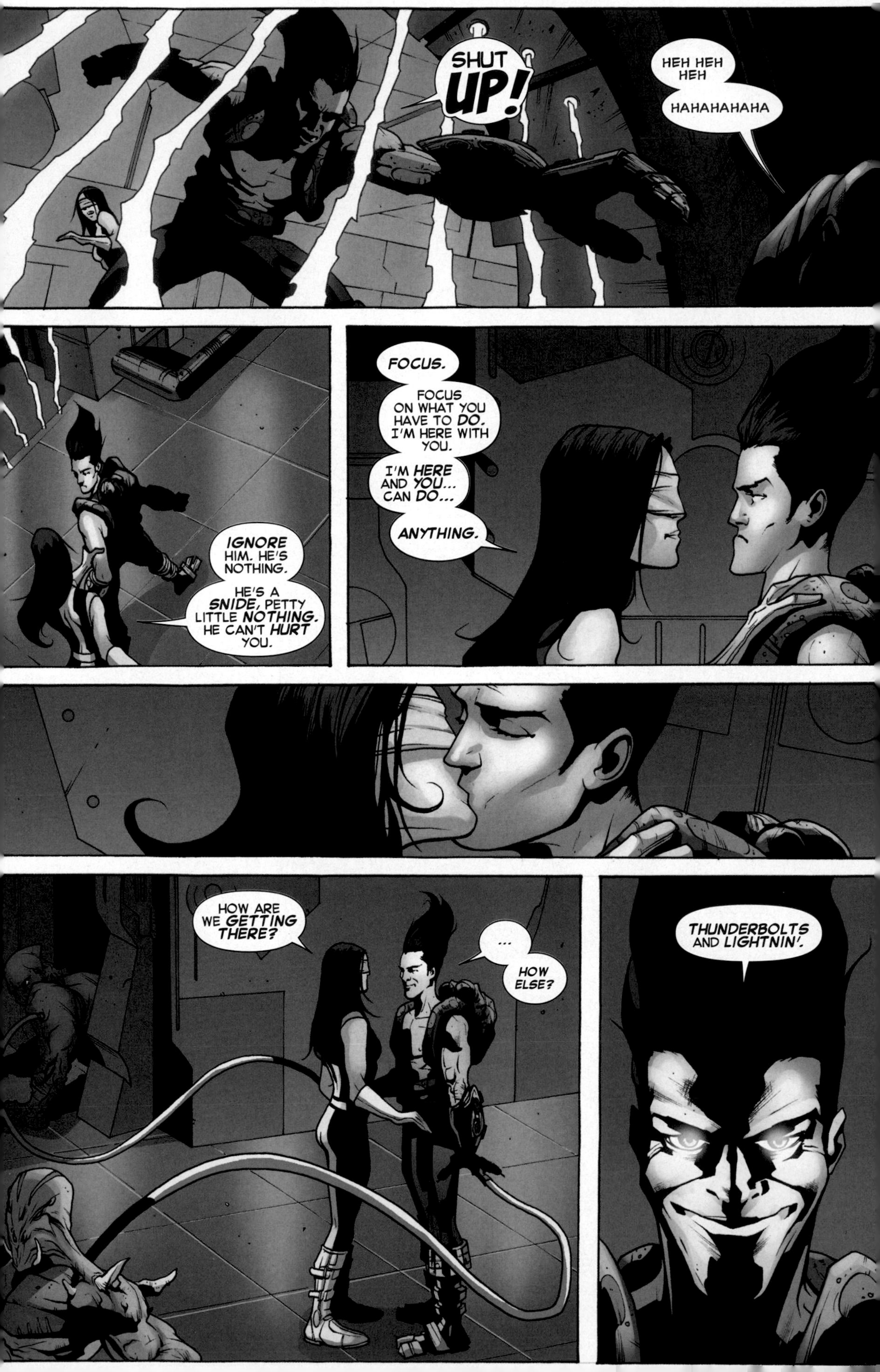
SHUT UP!
HEH HEH HEH
HAHAHAHAHA
IGNORE HIM. HE'S NOTHING.
HE'S A SNIDE, PETTY LITTLE NOTHING. HE CAN'T HURT YOU.
FOCUS.
FOCUS ON WHAT YOU HAVE TO DO. I'M HERE WITH YOU.
I'M HERE AND YOU... CAN DO...
ANYTHING.
HOW ARE WE GETTING THERE?
...
HOW ELSE?
THUNDERBOLTS AND LIGHTNIN'.

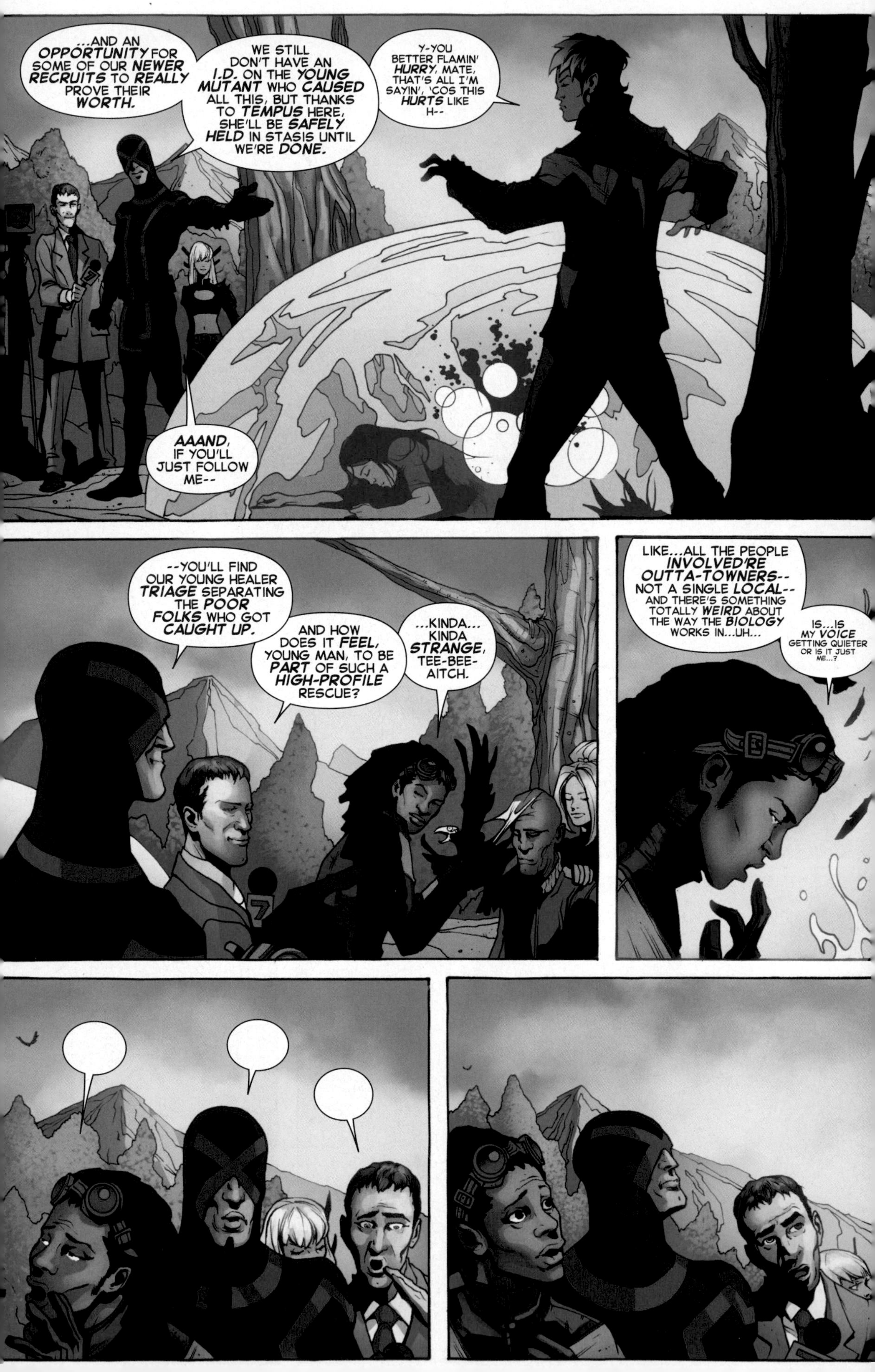
...AND AN OPPORTUNITY FOR SOME OF OUR NEWER RECRUITS TO REALLY PROVE THEIR WORTH.
WE STILL DON'T HAVE AN I.D. ON THE YOUNG MUTANT WHO CAUSED ALL THIS, BUT THANKS TO TEMPUS HERE, SHE'LL BE SAFELY HELD IN STASIS UNTIL WE'RE DONE.
Y-YOU BETTER FLAMIN' HURRY, MATE, THAT'S ALL I'M SAYIN', 'COS THIS HURTS LIKE H--
AAAND, IF YOU'LL JUST FOLLOW ME--
--YOU'LL FIND OUR YOUNG HEALER TRIAGE SEPARATING THE POOR FOLKS WHO GOT CAUGHT UP.
AND HOW DOES IT FEEL, YOUNG MAN, TO BE PART OF SUCH A HIGH-PROFILE RESCUE?
...KINDA... KINDA STRANGE, TEE-BEE-AITCH.
LIKE...ALL THE PEOPLE INVOLVED'RE OUTTA-TOWNERS-- NOT A SINGLE LOCAL-- AND THERE'S SOMETHING TOTALLY WEIRD ABOUT THE WAY THE BIOLOGY WORKS IN...UH...
IS...IS MY VOICE GETTING QUIETER OR IS IT JUST ME...?

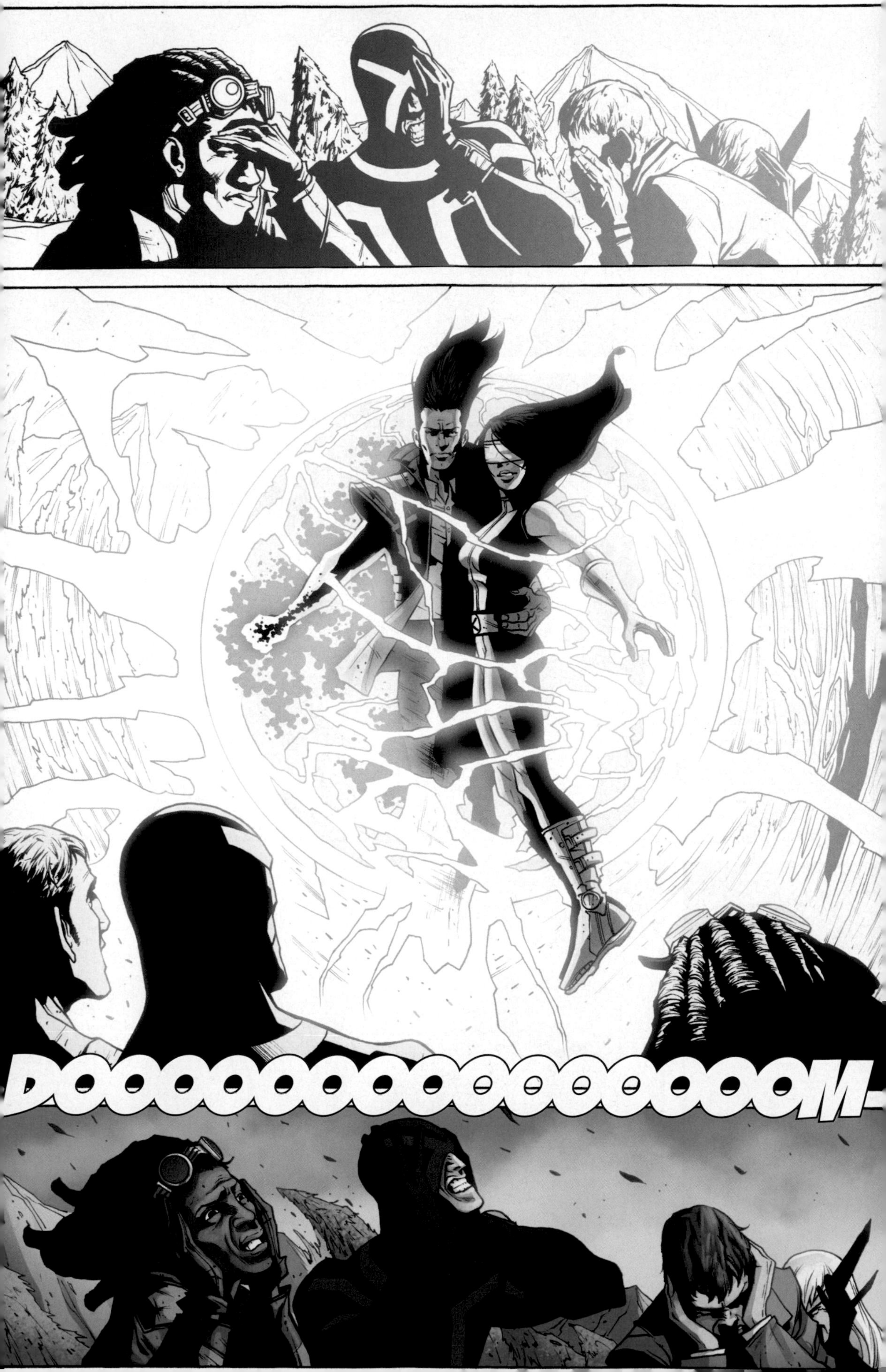
DOOOOOOOOOOOOOOOM-

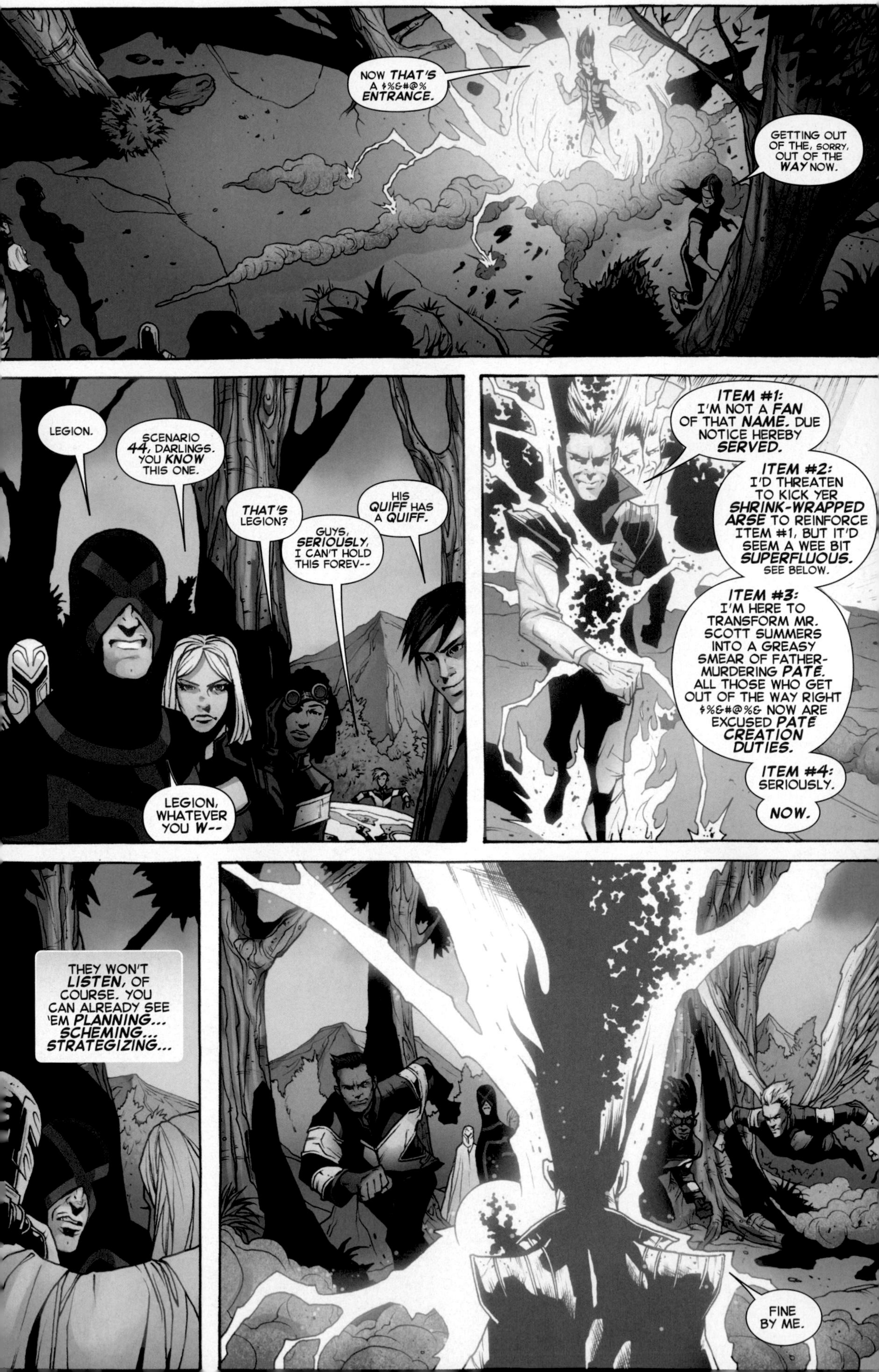
NOW THAT'S A $%&#@% ENTRANCE.
GETTING OUT OF THE, SORRY, OUT OF THE WAY NOW.
LEGION.
SCENARIO 44, DARLINGS. YOU KNOW THIS ONE.
THAT'S LEGION?
HIS QUIFF HAS A QUIFF.
GUYS, SERIOUSLY, I CAN'T HOLD THIS FOREV--
LEGION, WHATEVER YOU W--
ITEM #1: I'M NOT A FAN OF THAT NAME. DUE NOTICE HEREBY SERVED.
ITEM #2: I'D THREATEN TO KICK YER SHRINK-WRAPPED ARSE TO REINFORCE ITEM #1, BUT IT'D SEEM A WEE BIT SUPERFLUOUS. SEE BELOW.
ITEM #3: I'M HERE TO TRANSFORM MR. SCOTT SUMMERS INTO A GREASY SMEAR OF FATHER-MURDERING PATE. ALL THOSE WHO GET OUT OF THE WAY RIGHT $%&#@%& NOW ARE EXCUSED PATE CREATION DUTIES.
ITEM #4: SERIOUSLY.
NOW.
THEY WON'T LISTEN, OF COURSE. YOU CAN ALREADY SEE 'EM PLANNING... SCHEMING... STRATEGIZING...
FINE BY ME.

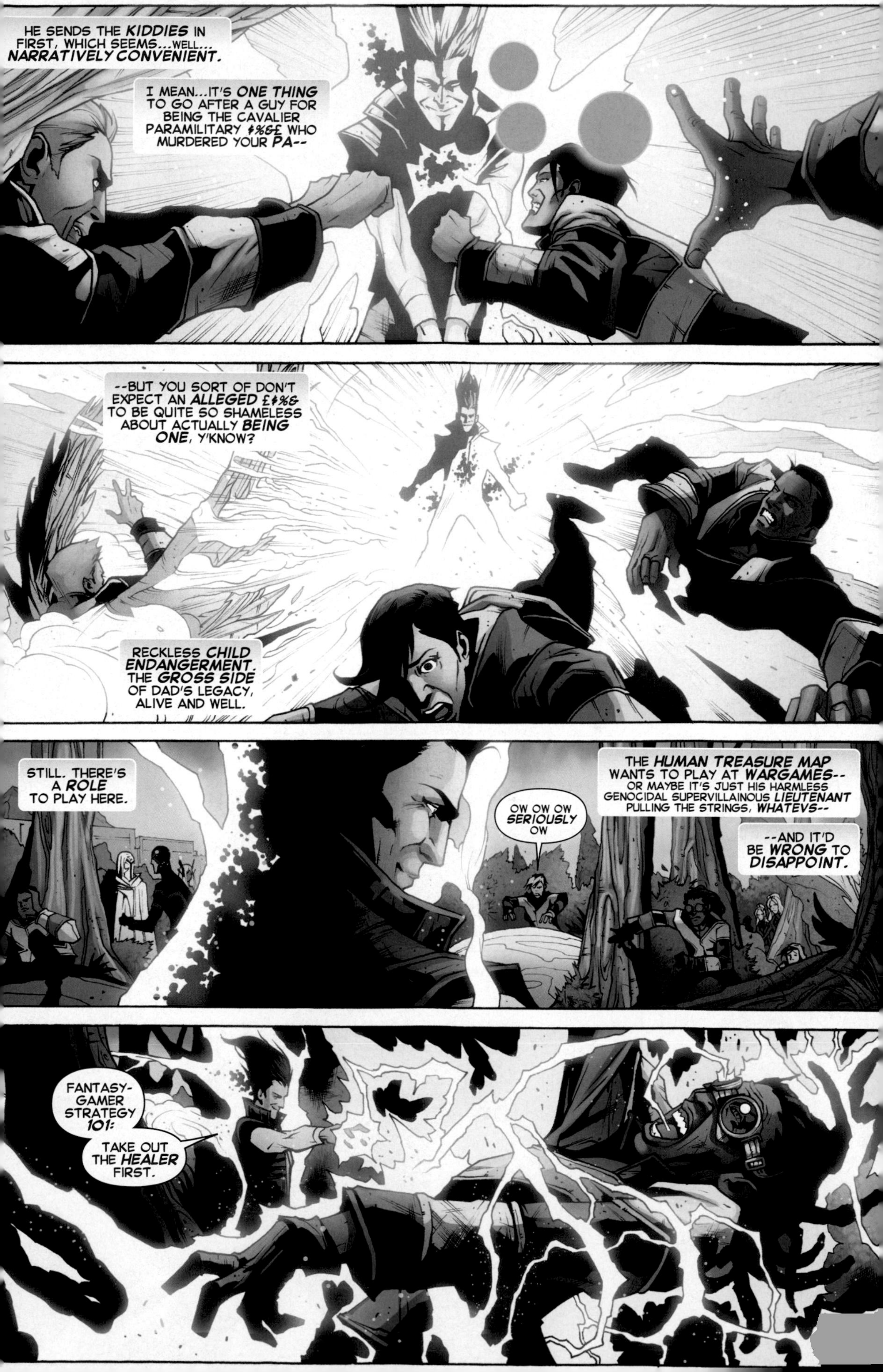
HE SENDS THE KIDDIES IN FIRST, WHICH SEEMS...WELL... NARRATIVELY CONVENIENT.
I MEAN...IT'S ONE THING TO GO AFTER A GUY FOR BEING THE CAVALIER PARAMILITARY ¢%&£ WHO MURDERED YOUR PA--
--BUT YOU SORT OF DON'T EXPECT AN ALLEGED £¢%& TO BE QUITE SO SHAMELESS ABOUT ACTUALLY BEING ONE, Y'KNOW?
RECKLESS CHILD ENDANGERMENT. THE GROSS SIDE OF DAD'S LEGACY, ALIVE AND WELL.
STILL. THERE'S A ROLE TO PLAY HERE.
OW OW OW SERIOUSLY OW
THE HUMAN TREASURE MAP WANTS TO PLAY AT WARGAMES-- OR MAYBE IT'S JUST HIS HARMLESS GENOCIDAL SUPERVILLAINOUS LIEUTENANT PULLING THE STRINGS, WHATEVS--
--AND IT'D BE WRONG TO DISAPPOINT.
FANTASY-GAMER STRATEGY 101:
TAKE OUT THE HEALER FIRST.

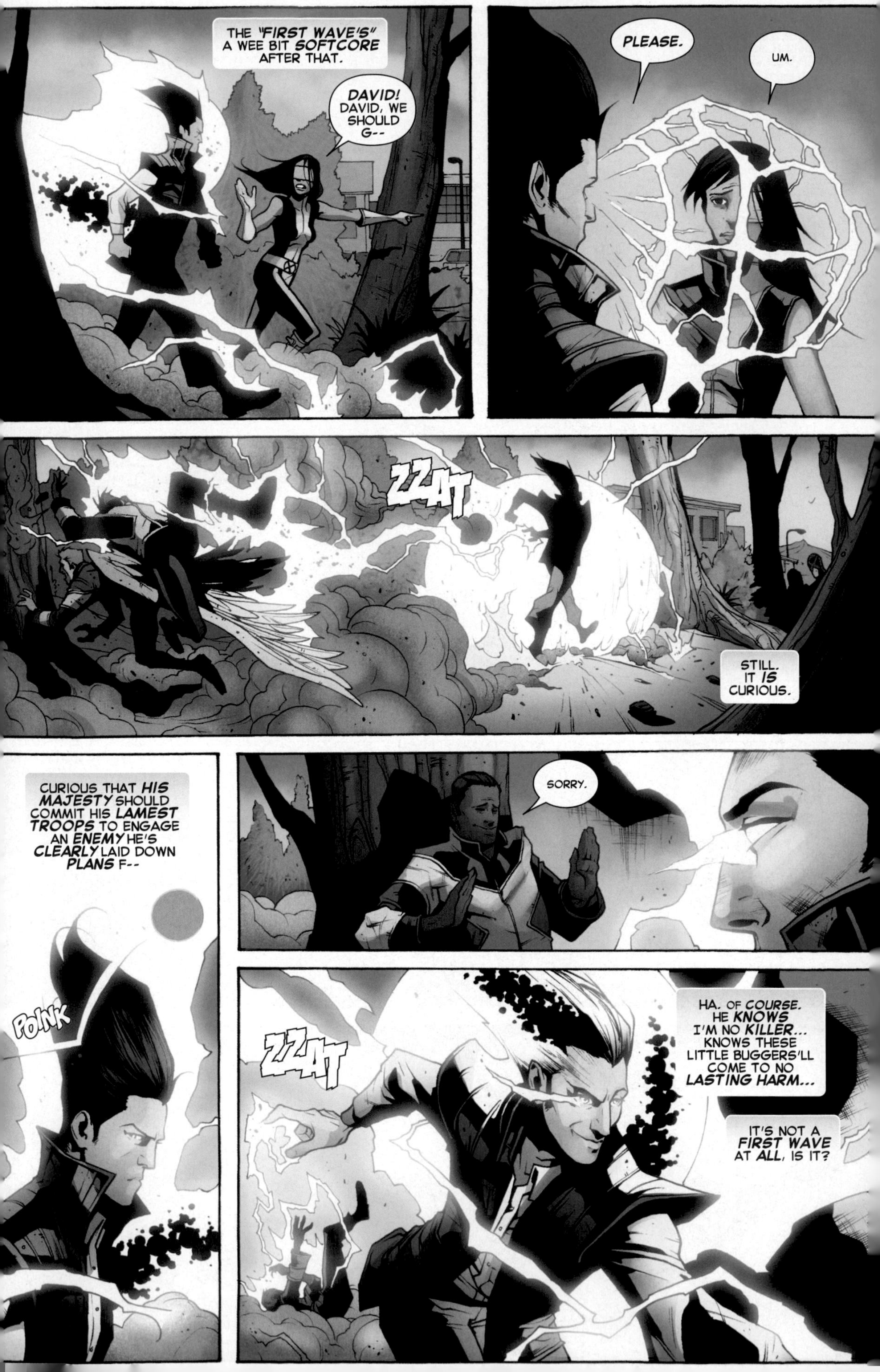
THE "FIRST WAVE'S" A WEE BIT SOFTCORE AFTER THAT.
DAVID! DAVID, WE SHOULD G--
PLEASE.
UM.
ZZAT
STILL. IT IS CURIOUS.
CURIOUS THAT HIS MAJESTY SHOULD COMMIT HIS LAMEST TROOPS TO ENGAGE AN ENEMY HE'S CLEARLY LAID DOWN PLANS F--
POINK
SORRY.
ZZAT
HA. OF COURSE. HE KNOWS I'M NO KILLER... KNOWS THESE LITTLE BUGGERS'LL COME TO NO LASTING HARM...
IT'S NOT A FIRST WAVE AT ALL, IS IT?

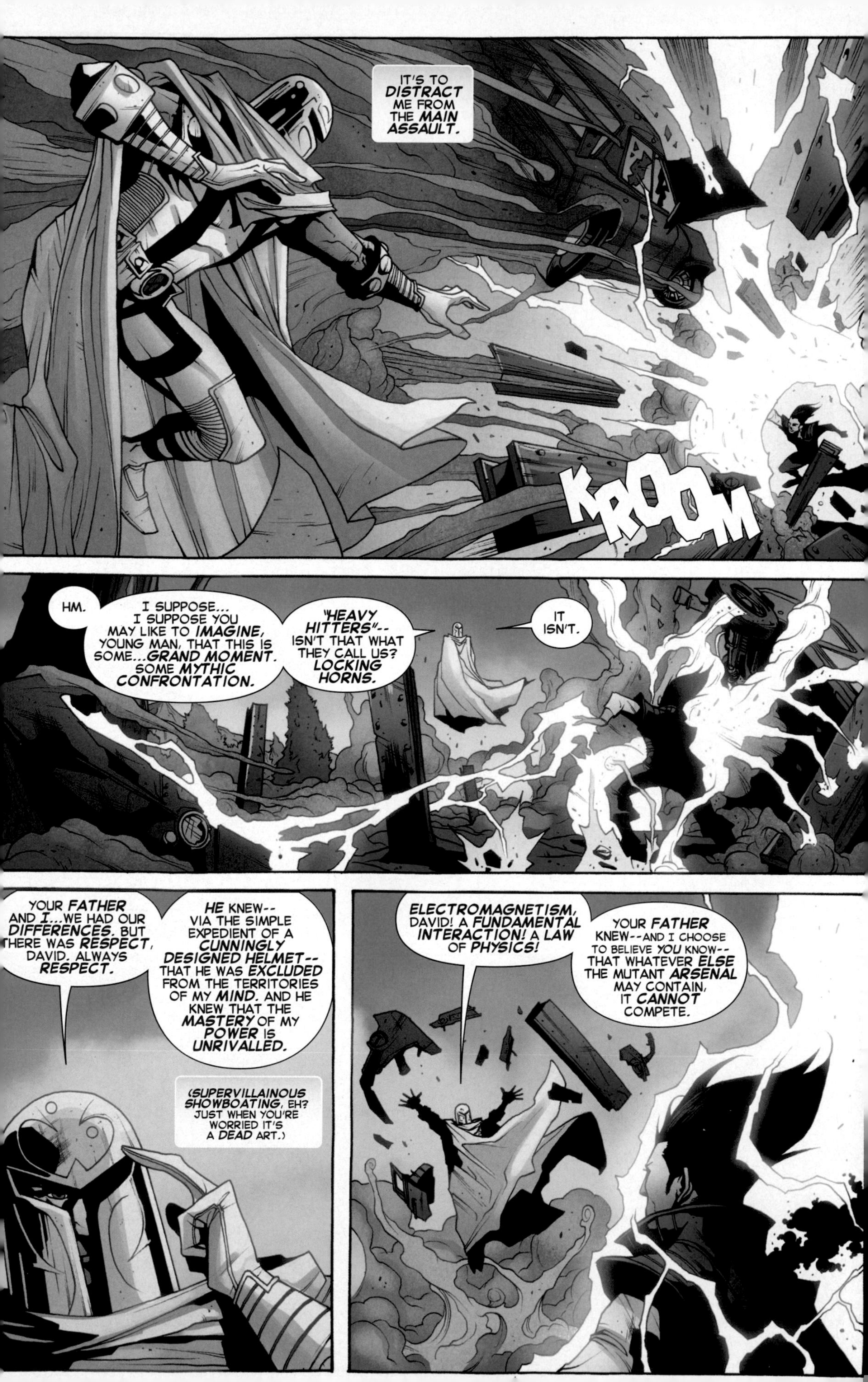
IT'S TO DISTRACT ME FROM THE MAIN ASSAULT.
KROOOM
HM.
I SUPPOSE... I SUPPOSE YOU MAY LIKE TO IMAGINE, YOUNG MAN, THAT THIS IS SOME...GRAND MOMENT. SOME MYTHIC CONFRONTATION.
"HEAVY HITTERS"-- ISN'T THAT WHAT THEY CALL US? LOCKING HORNS.
IT ISN'T.
YOUR FATHER AND I...WE HAD OUR DIFFERENCES. BUT THERE WAS RESPECT, DAVID. ALWAYS RESPECT.
HE KNEW-- VIA THE SIMPLE EXPEDIENT OF A CUNNINGLY DESIGNED HELMET-- THAT HE WAS EXCLUDED FROM THE TERRITORIES OF MY MIND. AND HE KNEW THAT THE MASTERY OF MY POWER IS UNRIVALLED.
(SUPERVILLAINOUS SHOWBOATING, EH? JUST WHEN YOU'RE WORRIED IT'S A DEAD ART.)
ELECTROMAGNETISM, DAVID! A FUNDAMENTAL INTERACTION! A LAW OF PHYSICS!
YOUR FATHER KNEW--AND I CHOOSE TO BELIEVE YOU KNOW-- THAT WHATEVER ELSE THE MUTANT ARSENAL MAY CONTAIN, IT CANNOT COMPETE.

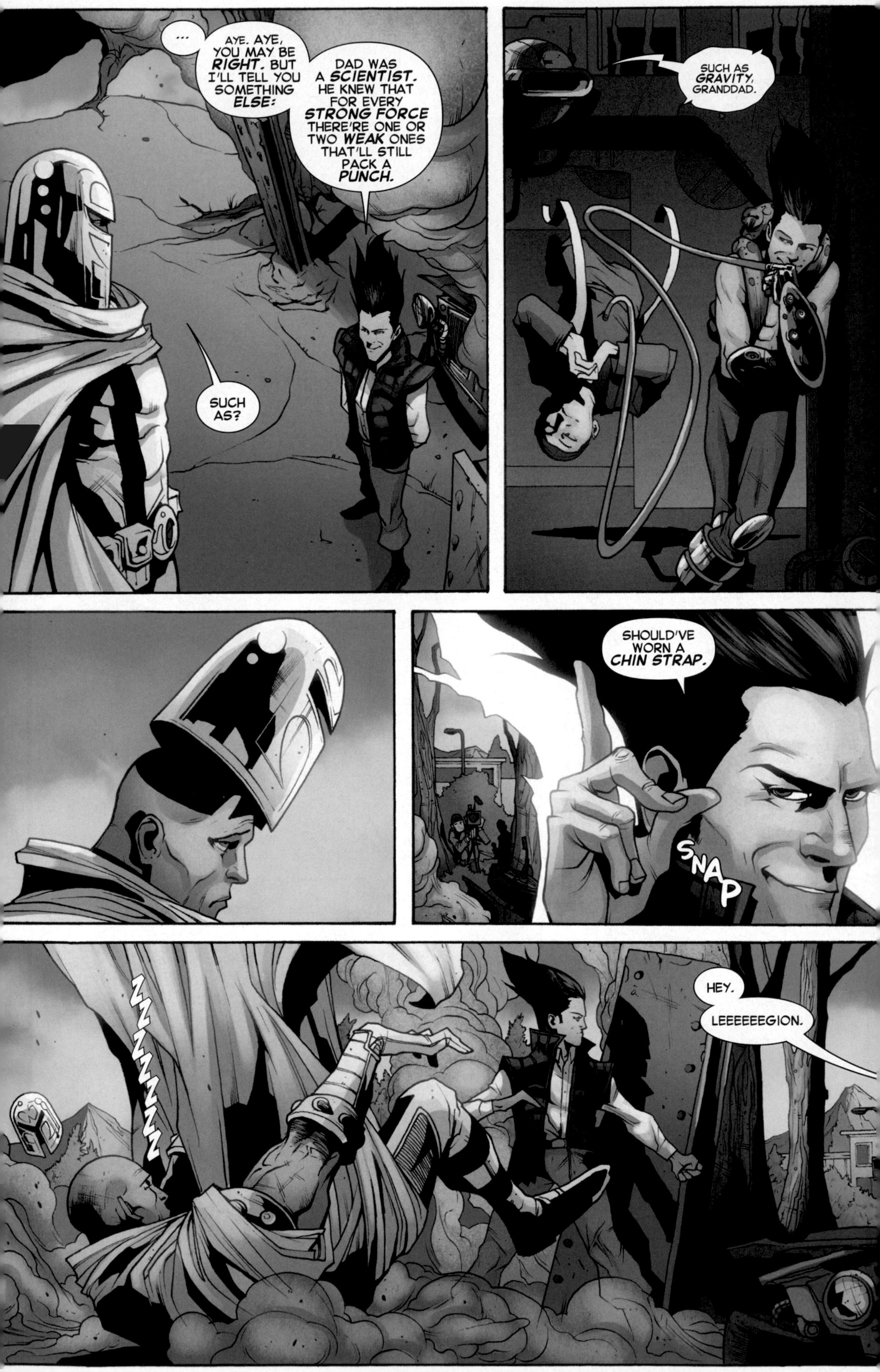
...
AYE. AYE, YOU MAY BE RIGHT. BUT I'LL TELL YOU SOMETHING ELSE:
DAD WAS A SCIENTIST. HE KNEW THAT FOR EVERY STRONG FORCE THERE'RE ONE OR TWO WEAK ONES THAT'LL STILL PACK A PUNCH.
SUCH AS?
SUCH AS GRAVITY, GRANDDAD.
SHOULD'VE WORN A CHIN STRAP.
SNAP
ZZZZZZZ
HEY.
LEEEEEEGION.

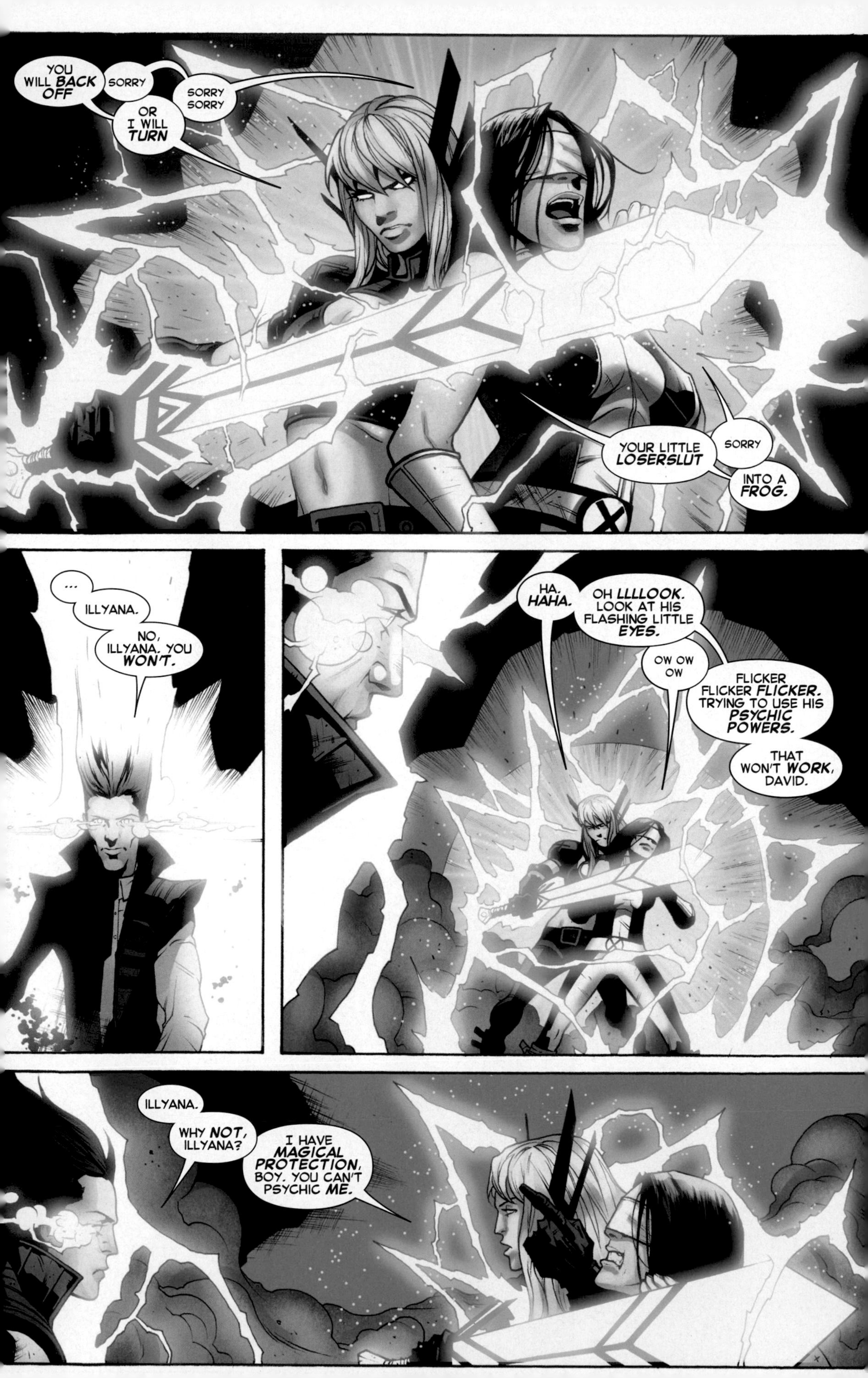
YOU WILL BACK OFF
SORRY
SORRY SORRY
OR I WILL TURN
YOUR LITTLE LOSERSLUT
SORRY
INTO A FROG.
...
ILLYANA.
NO, ILLYANA. YOU WON'T.
HA. HAHA.
OH LLLLOOK. LOOK AT HIS FLASHING LITTLE EYES.
OW OW OW
FLICKER FLICKER FLICKER. TRYING TO USE HIS PSYCHIC POWERS.
THAT WON'T WORK, DAVID.
ILLYANA.
WHY NOT, ILLYANA?
I HAVE MAGICAL PROTECTION, BOY. YOU CAN'T PSYCHIC ME.

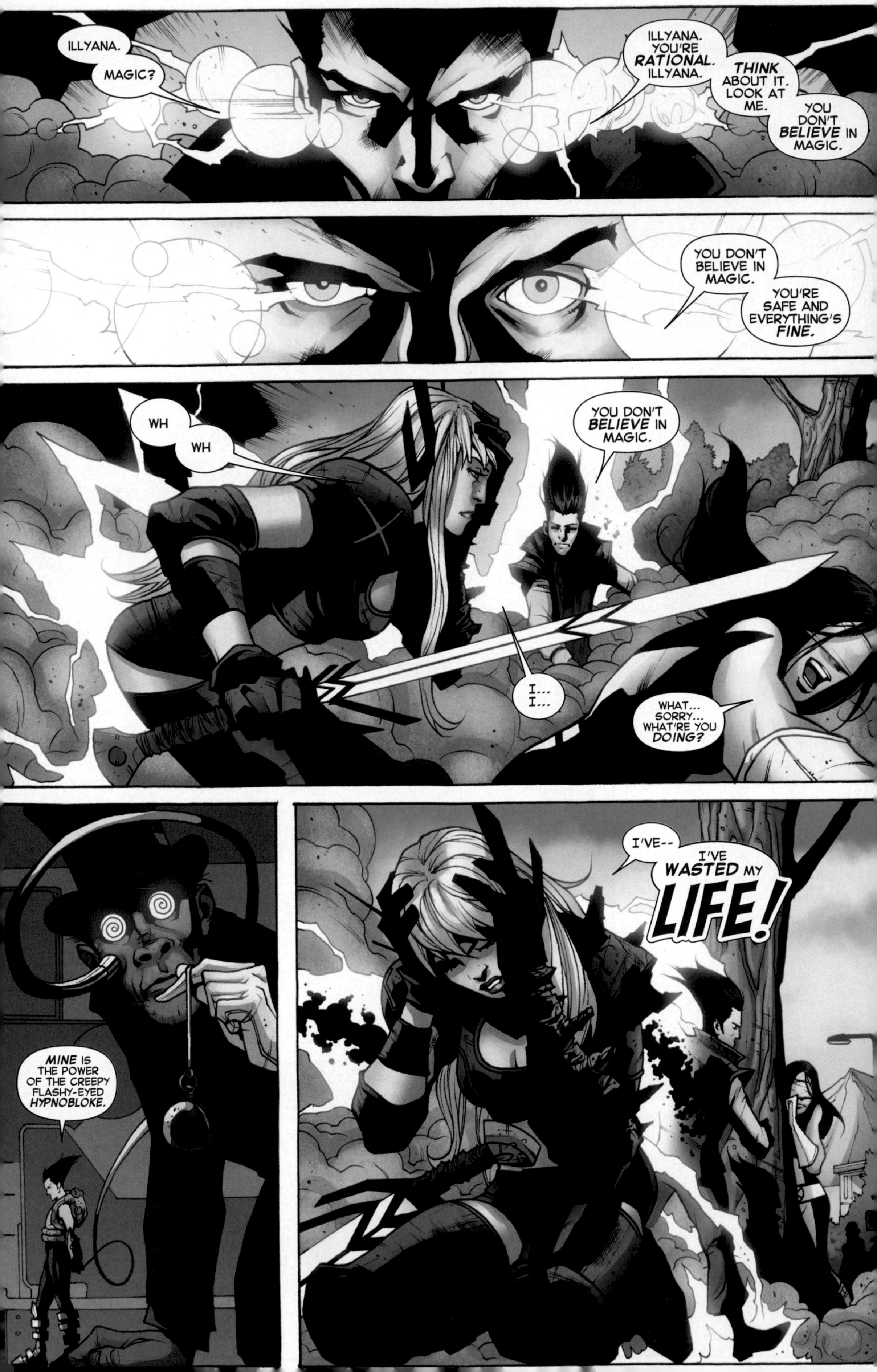
ILLYANA.
MAGIC?
ILLYANA. YOU'RE RATIONAL. ILLYANA.
THINK ABOUT IT. LOOK AT ME.
YOU DON'T BELIEVE IN MAGIC.
YOU DON'T BELIEVE IN MAGIC.
YOU'RE SAFE AND EVERYTHING'S FINE.
WH
WH
YOU DON'T BELIEVE IN MAGIC.
I... I...
WHAT... SORRY... WHAT'RE YOU DOING?
MINE IS THE POWER OF THE CREEPY FLASHY-EYED HYPNOBLOKE.
I'VE--
I'VE WASTED MY LIFE!

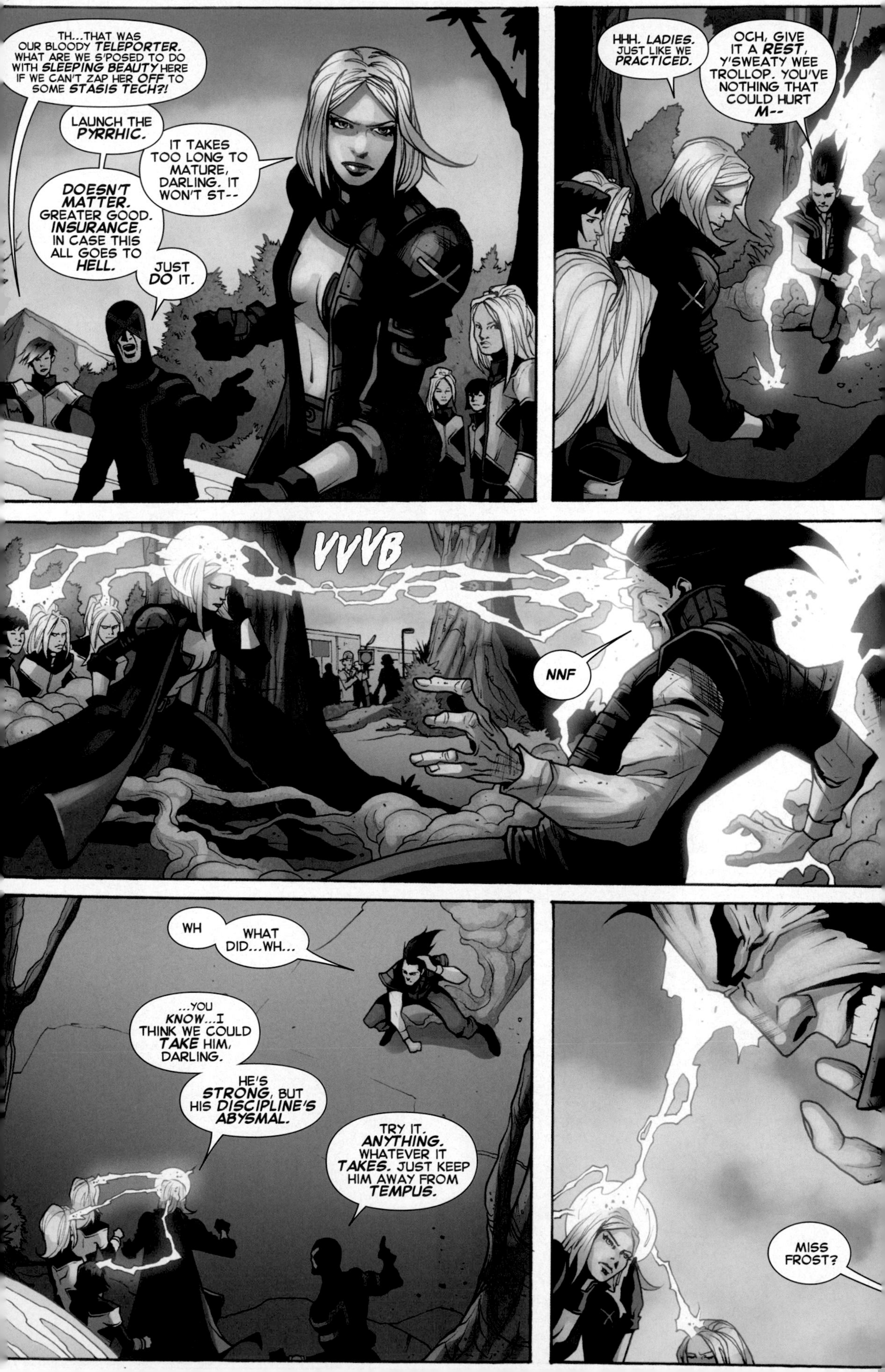

TH...THAT WAS OUR BLOODY TELEPORTER. WHAT ARE WE S'POSED TO DO WITH SLEEPING BEAUTY HERE IF WE CAN'T ZAP HER OFF TO SOME STASIS TECH?!
LAUNCH THE PYRRHIC.
IT TAKES TOO LONG TO MATURE, DARLING. IT WON'T ST--
DOESN'T MATTER. GREATER GOOD. INSURANCE, IN CASE THIS ALL GOES TO HELL.
JUST DO IT.
HHH. LADIES. JUST LIKE WE PRACTICED.
OCH, GIVE IT A REST, Y'SWEATY WEE TROLLOP. YOU'VE NOTHING THAT COULD HURT M--
VVVB
NNF
WH
WHAT DID...WH...
...YOU KNOW...I THINK WE COULD TAKE HIM, DARLING.
HE'S STRONG, BUT HIS DISCIPLINE'S ABYSMAL.
TRY IT. ANYTHING. WHATEVER IT TAKES. JUST KEEP HIM AWAY FROM TEMPUS.
MISS FROST?

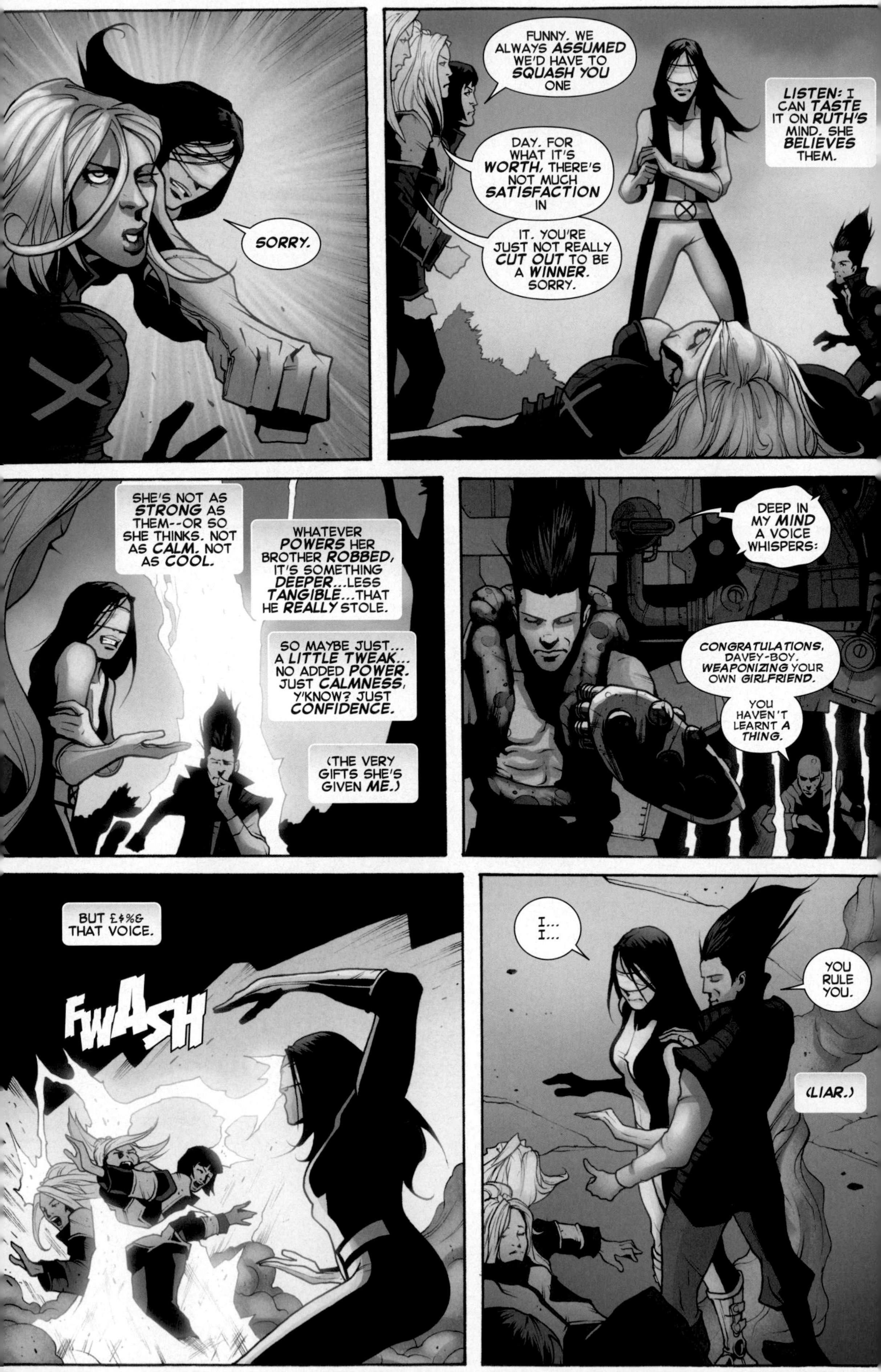
SORRY.
FUNNY. WE ALWAYS ASSUMED WE'D HAVE TO SQUASH YOU ONE
DAY. FOR WHAT IT'S WORTH, THERE'S NOT MUCH SATISFACTION IN
IT. YOU'RE JUST NOT REALLY CUT OUT TO BE A WINNER. SORRY.
LISTEN: I CAN TASTE IT ON RUTH'S MIND. SHE BELIEVES THEM.
SHE'S NOT AS STRONG AS THEM--OR SO SHE THINKS. NOT AS CALM. NOT AS COOL.
WHATEVER POWERS HER BROTHER ROBBED, IT'S SOMETHING DEEPER...LESS TANGIBLE...THAT HE REALLY STOLE.
SO MAYBE JUST... A LITTLE TWEAK... NO ADDED POWER. JUST CALMNESS, Y'KNOW? JUST CONFIDENCE.
(THE VERY GIFTS SHE'S GIVEN ME.)
DEEP IN MY MIND A VOICE WHISPERS:
CONGRATULATIONS, DAVEY-BOY. WEAPONIZING YOUR OWN GIRLFRIEND.
YOU HAVEN'T LEARNT A THING.
BUT £$%& THAT VOICE.
FWASH
I... I...
YOU RULE YOU.
(LIAR.)

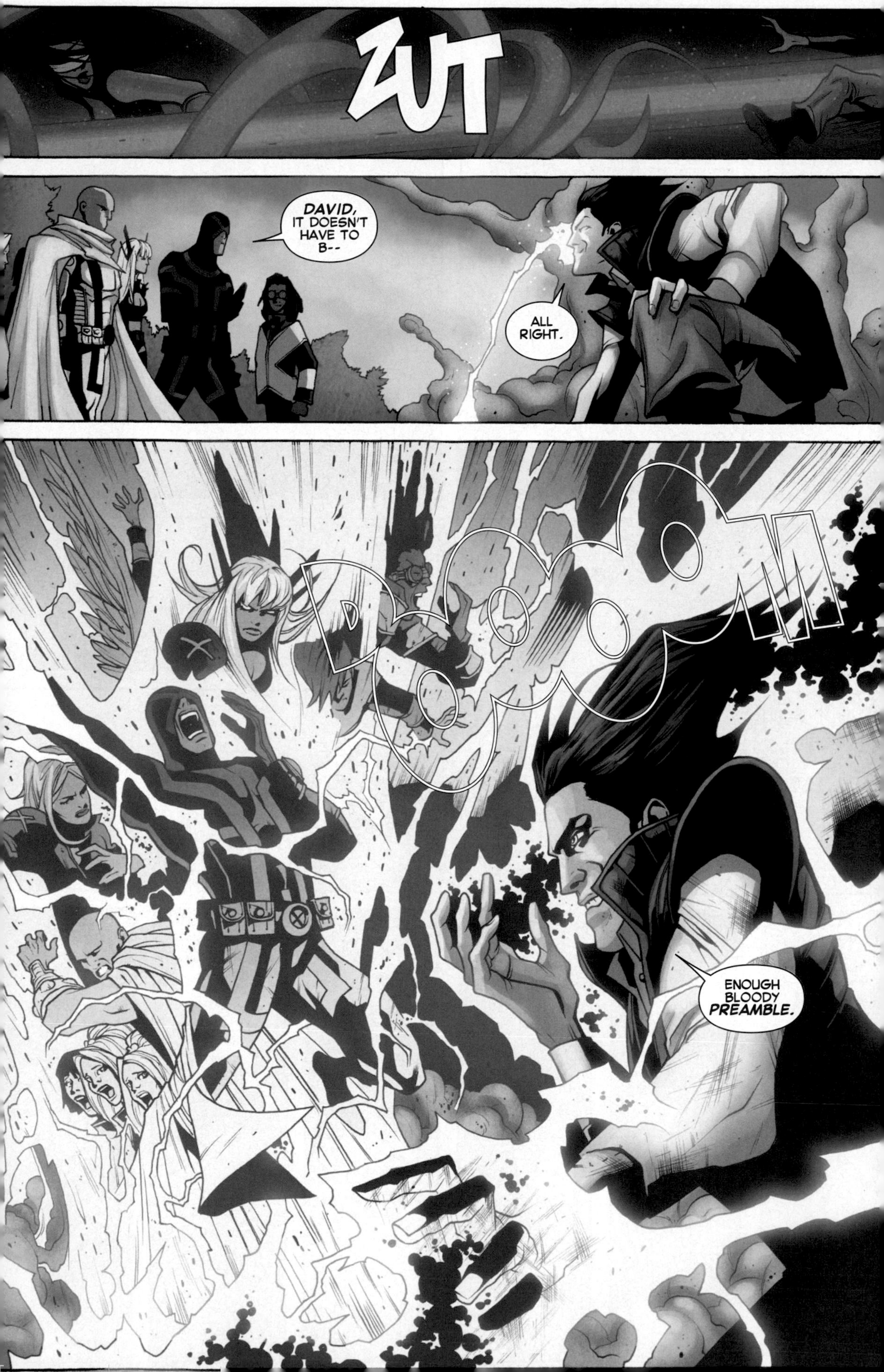
ZUT
DAVID, IT DOESN'T HAVE TO B--
ALL RIGHT.
DOOOOOM
ENOUGH BLOODY PREAMBLE.

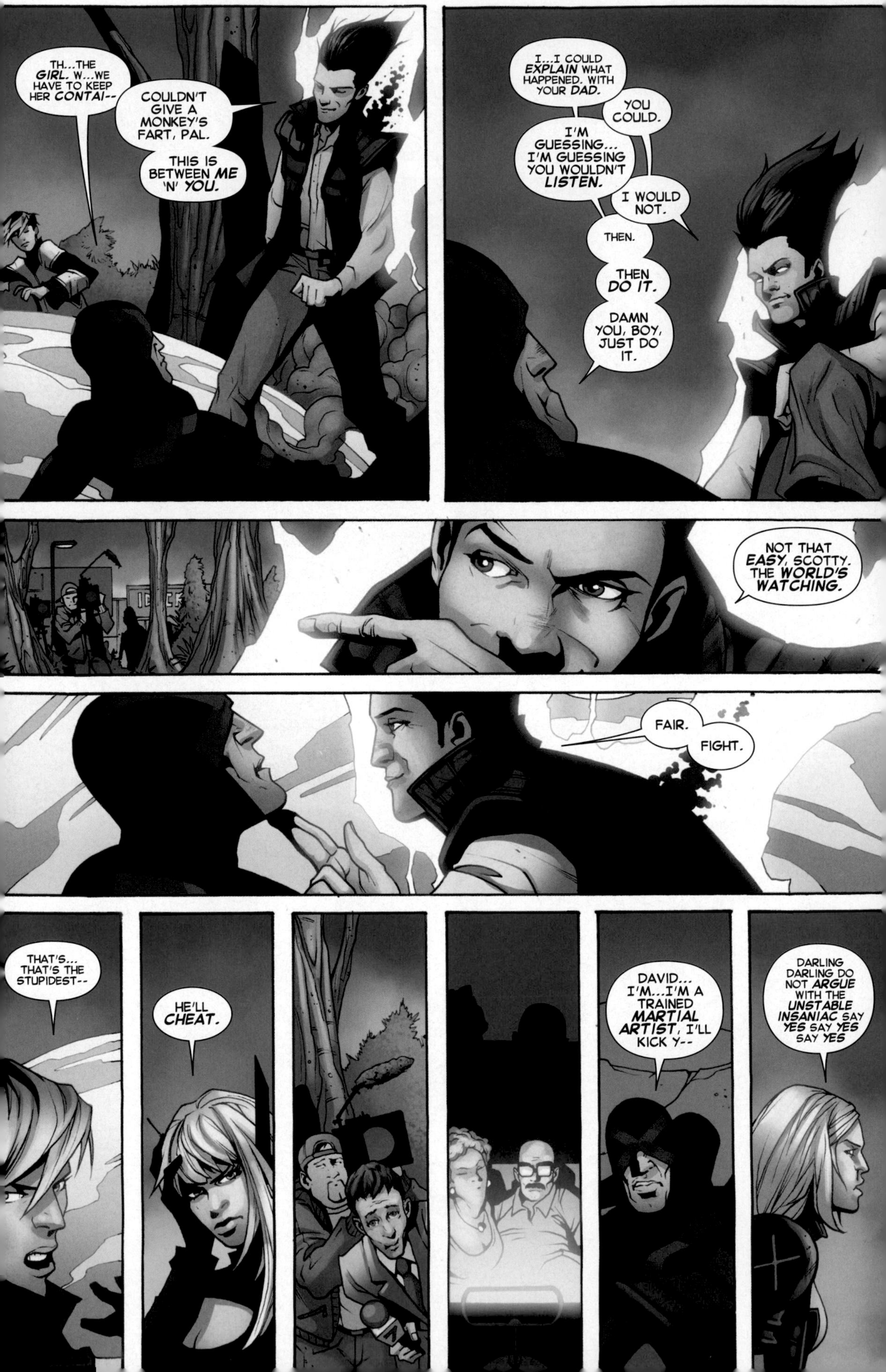

TH...THE GIRL. W...WE HAVE TO KEEP HER CONTAI--
COULDN'T GIVE A MONKEY'S FART, PAL.
THIS IS BETWEEN ME 'N' YOU.
I...I COULD EXPLAIN WHAT HAPPENED. WITH YOUR DAD.
YOU COULD.
I'M GUESSING... I'M GUESSING YOU WOULDN'T LISTEN.
I WOULD NOT.
THEN.
THEN DO IT.
DAMN YOU, BOY, JUST DO IT.
NOT THAT EASY, SCOTTY. THE WORLD'S WATCHING.
FAIR.
FIGHT.
THAT'S... THAT'S THE STUPIDEST--
HE'LL CHEAT.
DAVID... I'M...I'M A TRAINED MARTIAL ARTIST, I'LL KICK Y--
DARLING DARLING DO NOT ARGUE WITH THE UNSTABLE INSANIAC SAY YES SAY YES SAY YES

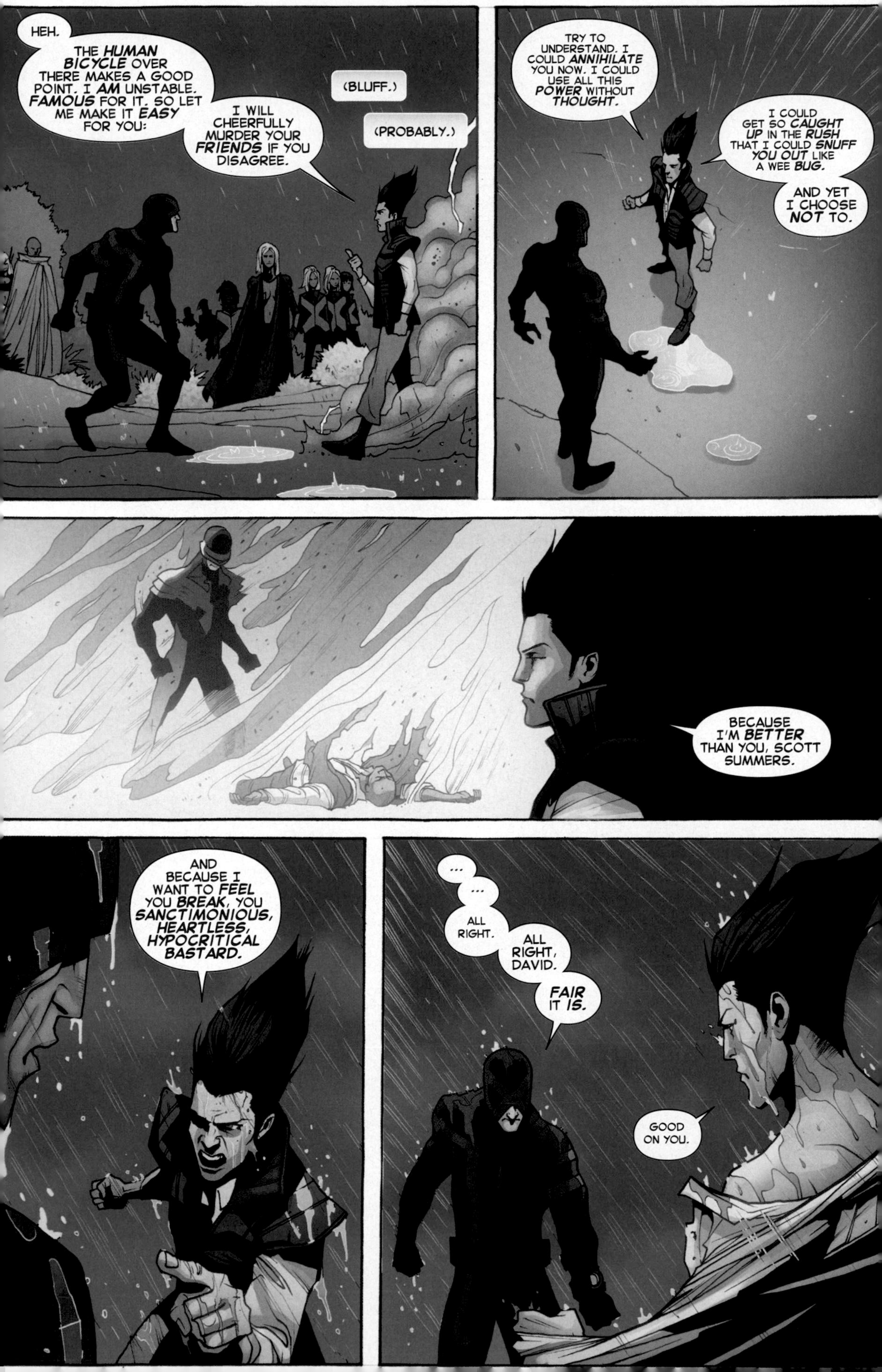
HEH.
THE HUMAN BICYCLE OVER THERE MAKES A GOOD POINT. I AM UNSTABLE. FAMOUS FOR IT. SO LET ME MAKE IT EASY FOR YOU:
I WILL CHEERFULLY MURDER YOUR FRIENDS IF YOU DISAGREE.
(BLUFF.)
(PROBABLY.)
TRY TO UNDERSTAND. I COULD ANNIHILATE YOU NOW. I COULD USE ALL THIS POWER WITHOUT THOUGHT.
I COULD GET SO CAUGHT UP IN THE RUSH THAT I COULD SNUFF YOU OUT LIKE A WEE BUG.
AND YET I CHOOSE NOT TO.
BECAUSE I'M BETTER THAN YOU, SCOTT SUMMERS.
AND BECAUSE I WANT TO FEEL YOU BREAK, YOU SANCTIMONIOUS, HEARTLESS, HYPOCRITICAL BASTARD.
...
...
ALL RIGHT.
ALL RIGHT, DAVID.
FAIR IT IS.
GOOD ON YOU.

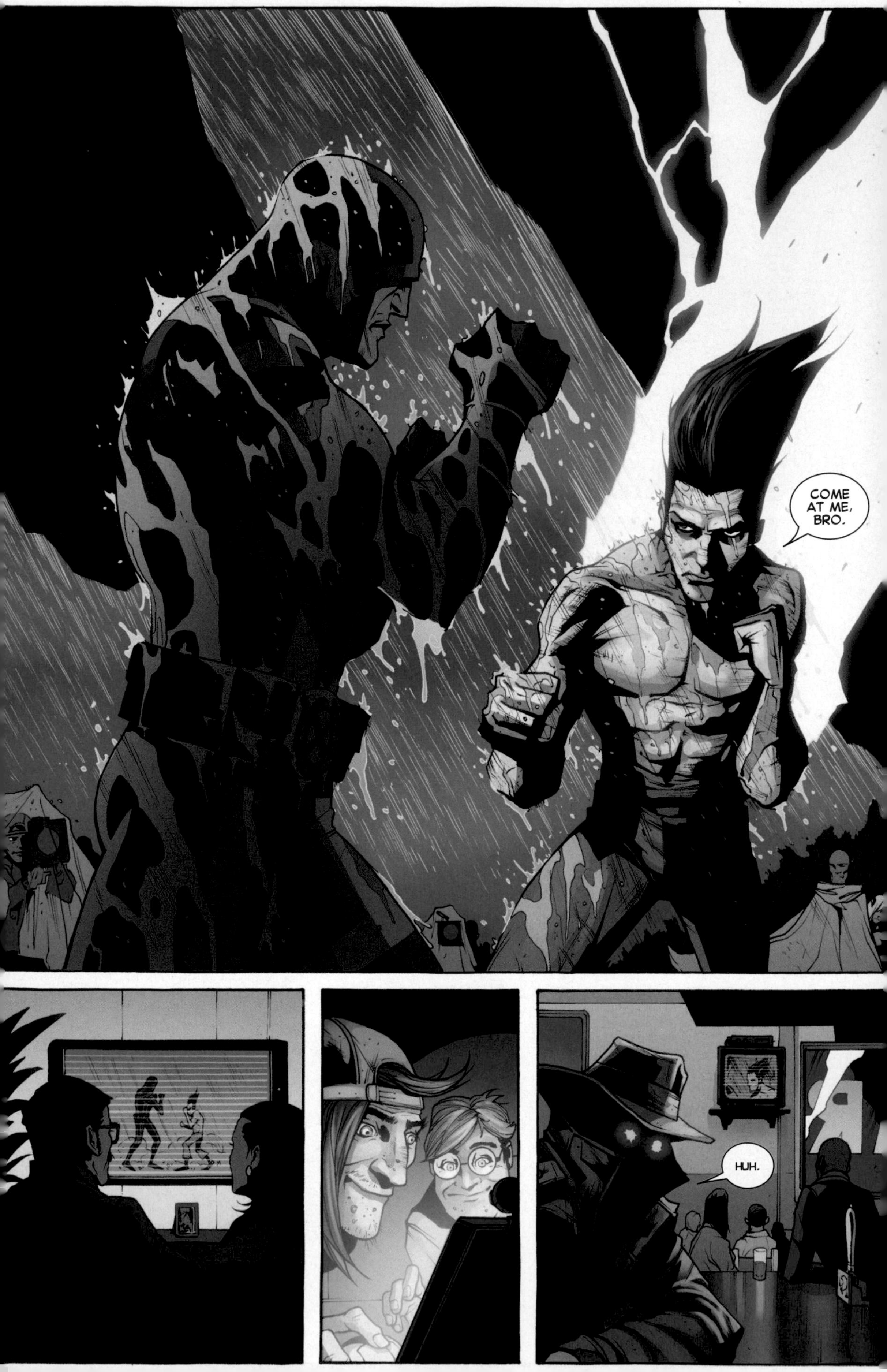
COME AT ME, BRO.
HUH.

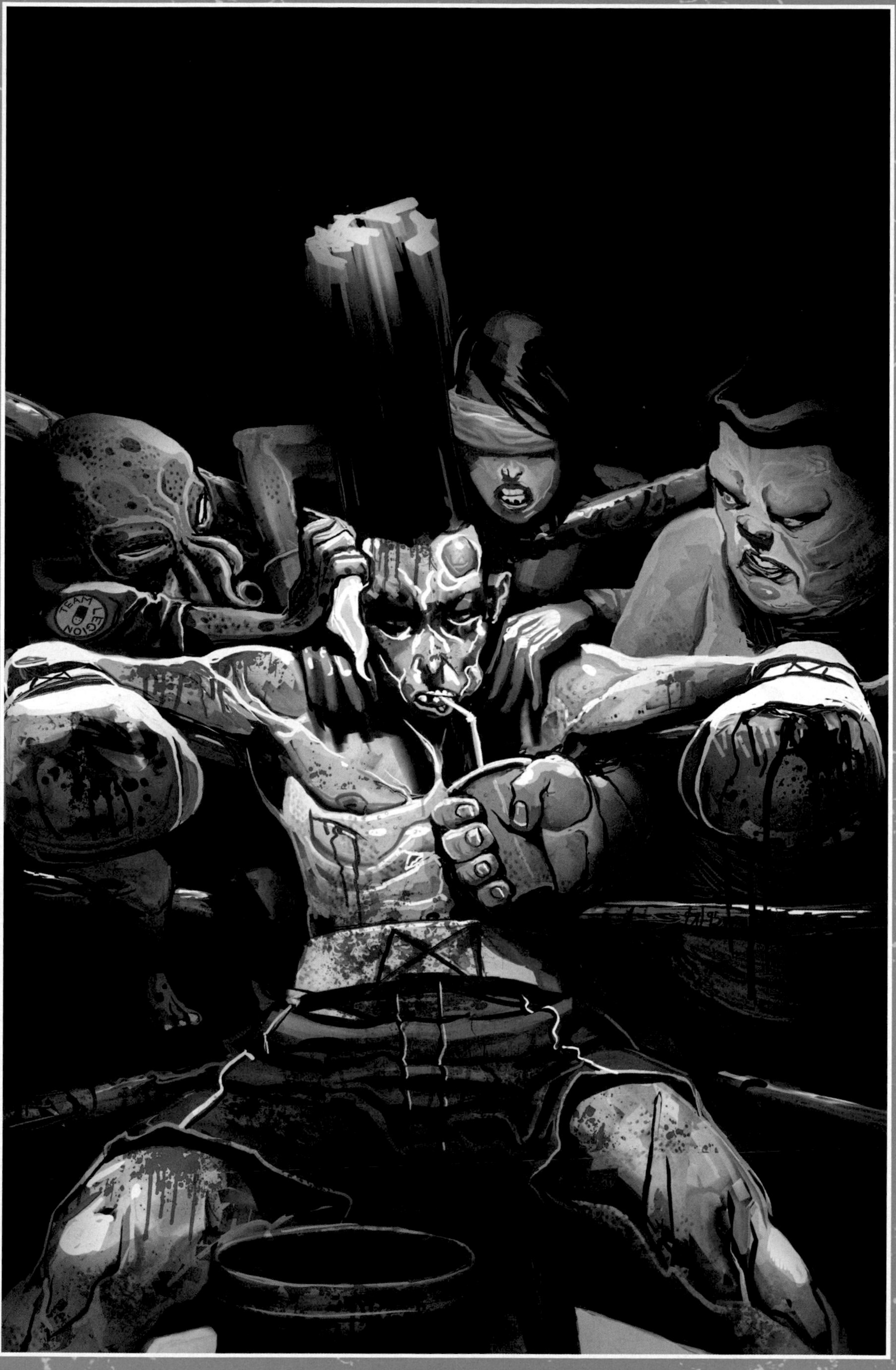
TEAM LEGION

SEVENTEEN

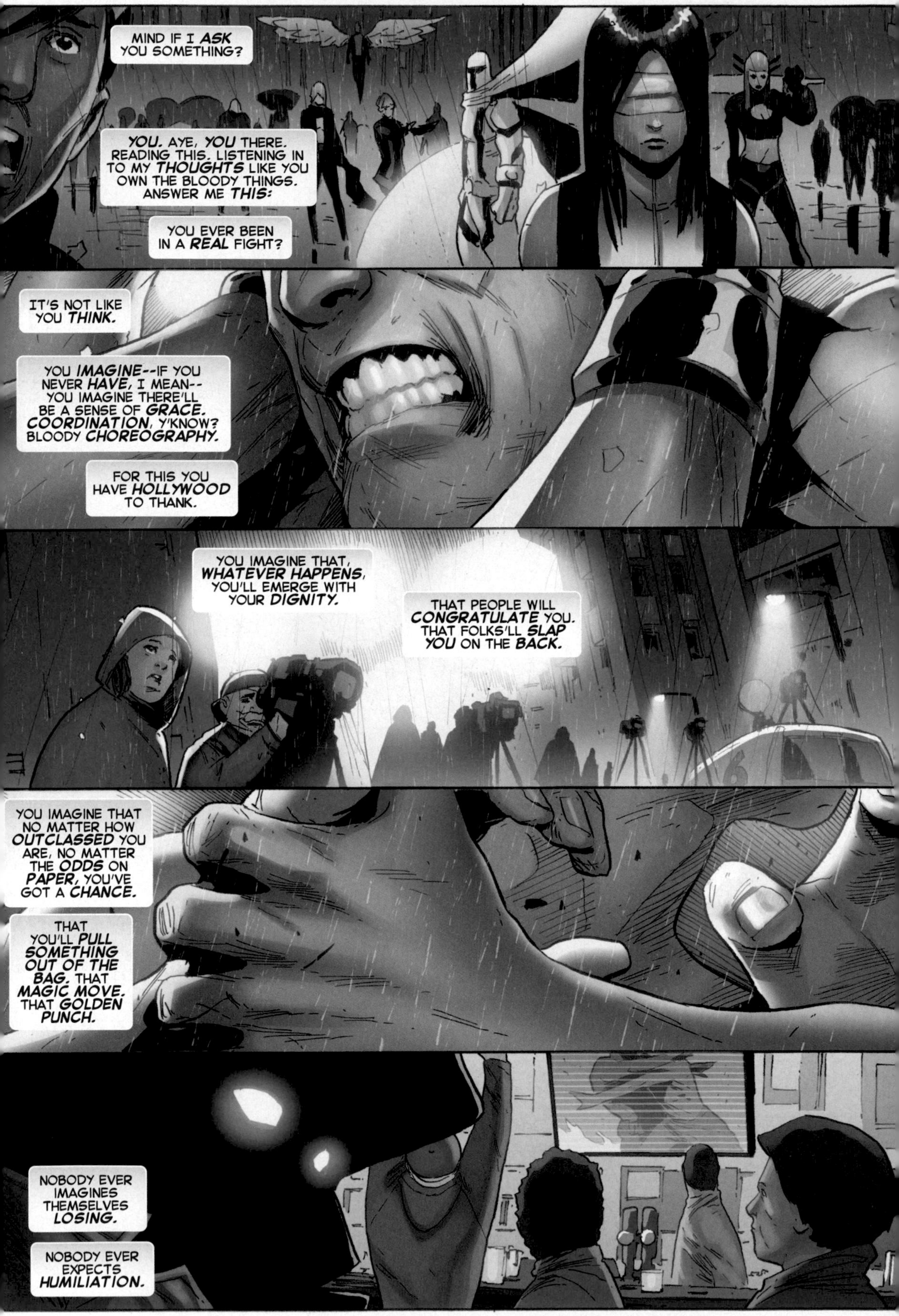
MIND IF I ASK YOU SOMETHING?
YOU. AYE, YOU THERE. READING THIS. LISTENING IN TO MY THOUGHTS LIKE YOU OWN THE BLOODY THINGS. ANSWER ME THIS:
YOU EVER BEEN IN A REAL FIGHT?
IT'S NOT LIKE YOU THINK.
YOU IMAGINE--IF YOU NEVER HAVE, I MEAN--YOU IMAGINE THERE'LL BE A SENSE OF GRACE. COORDINATION, Y'KNOW? BLOODY CHOREOGRAPHY.
FOR THIS YOU HAVE HOLLYWOOD TO THANK.
YOU IMAGINE THAT, WHATEVER HAPPENS, YOU'LL EMERGE WITH YOUR DIGNITY.
THAT PEOPLE WILL CONGRATULATE YOU. THAT FOLKS'LL SLAP YOU ON THE BACK.
YOU IMAGINE THAT NO MATTER HOW OUTCLASSED YOU ARE, NO MATTER THE ODDS ON PAPER, YOU'VE GOT A CHANCE.
THAT YOU'LL PULL SOMETHING OUT OF THE BAG. THAT MAGIC MOVE. THAT GOLDEN PUNCH.
NOBODY EVER IMAGINES THEMSELVES LOSING.
NOBODY EVER EXPECTS HUMILIATION.

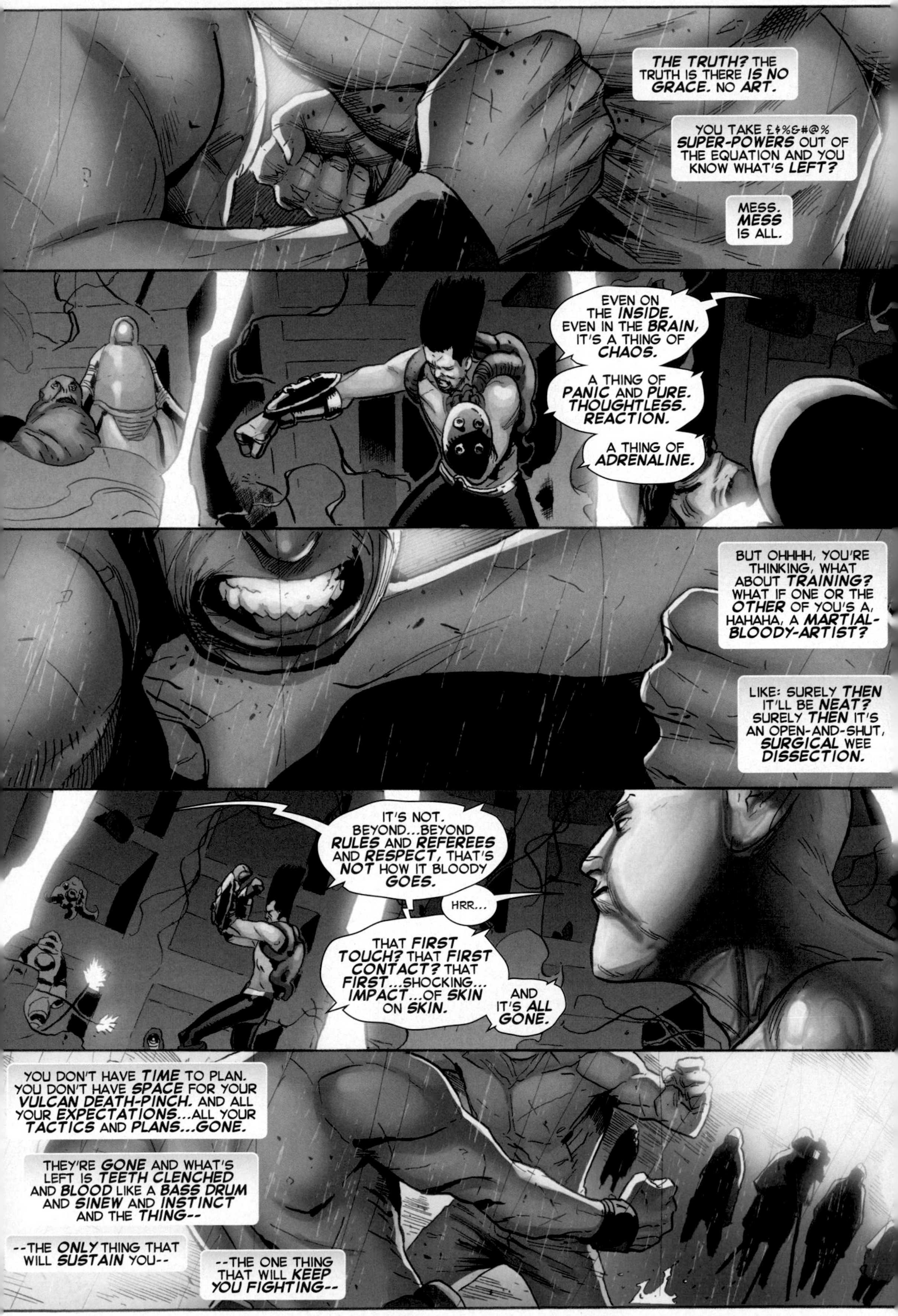
THE TRUTH? THE TRUTH IS THERE IS NO GRACE. NO ART.
YOU TAKE £$%&#@% SUPER-POWERS OUT OF THE EQUATION AND YOU KNOW WHAT'S LEFT?
MESS. MESS IS ALL.
EVEN ON THE INSIDE. EVEN IN THE BRAIN, IT'S A THING OF CHAOS.
A THING OF PANIC AND PURE. THOUGHTLESS. REACTION.
A THING OF ADRENALINE.
BUT OHHHH, YOU'RE THINKING, WHAT ABOUT TRAINING? WHAT IF ONE OR THE OTHER OF YOU'S A, HAHAHA, A MARTIAL-BLOODY-ARTIST?
LIKE: SURELY THEN IT'LL BE NEAT? SURELY THEN IT'S AN OPEN-AND-SHUT, SURGICAL WEE DISSECTION.
IT'S NOT. BEYOND...BEYOND RULES AND REFEREES AND RESPECT, THAT'S NOT HOW IT BLOODY GOES.
HRR...
THAT FIRST TOUCH? THAT FIRST CONTACT? THAT FIRST...SHOCKING... IMPACT...OF SKIN ON SKIN.
AND IT'S ALL GONE.
YOU DON'T HAVE TIME TO PLAN. YOU DON'T HAVE SPACE FOR YOUR VULCAN DEATH-PINCH. AND ALL YOUR EXPECTATIONS...ALL YOUR TACTICS AND PLANS...GONE.
THEY'RE GONE AND WHAT'S LEFT IS TEETH CLENCHED AND BLOOD LIKE A BASS DRUM AND SINEW AND INSTINCT AND THE THING--
--THE ONLY THING THAT WILL SUSTAIN YOU--
--THE ONE THING THAT WILL KEEP YOU FIGHTING--

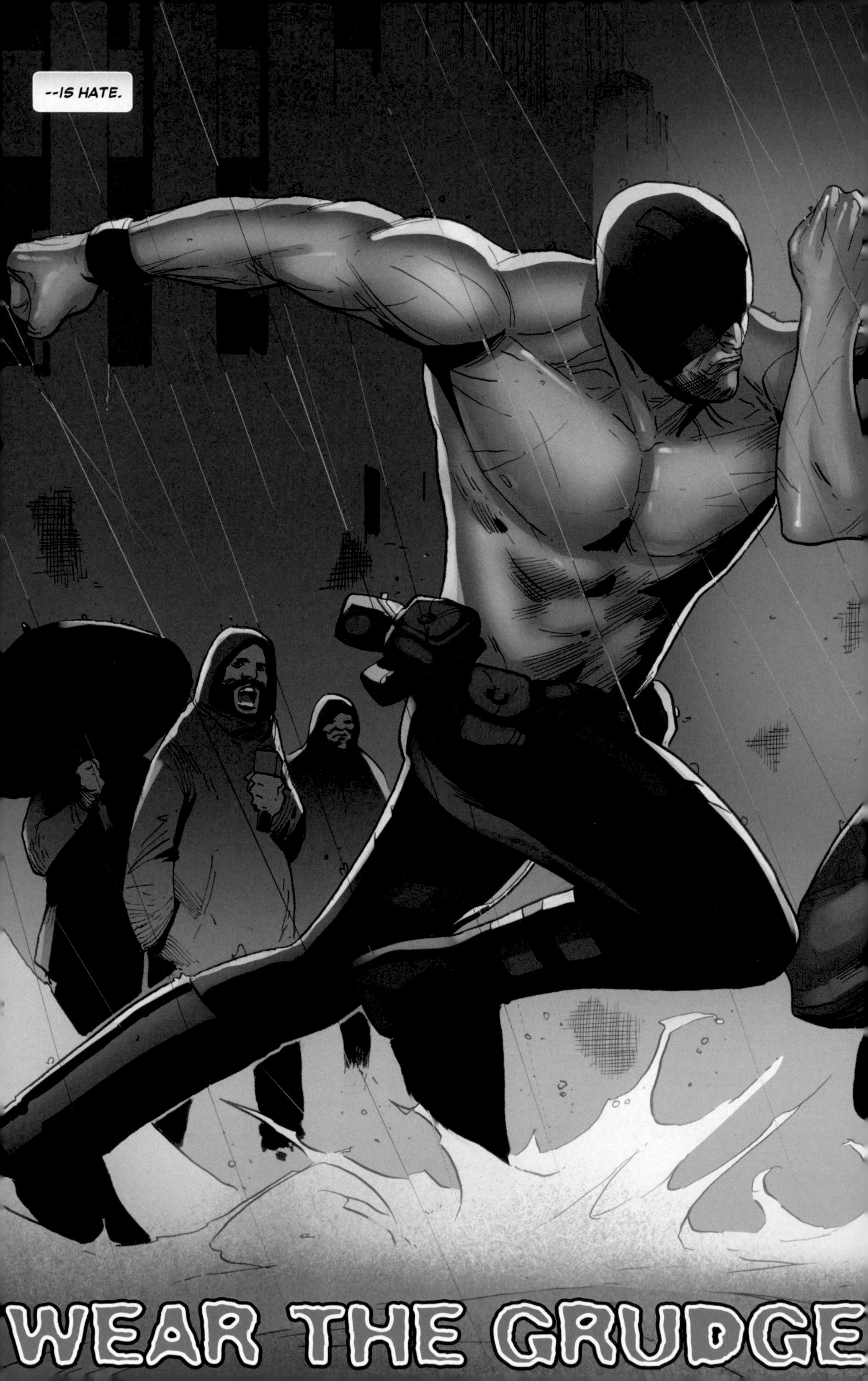
--IS HATE.
WEAR THE GRUDGE

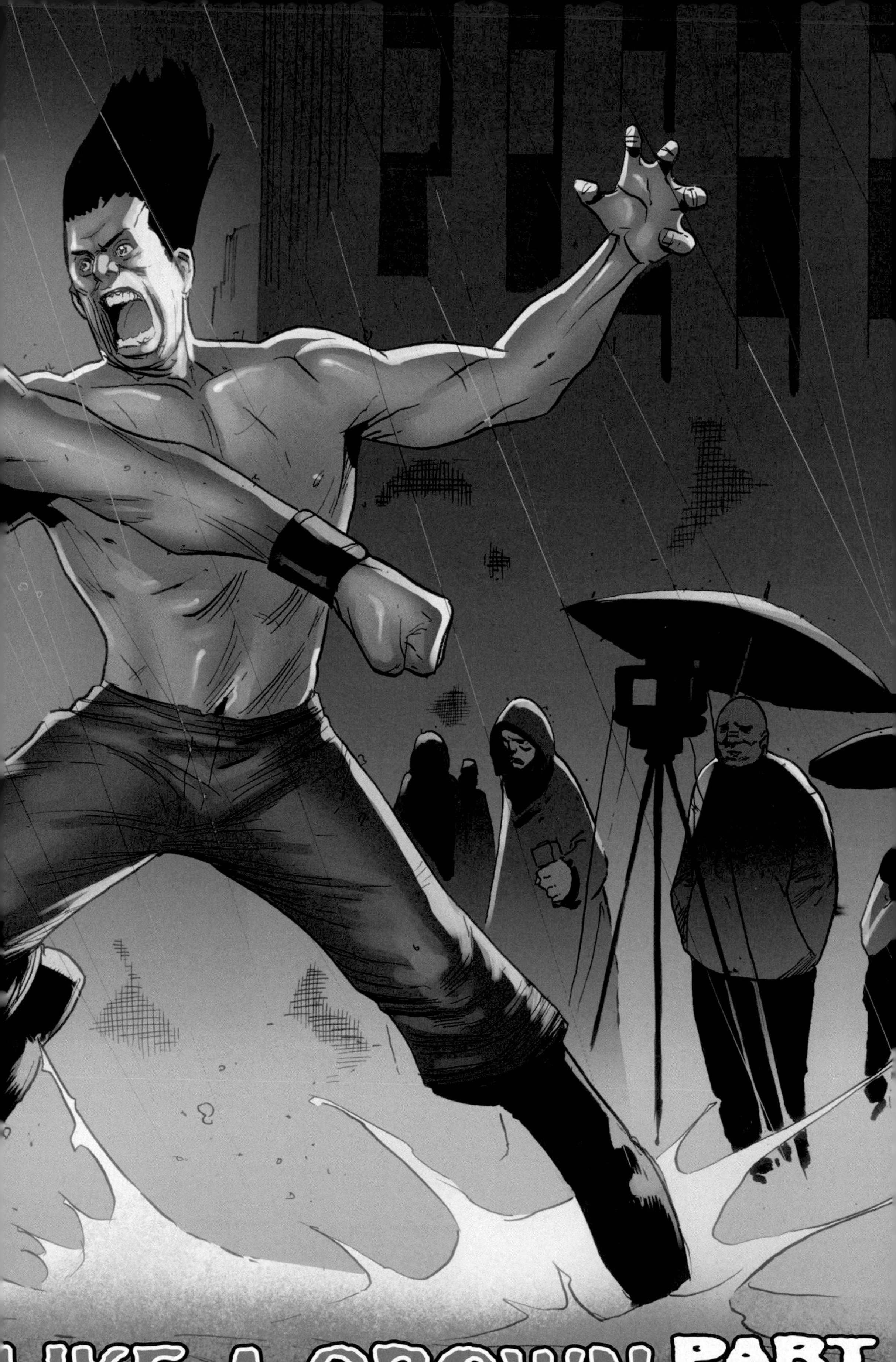

LIKE A CROWN PART TWO

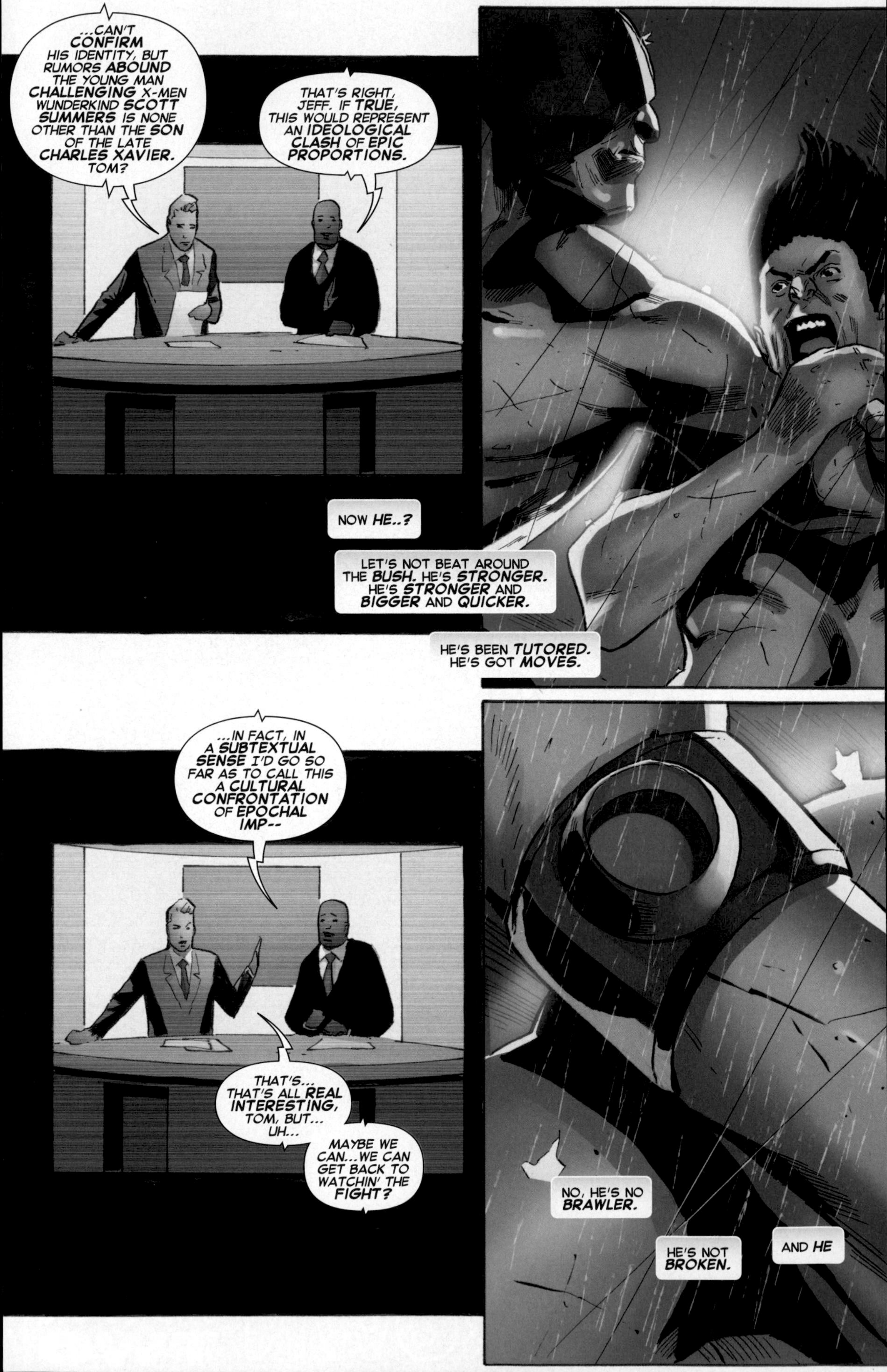
...CAN'T CONFIRM HIS IDENTITY, BUT RUMORS ABOUND THE YOUNG MAN CHALLENGING X-MEN WUNDERKIND SCOTT SUMMERS IS NONE OTHER THAN THE SON OF THE LATE CHARLES XAVIER. TOM?
THAT'S RIGHT, JEFF. IF TRUE, THIS WOULD REPRESENT AN IDEOLOGICAL CLASH OF EPIC PROPORTIONS.
NOW HE..?
LET'S NOT BEAT AROUND THE BUSH. HE'S STRONGER. HE'S STRONGER AND BIGGER AND QUICKER.
HE'S BEEN TUTORED. HE'S GOT MOVES.
...IN FACT, IN A SUBTEXTUAL SENSE I'D GO SO FAR AS TO CALL THIS A CULTURAL CONFRONTATION OF EPOCHAL IMP--
THAT'S... THAT'S ALL REAL INTERESTING, TOM, BUT... UH...
MAYBE WE CAN...WE CAN GET BACK TO WATCHIN' THE FIGHT?
NO, HE'S NO BRAWLER.
HE'S NOT BROKEN.
AND HE

--REALLY HAVE TO *SEE* ALL THIS IN LIGHT OF ONGOING *EVENTS* IN THE *MUTANT* SPHERE. WITH TENSIONS BETWEEN *RIVAL* GROUPS AT AN ALL TIME *LOW* AND THIS SPATE OF "X-BEAST" ATROCITIES STILL ON FRONT PAGES--

--IN WHICH *PRO-MUTANT* INDIVIDUALS HAVE BEEN FOUND *MURDERED* NEAR *ENIGMATIC GRAFFITI*--

LIVE

--THESE EPISODES OF INTERNAL *DISHARMONY* TAKE ON A PARTICULARLY *DESTRUCTIVE* ASPECT.

...AYE: I'M *OUTCLASSED*--BUT THE *WEE BOY SCOUT'S* OFF HIS OWN *MAP* TOO. HE'S *ACCUSTOMED* TO *SUPERDUPERS*; TO *POSTURING PILLOCKS* LETTIN' RIP FROM THEIR *COSMIC ARMPITS*.

HE'S NO *BRAWLER.* AND *WORSE?* HE'S FULL TO THE BRIM WITH *HONOR.*

DAVID.

I DON'T WANT TO *HURT* YOU.

(SANCTIMONIOUS GIT.)

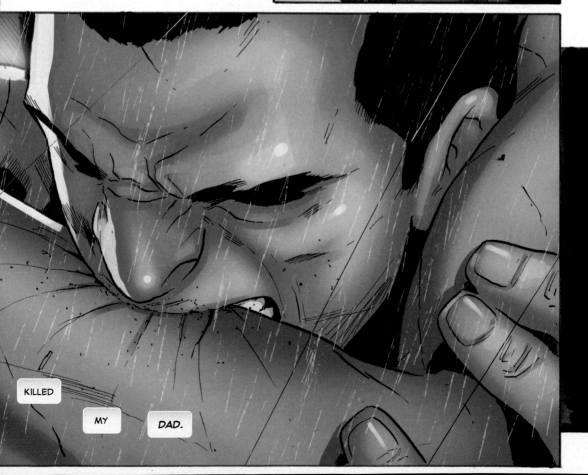

KILLED

MY

DAD.

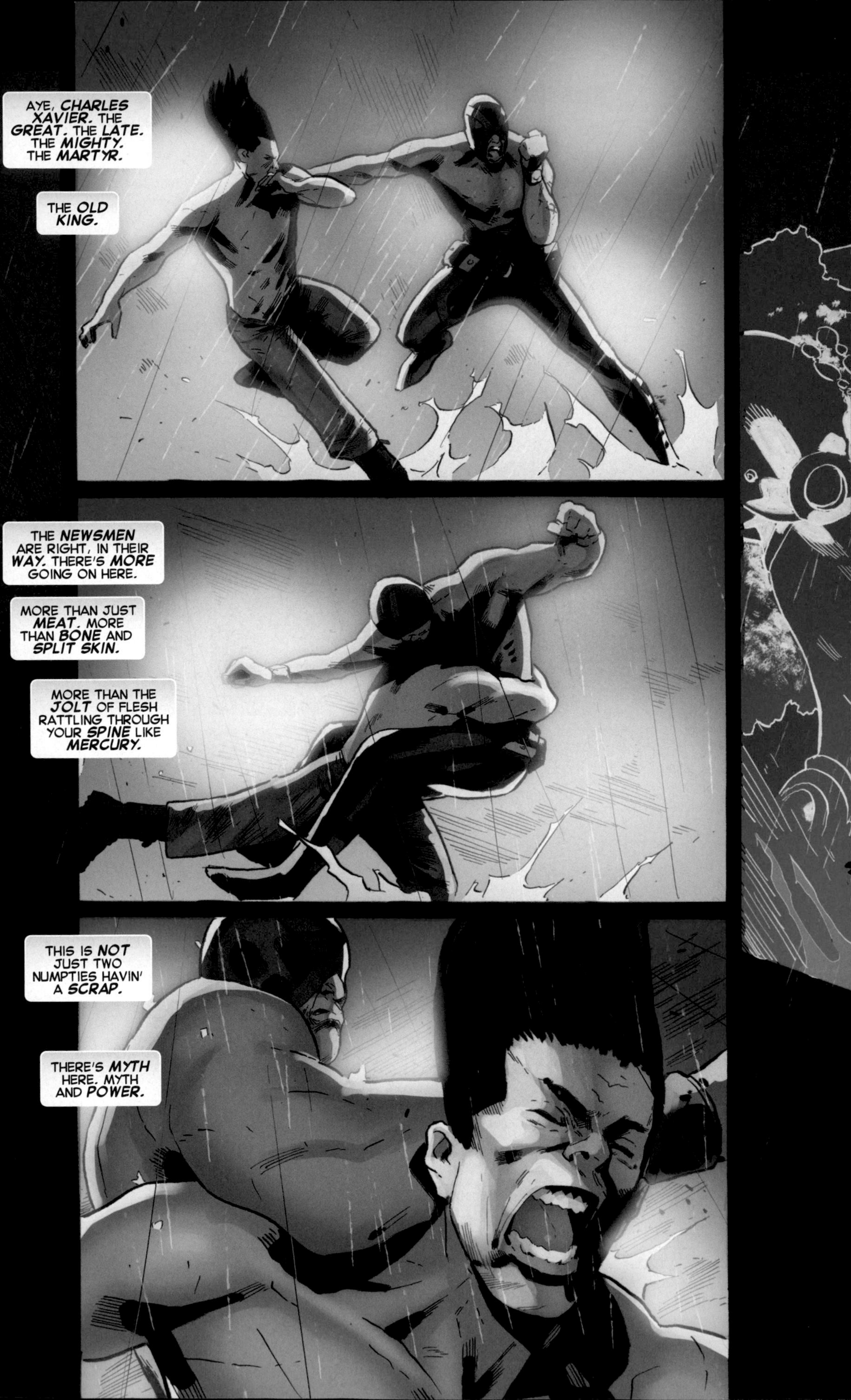
AYE, CHARLES XAVIER. THE GREAT. THE LATE. THE MIGHTY. THE MARTYR.
THE OLD KING.
THE NEWSMEN ARE RIGHT, IN THEIR WAY. THERE'S MORE GOING ON HERE.
MORE THAN JUST MEAT. MORE THAN BONE AND SPLIT SKIN.
MORE THAN THE JOLT OF FLESH RATTLING THROUGH YOUR SPINE LIKE MERCURY.
THIS IS NOT JUST TWO NUMPTIES HAVIN' A SCRAP.
THERE'S MYTH HERE. MYTH AND POWER.

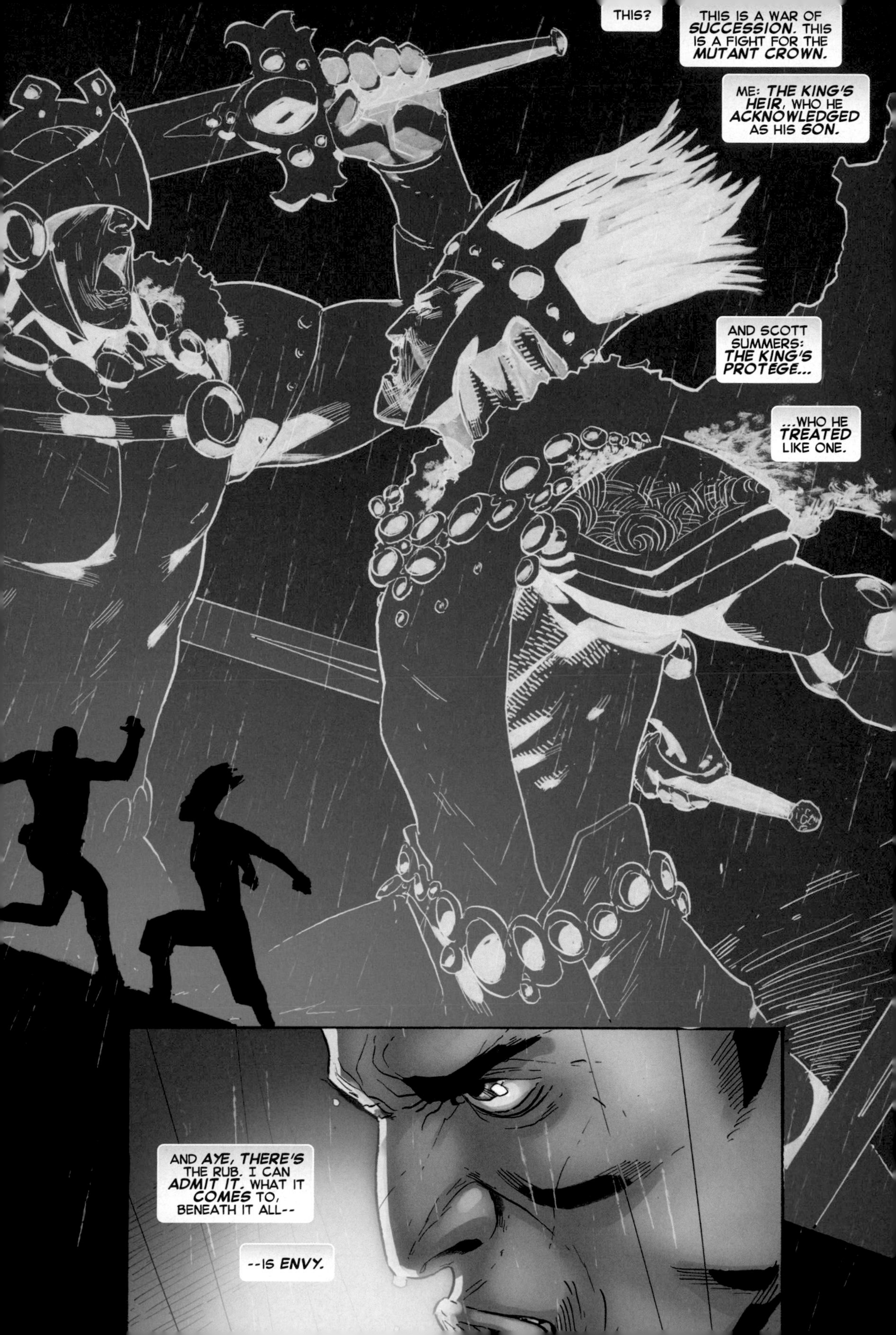
THIS?
THIS IS A WAR OF SUCCESSION. THIS IS A FIGHT FOR THE MUTANT CROWN.
ME: THE KING'S HEIR, WHO HE ACKNOWLEDGED AS HIS SON.
AND SCOTT SUMMERS: THE KING'S PROTEGE...
...WHO HE TREATED LIKE ONE.
AND AYE, THERE'S THE RUB. I CAN ADMIT IT. WHAT IT COMES TO, BENEATH IT ALL--
--IS ENVY.

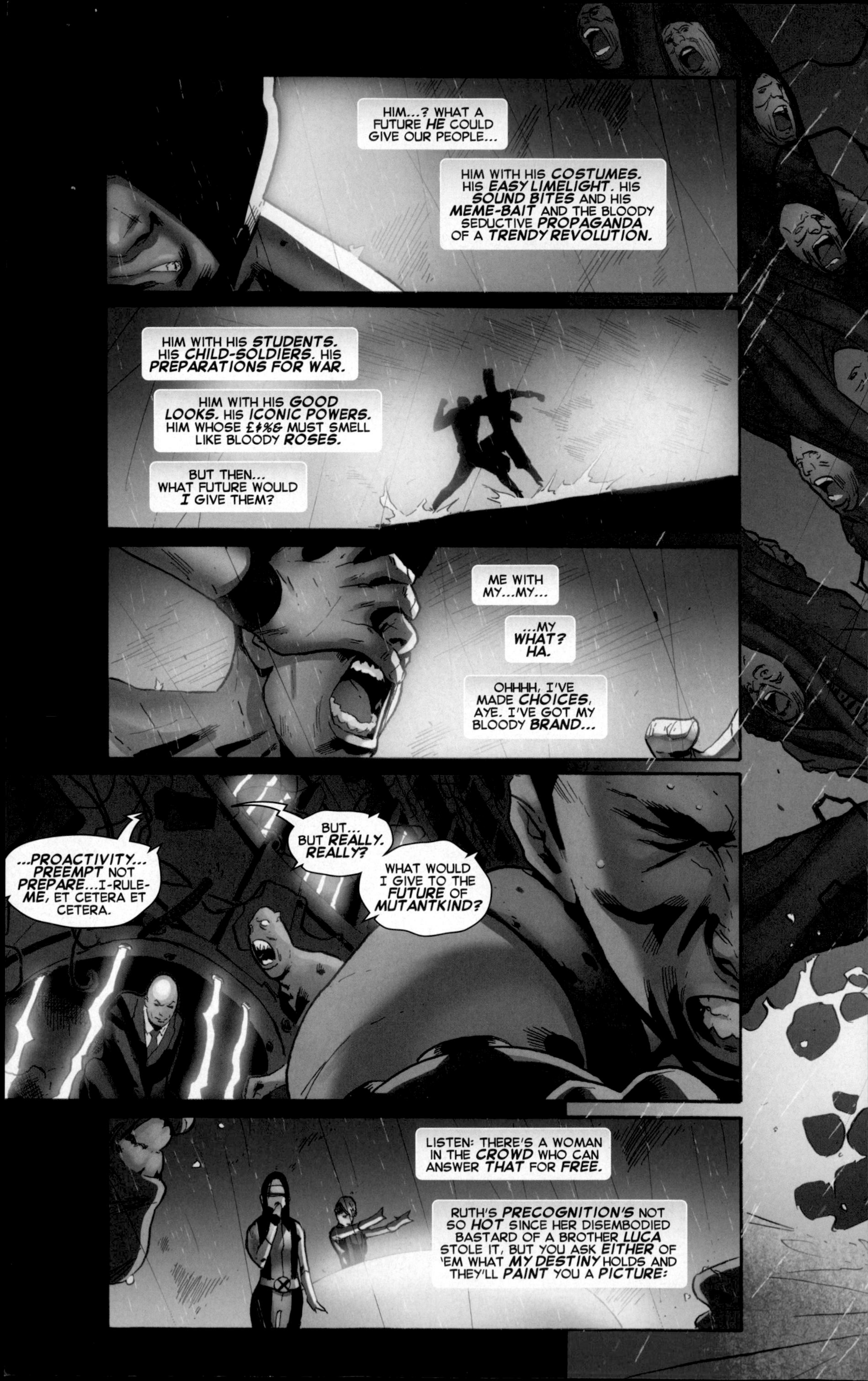
HIM...? WHAT A FUTURE HE COULD GIVE OUR PEOPLE...
HIM WITH HIS COSTUMES. HIS EASY LIMELIGHT. HIS SOUND BITES AND HIS MEME-BAIT AND THE BLOODY SEDUCTIVE PROPAGANDA OF A TRENDY REVOLUTION.
HIM WITH HIS STUDENTS. HIS CHILD-SOLDIERS. HIS PREPARATIONS FOR WAR.
HIM WITH HIS GOOD LOOKS. HIS ICONIC POWERS. HIM WHOSE £$%& MUST SMELL LIKE BLOODY ROSES.
BUT THEN... WHAT FUTURE WOULD I GIVE THEM?
ME WITH MY...MY...
...MY WHAT? HA.
OHHHH, I'VE MADE CHOICES, AYE. I'VE GOT MY BLOODY BRAND...
...PROACTIVITY... PREEMPT NOT PREPARE...I-RULE-ME, ET CETERA ET CETERA.
BUT... BUT REALLY. REALLY?
WHAT WOULD I GIVE TO THE FUTURE OF MUTANTKIND?
LISTEN: THERE'S A WOMAN IN THE CROWD WHO CAN ANSWER THAT FOR FREE.
RUTH'S PRECOGNITION'S NOT SO HOT SINCE HER DISEMBODIED BASTARD OF A BROTHER LUCA STOLE IT, BUT YOU ASK EITHER OF 'EM WHAT MY DESTINY HOLDS AND THEY'LL PAINT YOU A PICTURE:

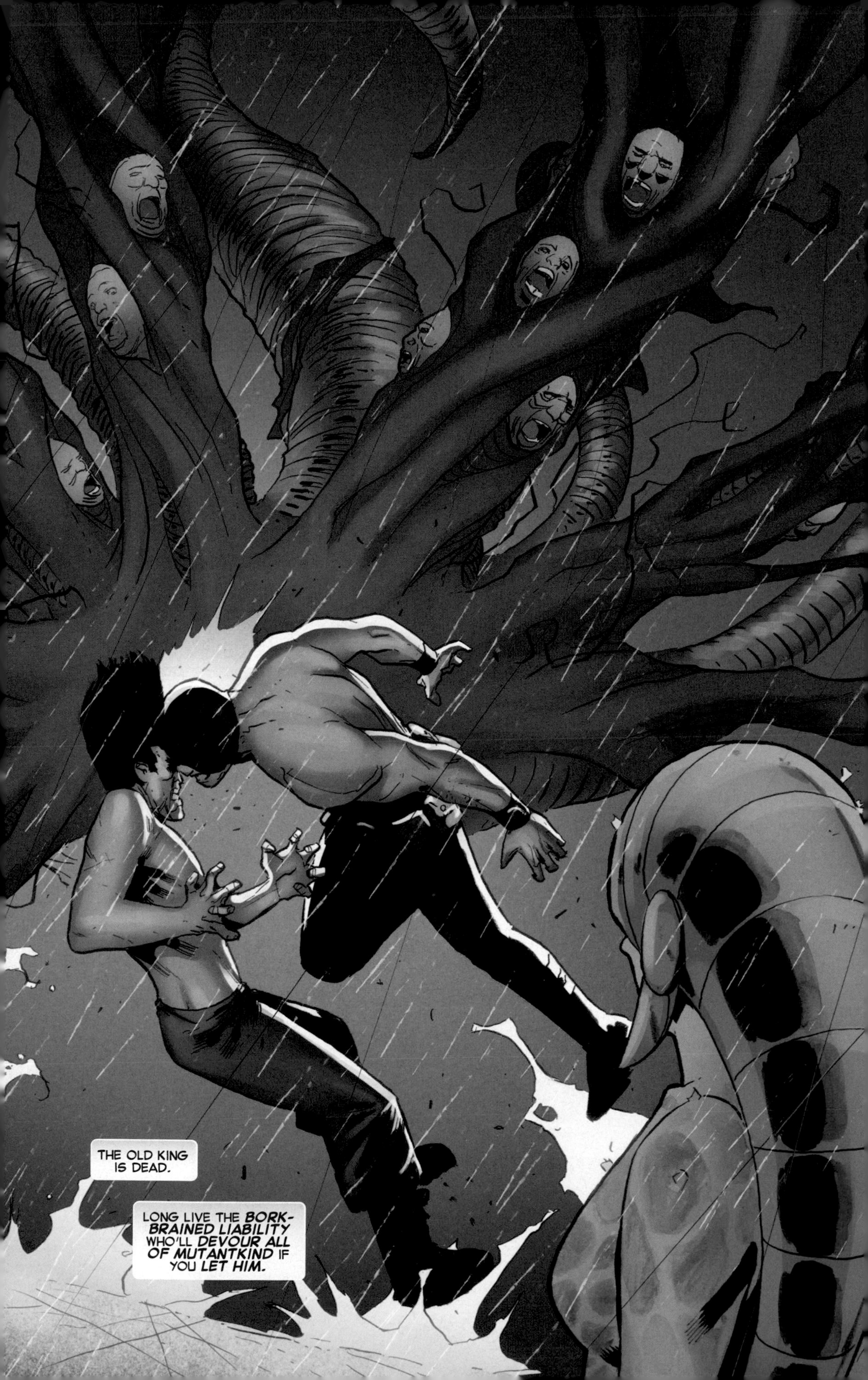
THE OLD KING IS DEAD.
LONG LIVE THE BORK-BRAINED LIABILITY WHO'LL DEVOUR ALL OF MUTANTKIND IF YOU LET HIM.

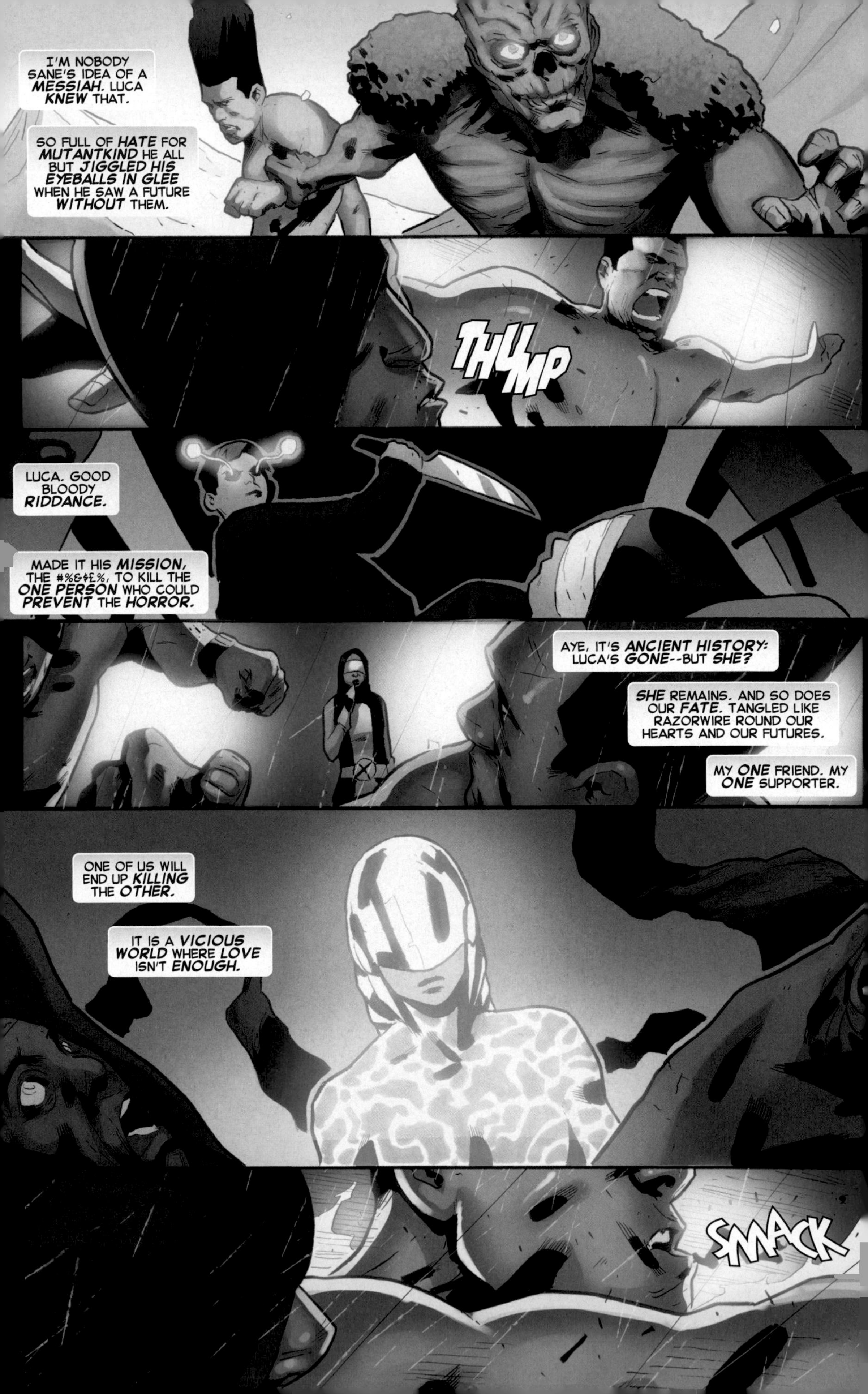

I'M NOBODY SANE'S IDEA OF A MESSIAH. LUCA KNEW THAT.
SO FULL OF HATE FOR MUTANTKIND HE ALL BUT JIGGLED HIS EYEBALLS IN GLEE WHEN HE SAW A FUTURE WITHOUT THEM.
THUMP
LUCA. GOOD BLOODY RIDDANCE.
MADE IT HIS MISSION, THE #%&$£%, TO KILL THE ONE PERSON WHO COULD PREVENT THE HORROR.
AYE, IT'S ANCIENT HISTORY: LUCA'S GONE--BUT SHE?
SHE REMAINS. AND SO DOES OUR FATE. TANGLED LIKE RAZORWIRE ROUND OUR HEARTS AND OUR FUTURES.
MY ONE FRIEND. MY ONE SUPPORTER.
ONE OF US WILL END UP KILLING THE OTHER.
IT IS A VICIOUS WORLD WHERE LOVE ISN'T ENOUGH.
SMACK

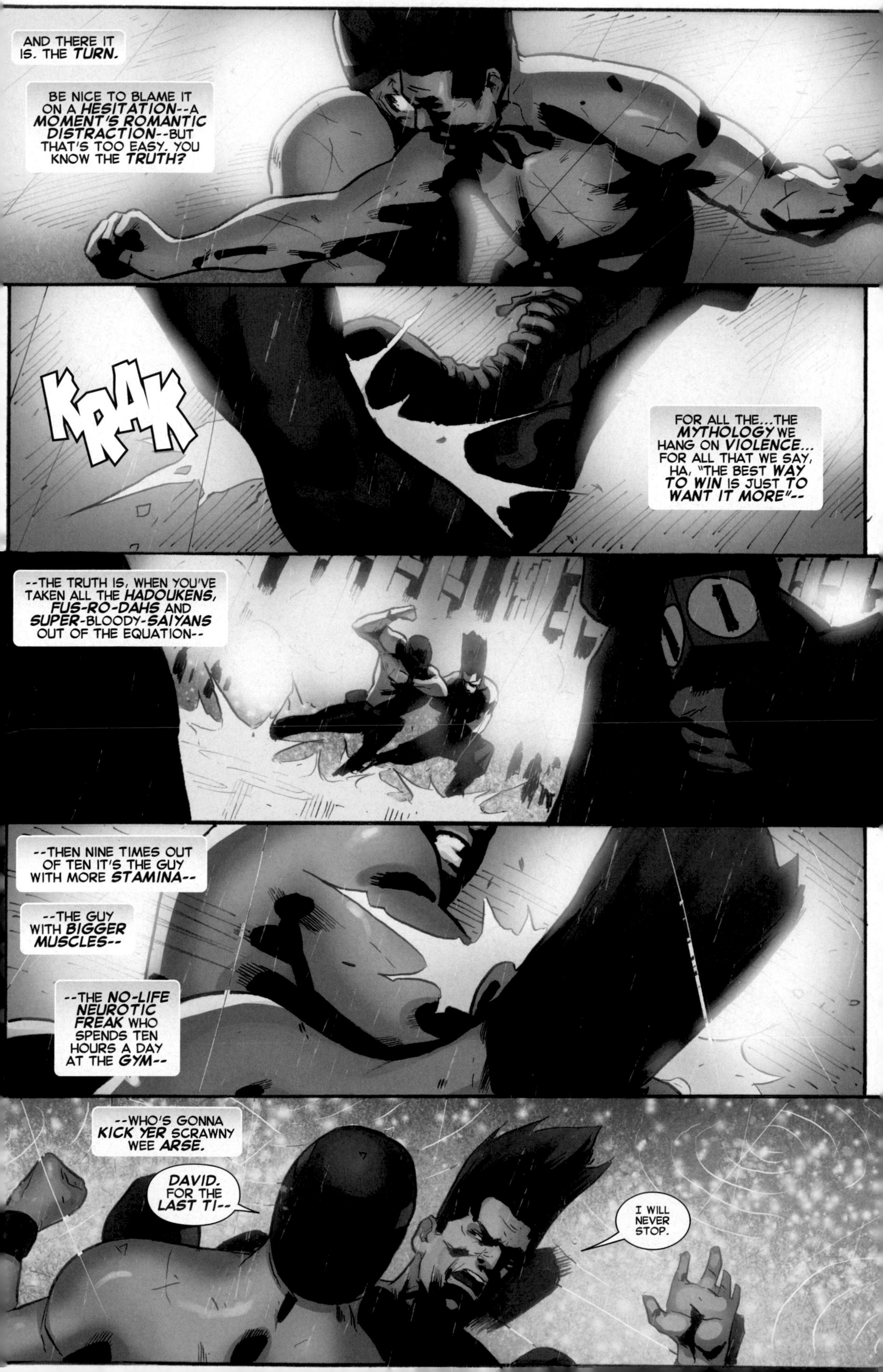
AND THERE IT IS. THE TURN.
BE NICE TO BLAME IT ON A HESITATION--A MOMENT'S ROMANTIC DISTRACTION--BUT THAT'S TOO EASY. YOU KNOW THE TRUTH?
KRAK
FOR ALL THE...THE MYTHOLOGY WE HANG ON VIOLENCE... FOR ALL THAT WE SAY, HA, "THE BEST WAY TO WIN IS JUST TO WANT IT MORE"--
--THE TRUTH IS, WHEN YOU'VE TAKEN ALL THE HADOUKENS, FUS-RO-DAHS AND SUPER-BLOODY-SAIYANS OUT OF THE EQUATION--
--THEN NINE TIMES OUT OF TEN IT'S THE GUY WITH MORE STAMINA--
--THE GUY WITH BIGGER MUSCLES--
--THE NO-LIFE NEUROTIC FREAK WHO SPENDS TEN HOURS A DAY AT THE GYM--
--WHO'S GONNA KICK YER SCRAWNY WEE ARSE.
DAVID. FOR THE LAST TI--
I WILL NEVER STOP.

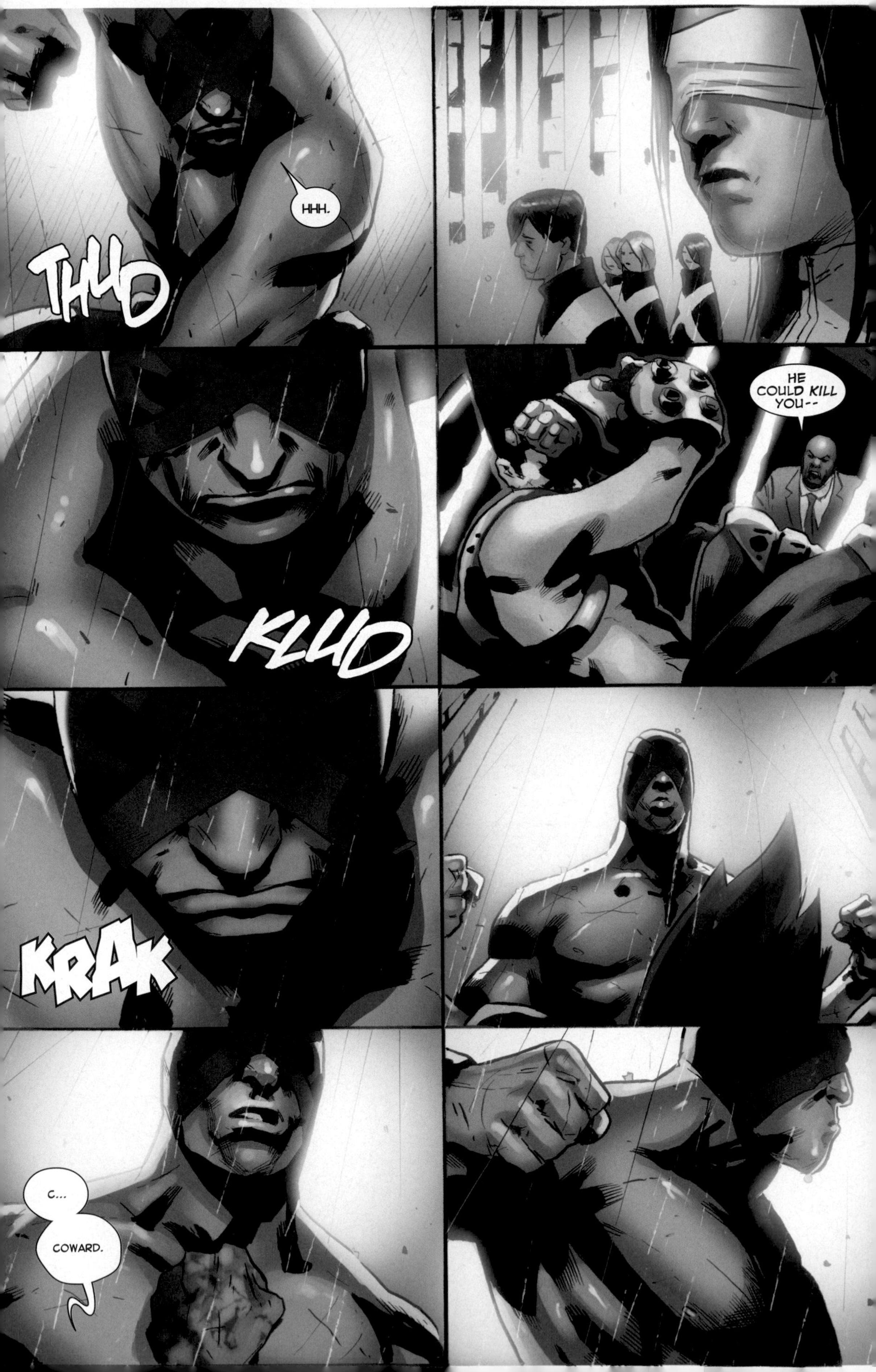
HHH.
THUD
KLUD
HE COULD KILL YOU--
KRAK
C...
COWARD.

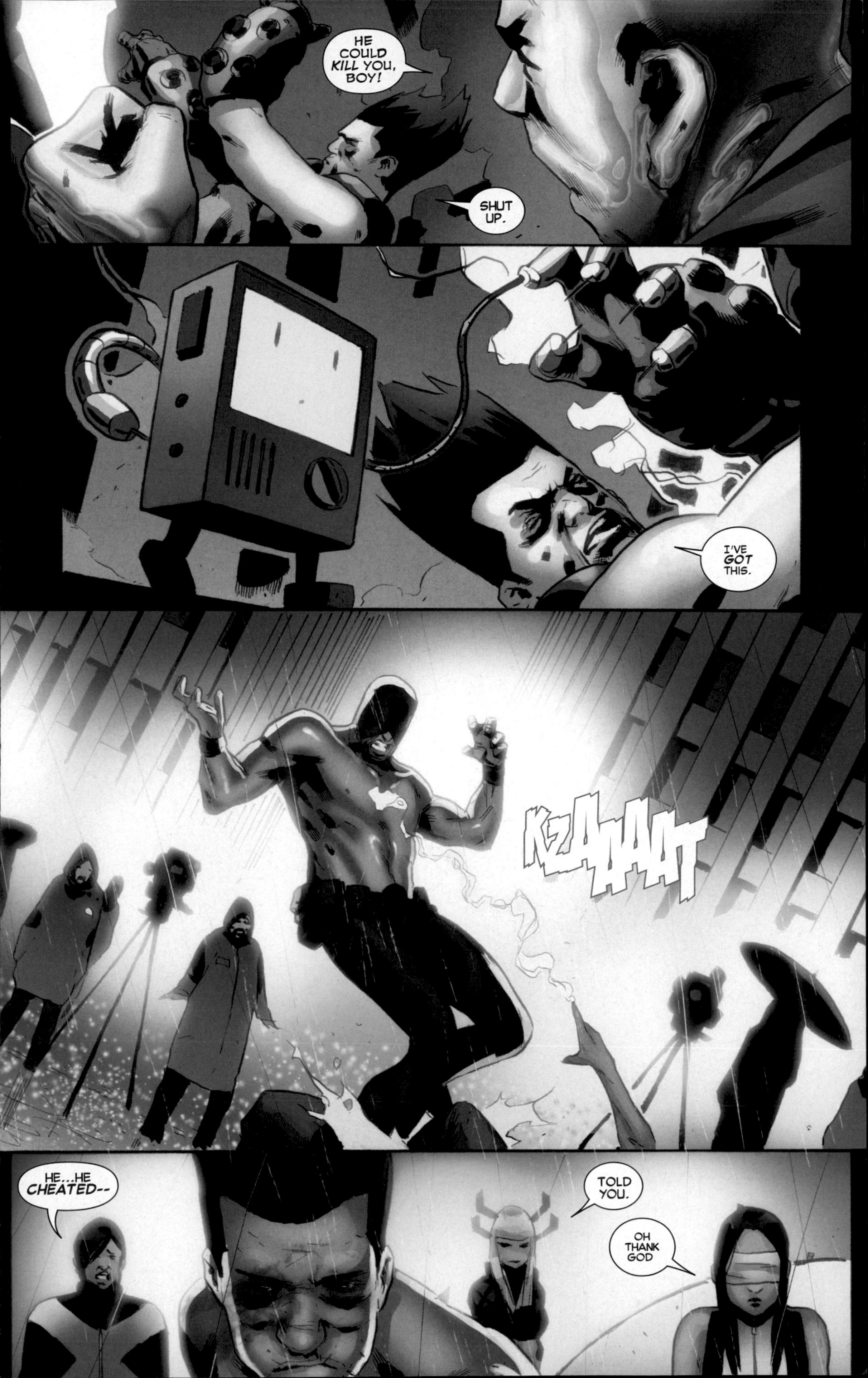
HE COULD KILL YOU, BOY!
SHUT UP.
I'VE GOT THIS.
KZAAAAT
HE...HE CHEATED--
TOLD YOU.
OH THANK GOD

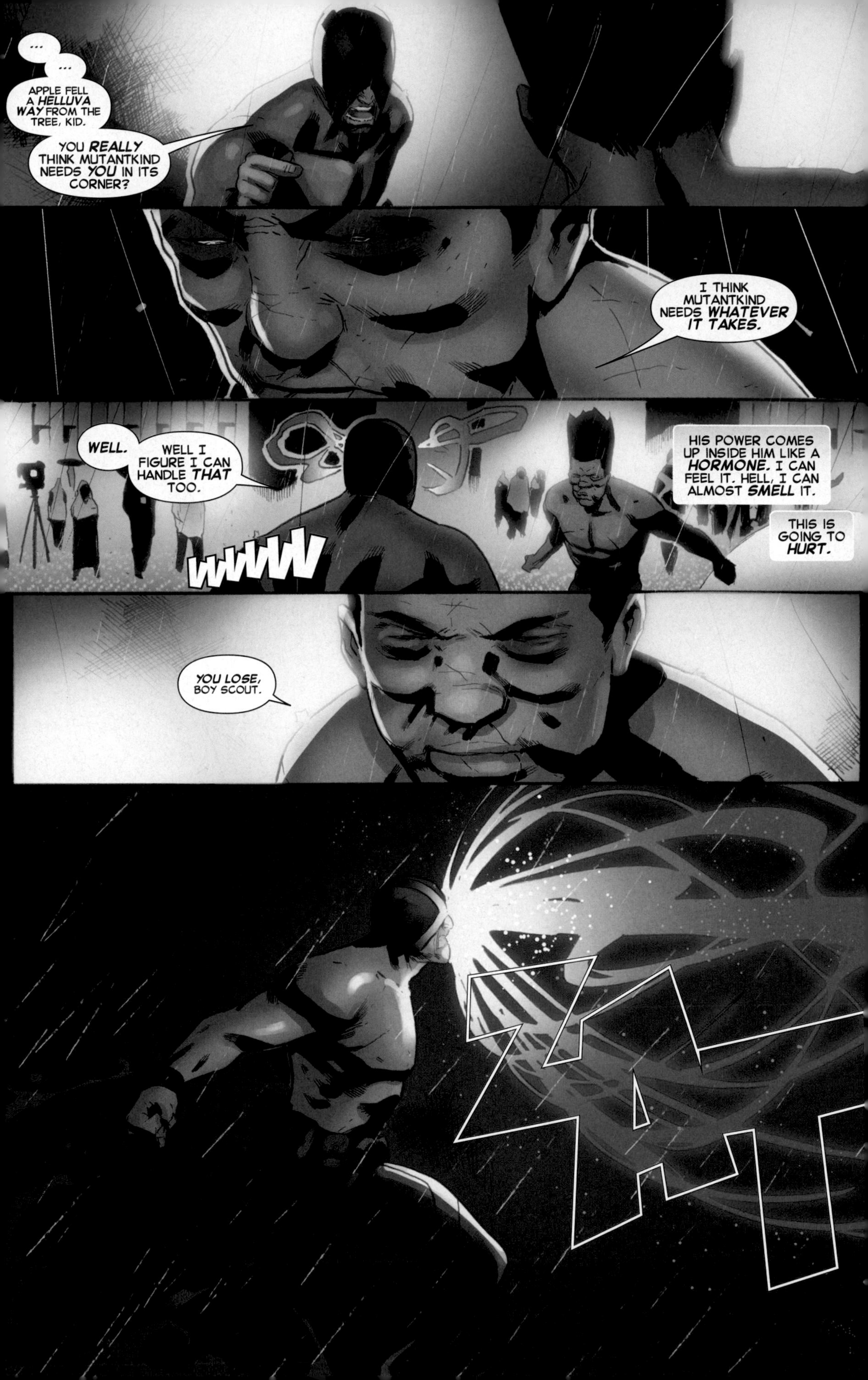
...
...
APPLE FELL A HELLUVA WAY FROM THE TREE, KID.
YOU REALLY THINK MUTANTKIND NEEDS YOU IN ITS CORNER?
I THINK MUTANTKIND NEEDS WHATEVER IT TAKES.
WELL.
WELL I FIGURE I CAN HANDLE THAT TOO.
WWWW
HIS POWER COMES UP INSIDE HIM LIKE A HORMONE. I CAN FEEL IT. HELL, I CAN ALMOST SMELL IT.
THIS IS GOING TO HURT.
YOU LOSE, BOY SCOUT.
ZAT

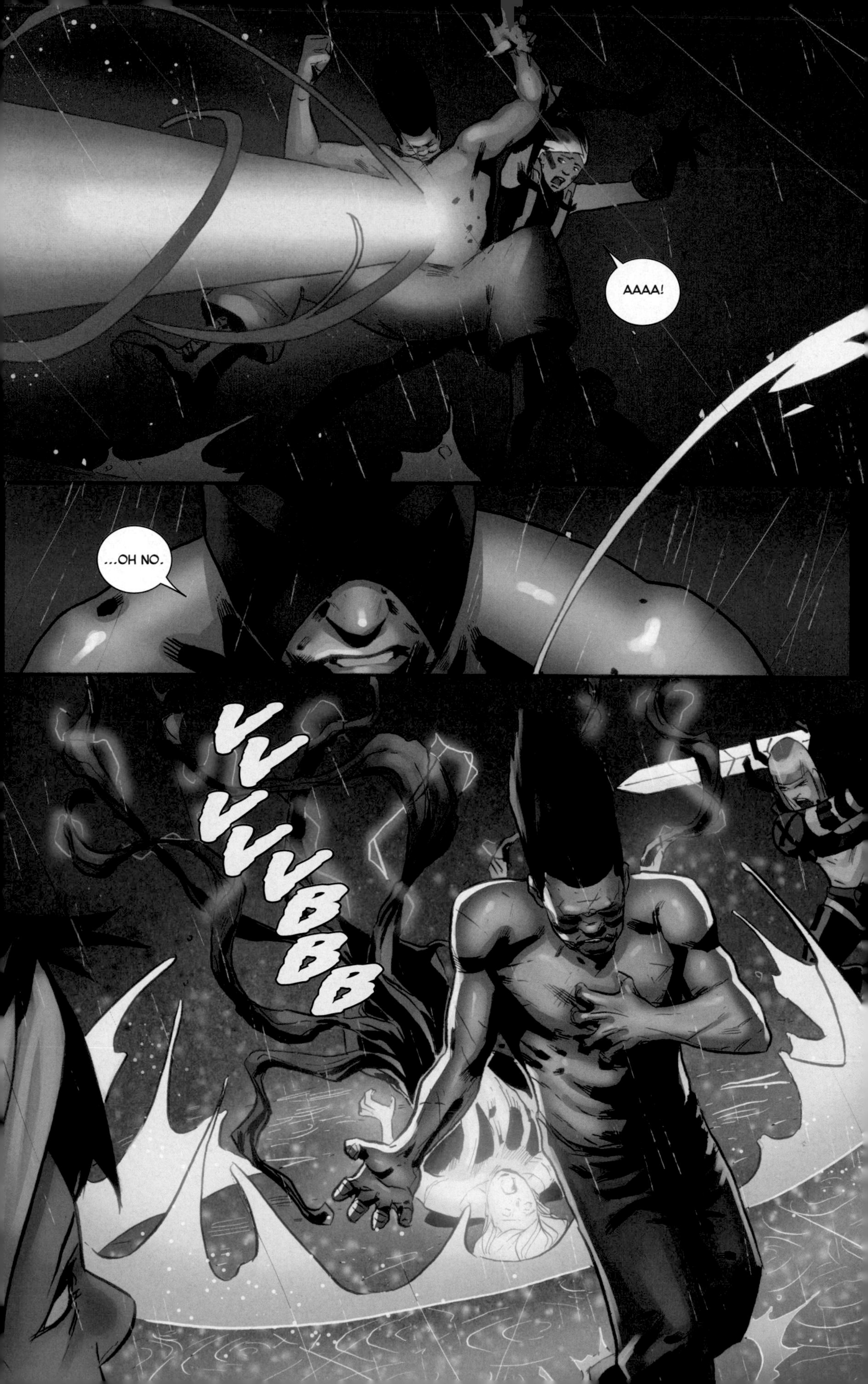
AAAA!
...OH NO.
VVVVVBBB

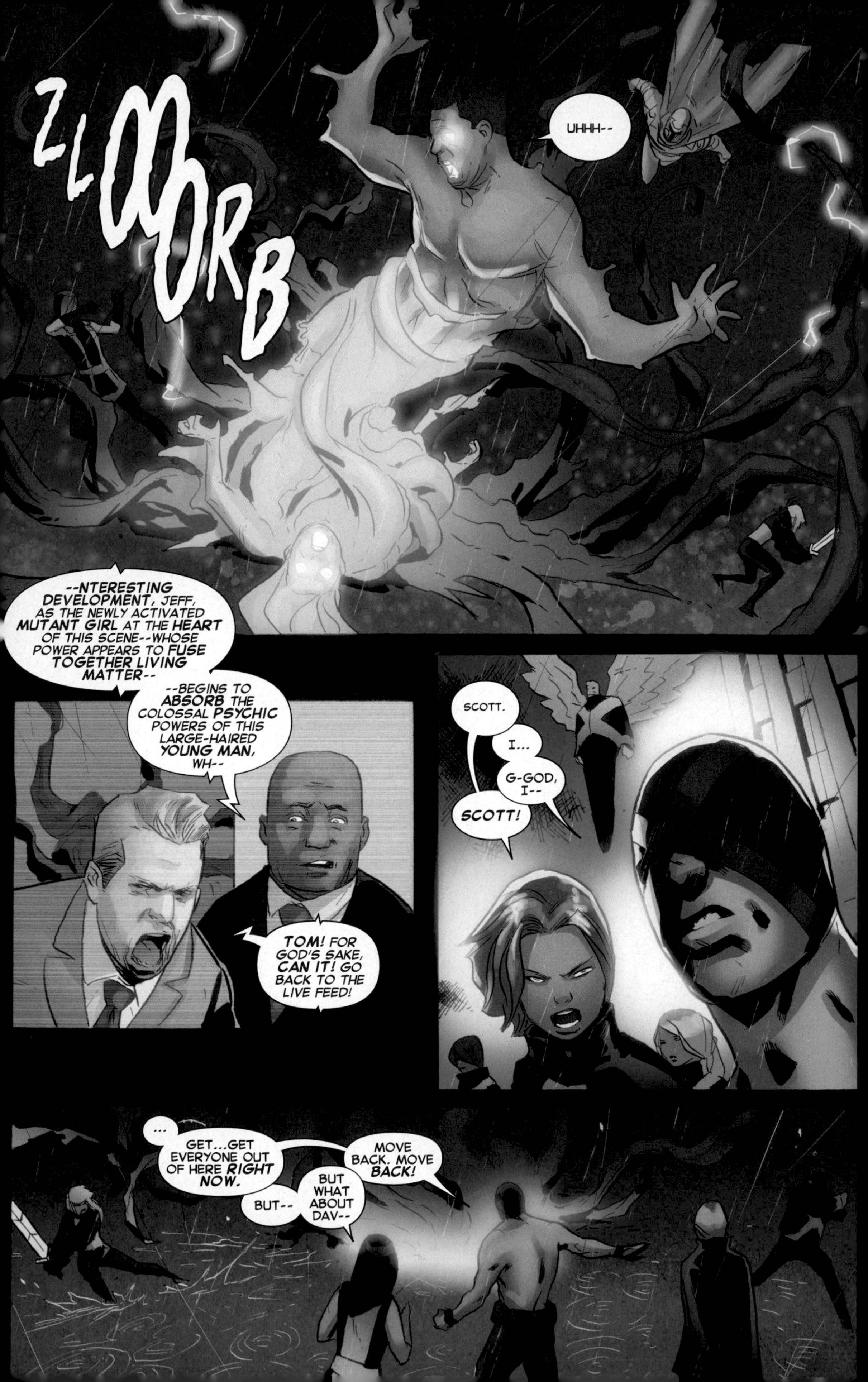
ZLOOORB
UHHH--
--NTERESTING DEVELOPMENT, JEFF, AS THE NEWLY ACTIVATED MUTANT GIRL AT THE HEART OF THIS SCENE--WHOSE POWER APPEARS TO FUSE TOGETHER LIVING MATTER--
--BEGINS TO ABSORB THE COLOSSAL PSYCHIC POWERS OF THIS LARGE-HAIRED YOUNG MAN, WH--
TOM! FOR GOD'S SAKE, CAN IT! GO BACK TO THE LIVE FEED!
SCOTT.
I...
G-GOD, I--
SCOTT!
...
GET...GET EVERYONE OUT OF HERE RIGHT NOW.
MOVE BACK. MOVE BACK!
BUT--
BUT WHAT ABOUT DAV--

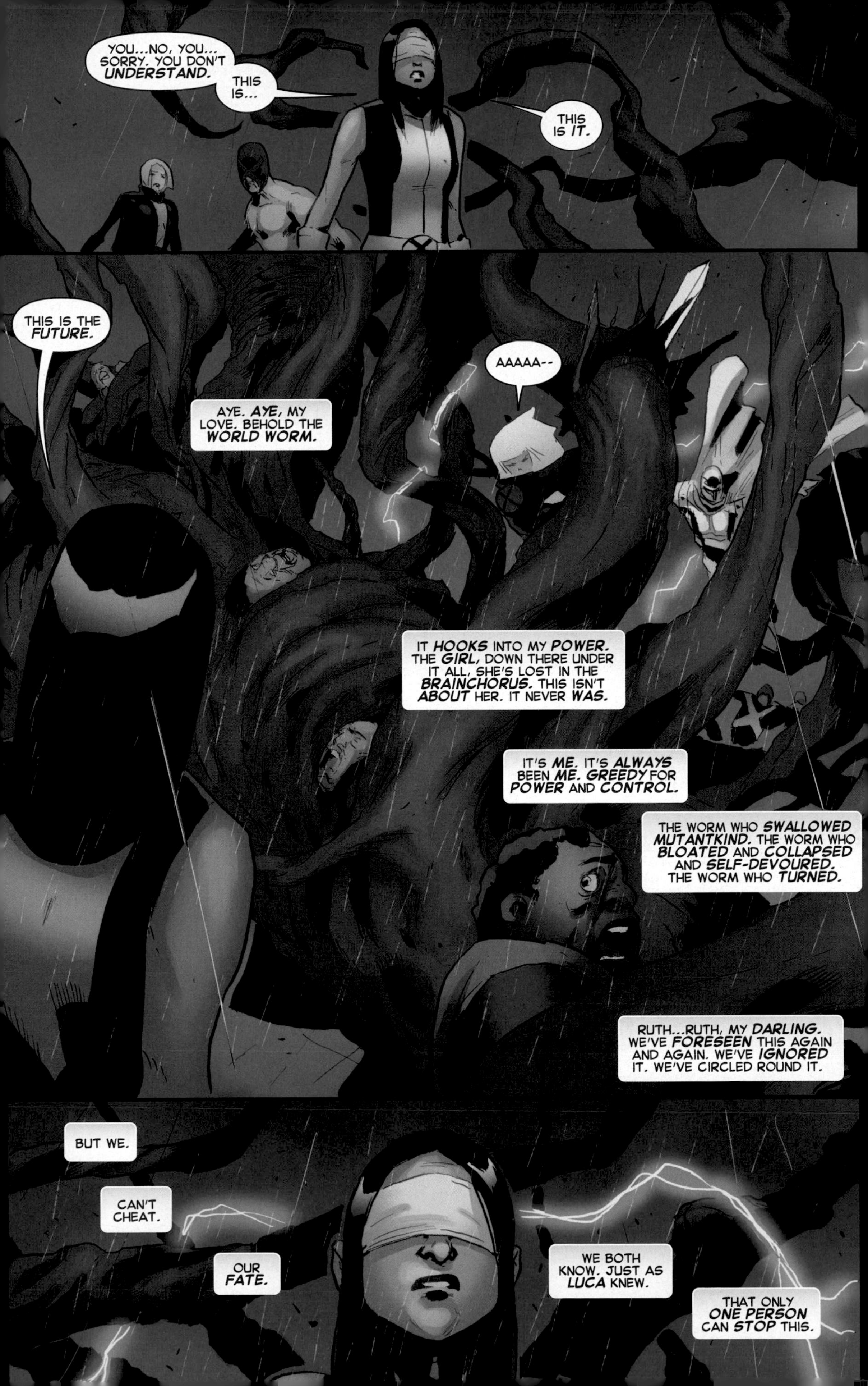

YOU...NO, YOU... SORRY. YOU DON'T UNDERSTAND.
THIS IS...
THIS IS IT.
THIS IS THE FUTURE.
AAAAA--
AYE. AYE, MY LOVE. BEHOLD THE WORLD WORM.
IT HOOKS INTO MY POWER. THE GIRL, DOWN THERE UNDER IT ALL, SHE'S LOST IN THE BRAINCHORUS. THIS ISN'T ABOUT HER. IT NEVER WAS.
IT'S ME. IT'S ALWAYS BEEN ME. GREEDY FOR POWER AND CONTROL.
THE WORM WHO SWALLOWED MUTANTKIND. THE WORM WHO BLOATED AND COLLAPSED AND SELF-DEVOURED. THE WORM WHO TURNED.
RUTH...RUTH, MY DARLING. WE'VE FORESEEN THIS AGAIN AND AGAIN. WE'VE IGNORED IT. WE'VE CIRCLED ROUND IT.
BUT WE.
CAN'T CHEAT.
OUR FATE.
WE BOTH KNOW. JUST AS LUCA KNEW.
THAT ONLY ONE PERSON CAN STOP THIS.

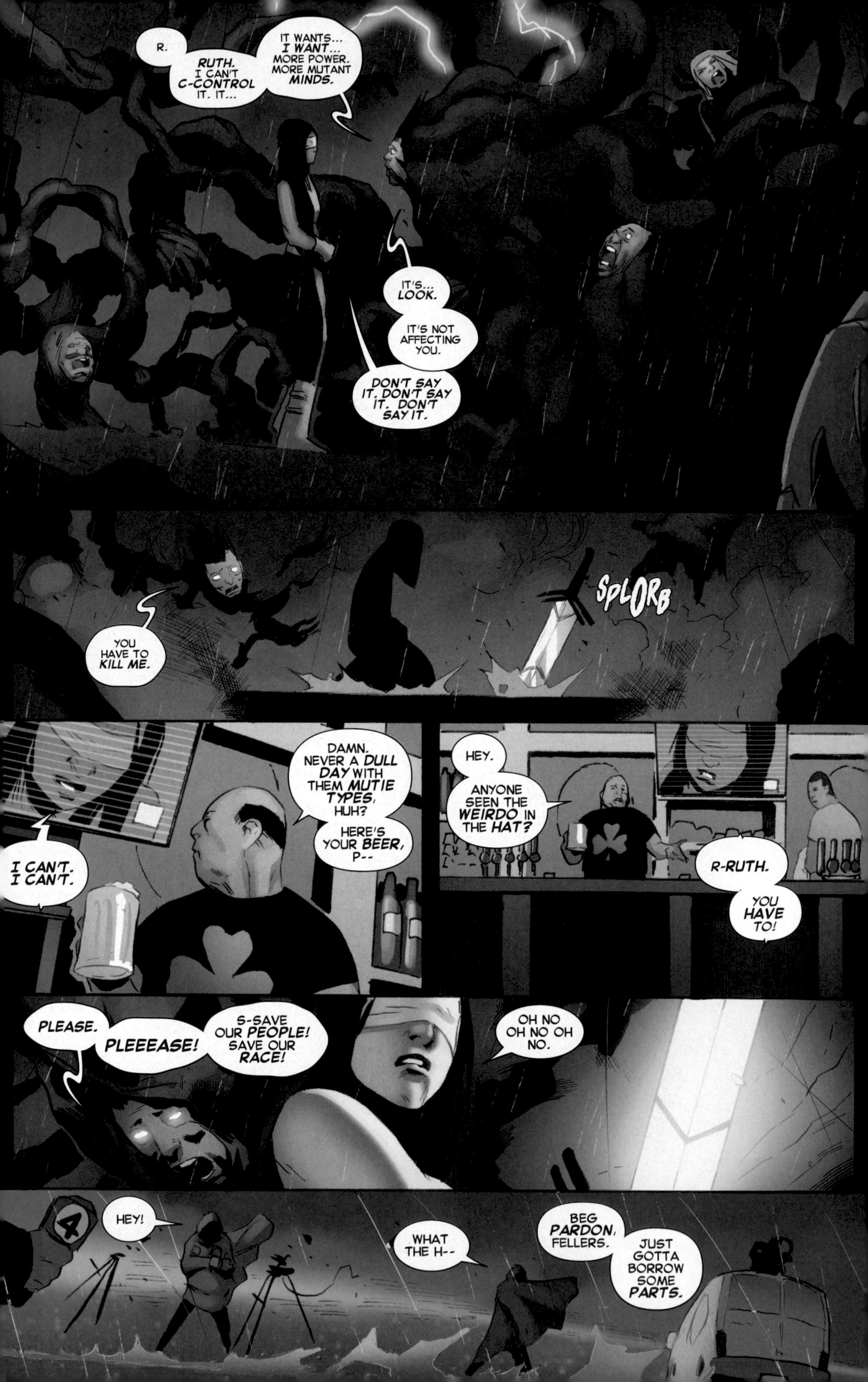

R.
RUTH. I CAN'T C-CONTROL IT. IT...
IT WANTS... I WANT... MORE POWER. MORE MUTANT MINDS.
IT'S... LOOK.
IT'S NOT AFFECTING YOU.
DON'T SAY IT. DON'T SAY IT. DON'T SAY IT.
YOU HAVE TO KILL ME.
SPLORB
I CAN'T. I CAN'T.
DAMN. NEVER A DULL DAY WITH THEM MUTIE TYPES, HUH?
HERE'S YOUR BEER, P--
HEY.
ANYONE SEEN THE WEIRDO IN THE HAT?
R-RUTH.
YOU HAVE TO!
PLEASE.
PLEEEASE!
S-SAVE OUR PEOPLE! SAVE OUR RACE!
OH NO OH NO OH NO.
4
HEY!
WHAT THE H--
BEG PARDON, FELLERS.
JUST GOTTA BORROW SOME PARTS.

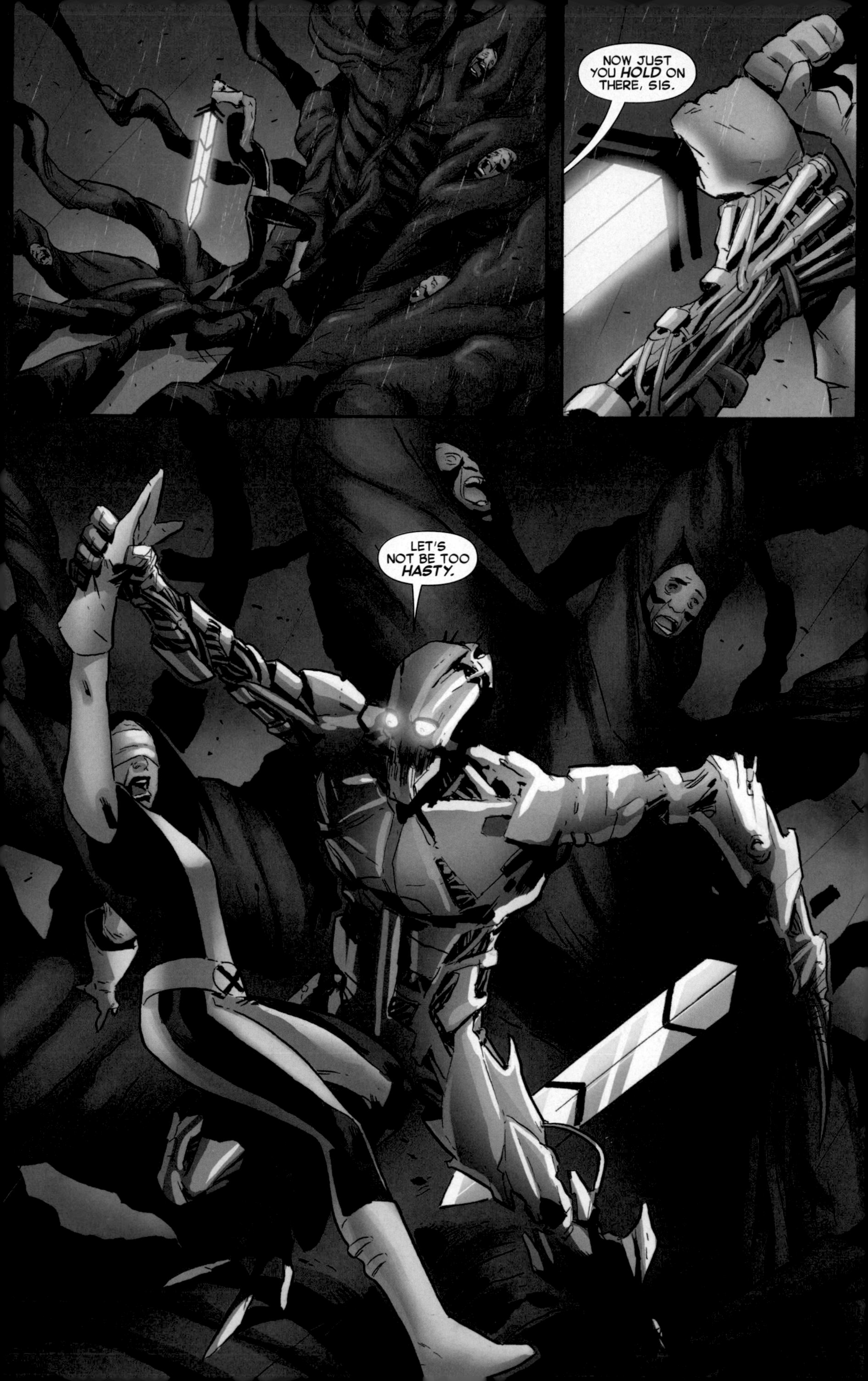
NOW JUST YOU HOLD ON THERE, SIS.
LET'S NOT BE TOO HASTY.

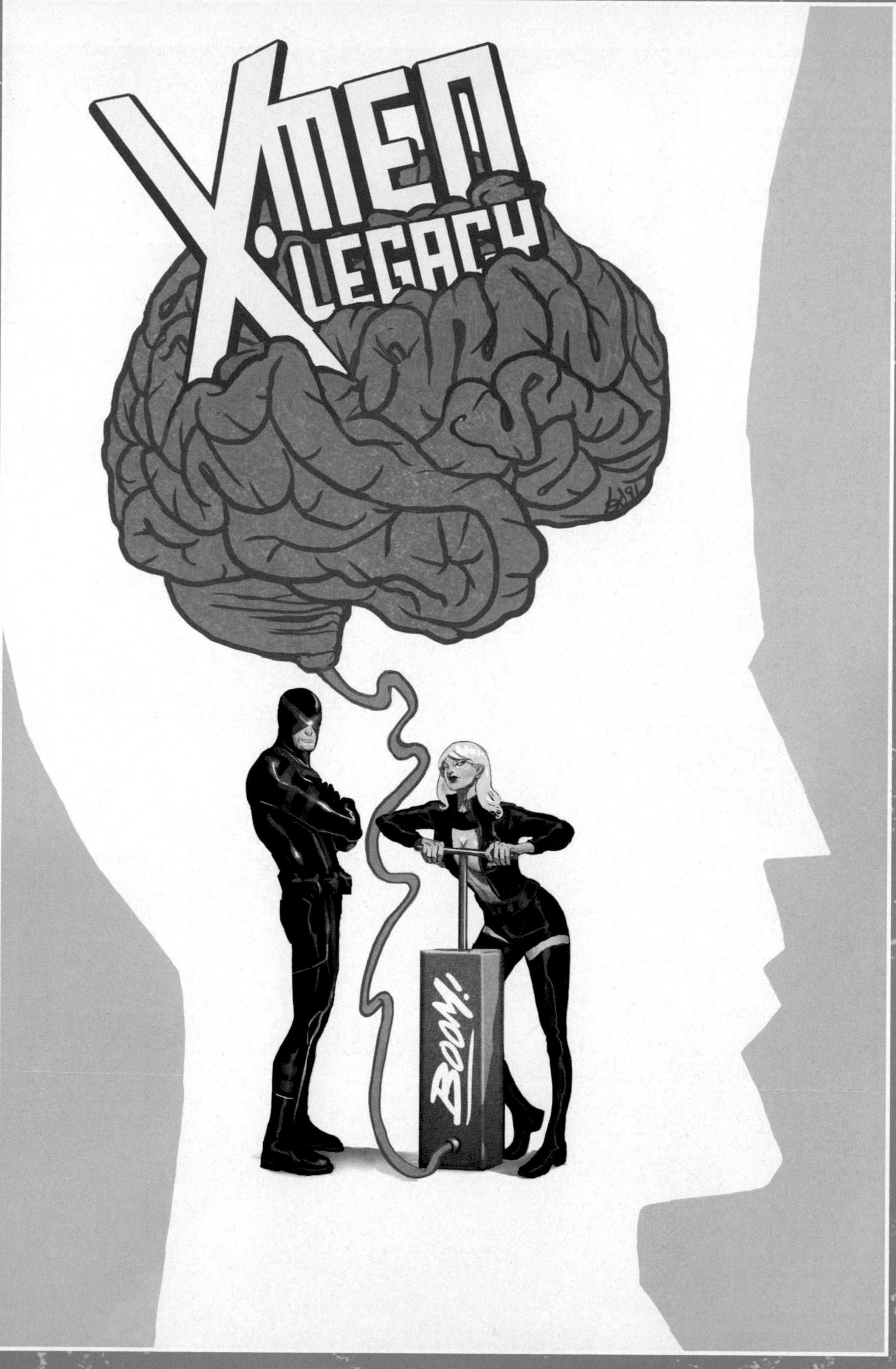
X-MEN
LEGACY
BOOM!

EIGHTEEN

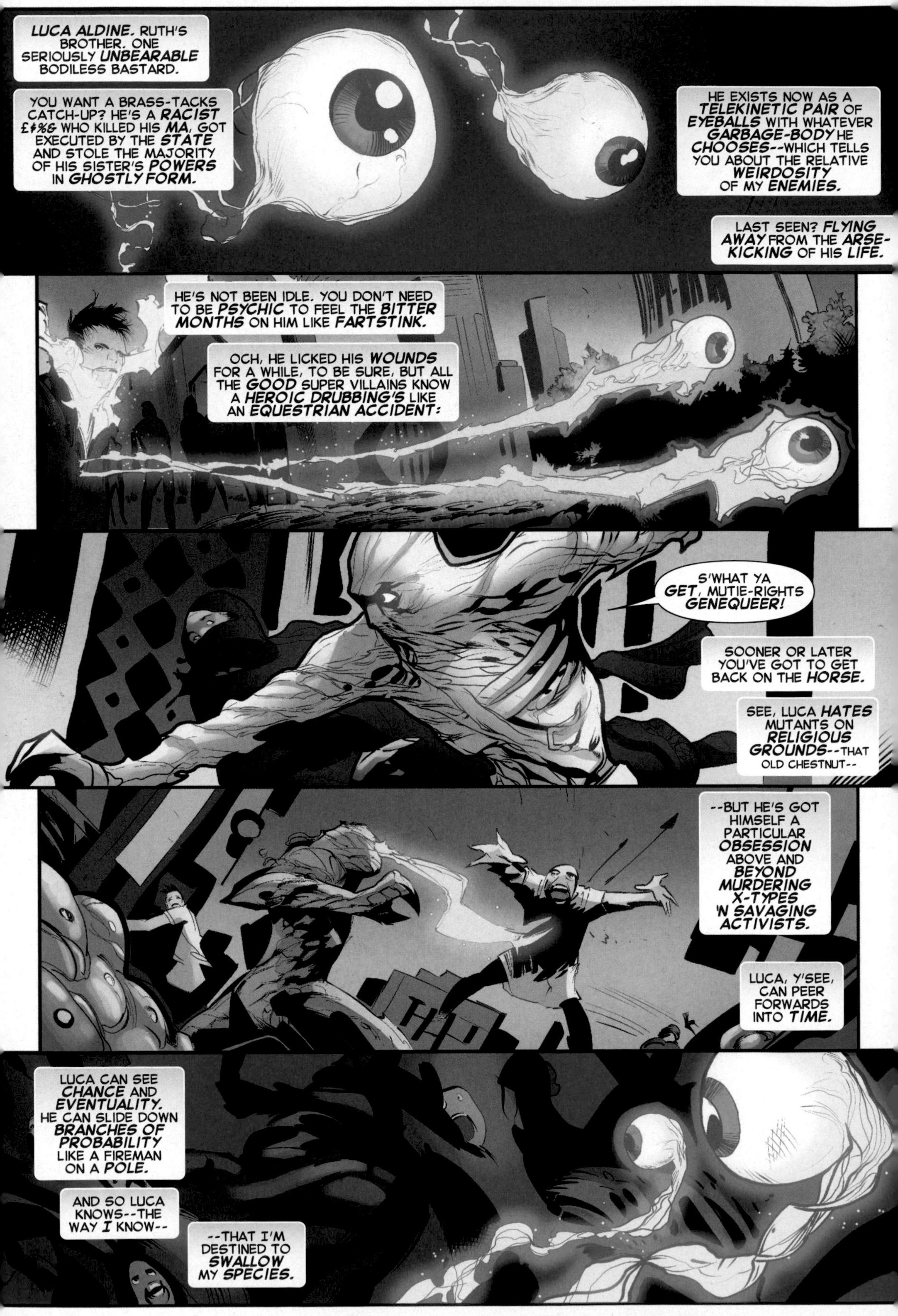
LUCA ALDINE. RUTH'S BROTHER. ONE SERIOUSLY UNBEARABLE BODILESS BASTARD.
YOU WANT A BRASS-TACKS CATCH-UP? HE'S A RACIST £$%& WHO KILLED HIS MA, GOT EXECUTED BY THE STATE AND STOLE THE MAJORITY OF HIS SISTER'S POWERS IN GHOSTLY FORM.
HE EXISTS NOW AS A TELEKINETIC PAIR OF EYEBALLS WITH WHATEVER GARBAGE-BODY HE CHOOSES--WHICH TELLS YOU ABOUT THE RELATIVE WEIRDOSITY OF MY ENEMIES.
LAST SEEN? FLYING AWAY FROM THE ARSE-KICKING OF HIS LIFE.
HE'S NOT BEEN IDLE. YOU DON'T NEED TO BE PSYCHIC TO FEEL THE BITTER MONTHS ON HIM LIKE FARTSTINK.
OCH, HE LICKED HIS WOUNDS FOR A WHILE, TO BE SURE, BUT ALL THE GOOD SUPER VILLAINS KNOW A HEROIC DRUBBING'S LIKE AN EQUESTRIAN ACCIDENT:
S'WHAT YA GET, MUTIE-RIGHTS GENEQUEER!
SOONER OR LATER YOU'VE GOT TO GET BACK ON THE HORSE.
SEE, LUCA HATES MUTANTS ON RELIGIOUS GROUNDS--THAT OLD CHESTNUT--
--BUT HE'S GOT HIMSELF A PARTICULAR OBSESSION ABOVE AND BEYOND MURDERING X-TYPES 'N SAVAGING ACTIVISTS.
LUCA, Y'SEE, CAN PEER FORWARDS INTO TIME.
LUCA CAN SEE CHANCE AND EVENTUALITY. HE CAN SLIDE DOWN BRANCHES OF PROBABILITY LIKE A FIREMAN ON A POLE.
AND SO LUCA KNOWS--THE WAY I KNOW--
--THAT I'M DESTINED TO SWALLOW MY SPECIES.

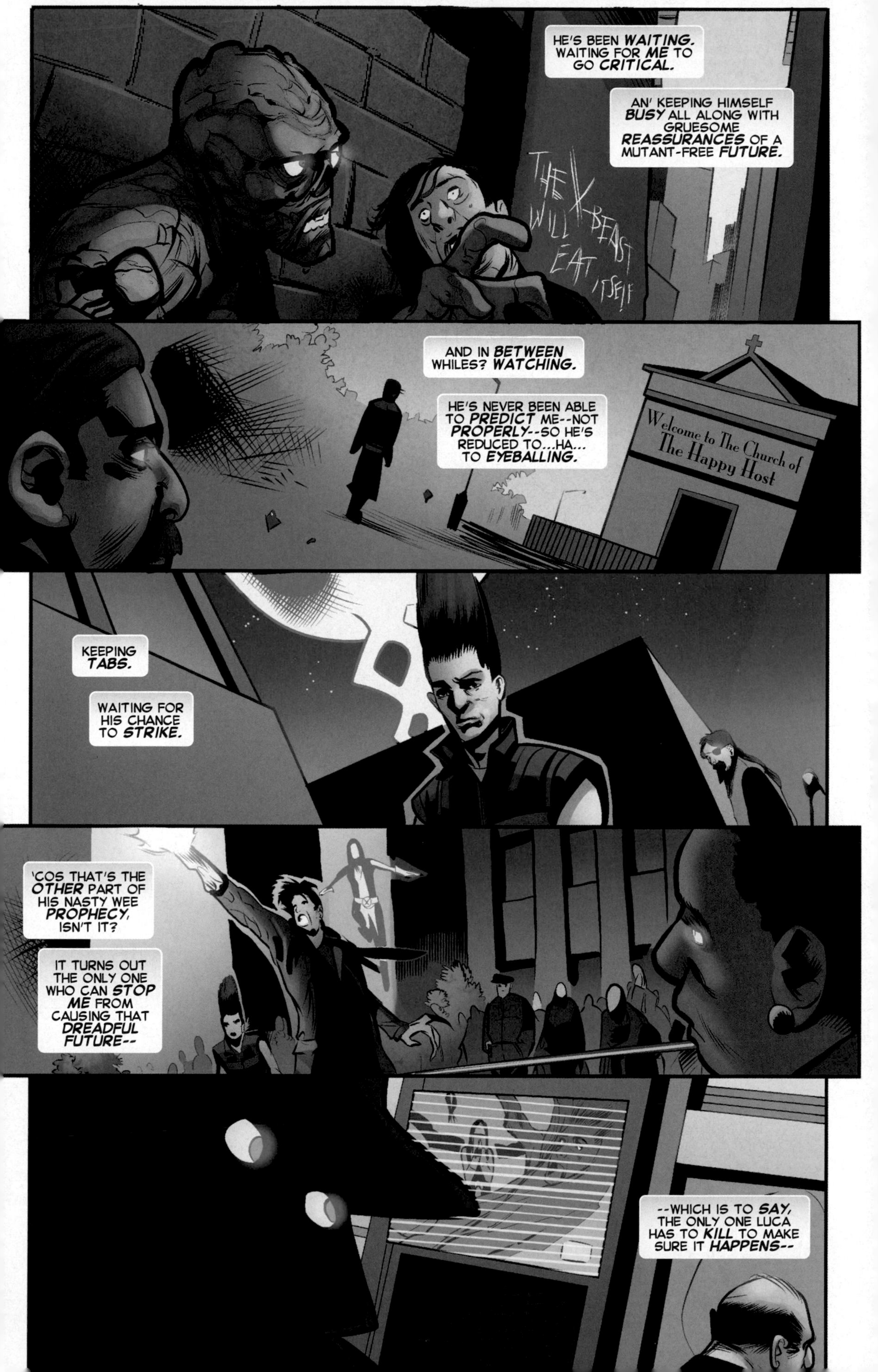
HE'S BEEN WAITING. WAITING FOR ME TO GO CRITICAL.
AN' KEEPING HIMSELF BUSY ALL ALONG WITH GRUESOME REASSURANCES OF A MUTANT-FREE FUTURE.
THE X-BEAST WILL EAT ITSELF!
AND IN BETWEEN WHILES? WATCHING.
HE'S NEVER BEEN ABLE TO PREDICT ME--NOT PROPERLY--SO HE'S REDUCED TO...HA... TO EYEBALLING.
Welcome to The Church of The Happy Host
KEEPING TABS.
WAITING FOR HIS CHANCE TO STRIKE.
'COS THAT'S THE OTHER PART OF HIS NASTY WEE PROPHECY, ISN'T IT?
IT TURNS OUT THE ONLY ONE WHO CAN STOP ME FROM CAUSING THAT DREADFUL FUTURE--
--WHICH IS TO SAY, THE ONLY ONE LUCA HAS TO KILL TO MAKE SURE IT HAPPENS--

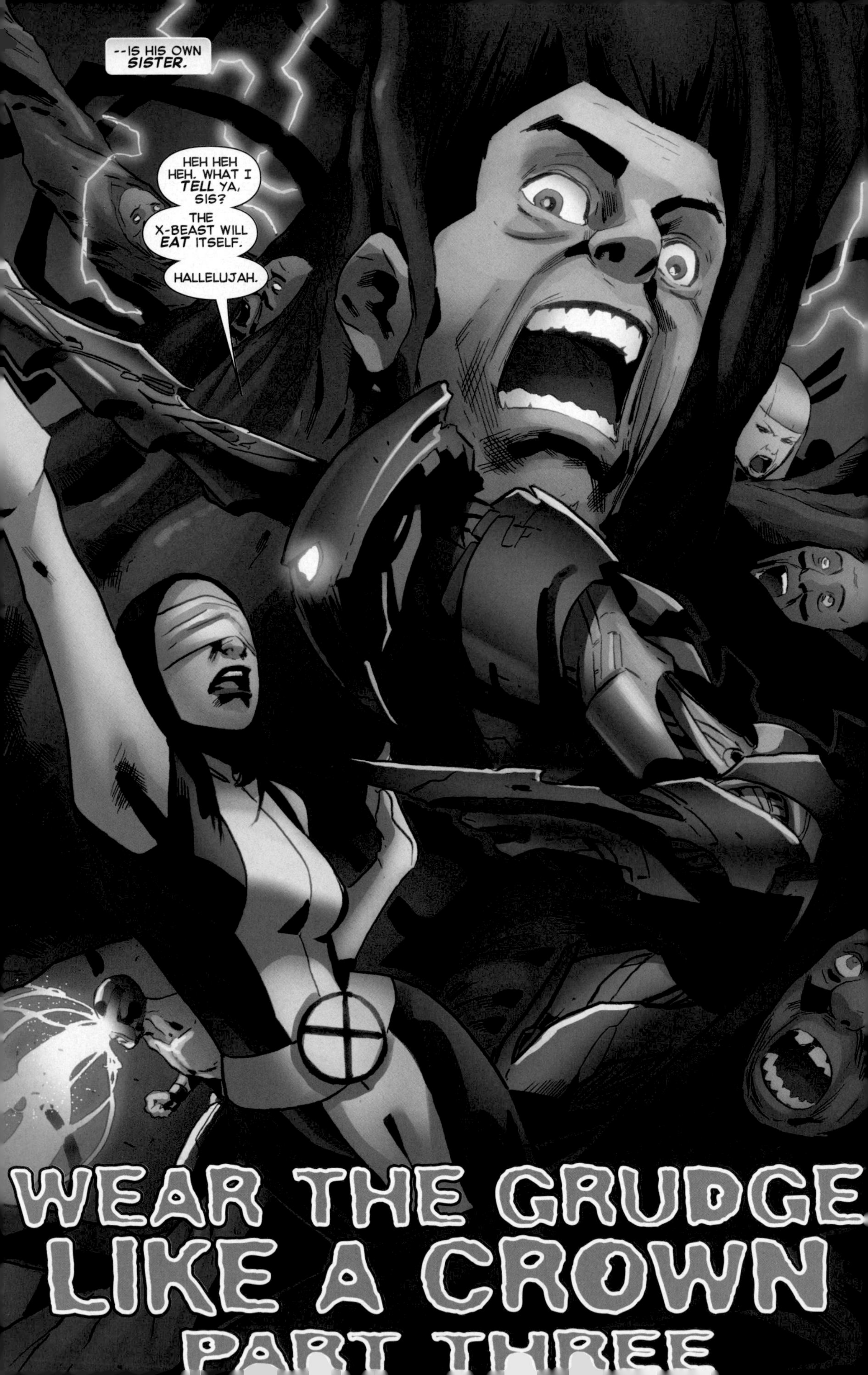
--IS HIS OWN SISTER.
HEH HEH HEH. WHAT I TELL YA, SIS?
THE X-BEAST WILL EAT ITSELF.
HALLELUJAH.
WEAR THE GRUDGE LIKE A CROWN
PART THREE

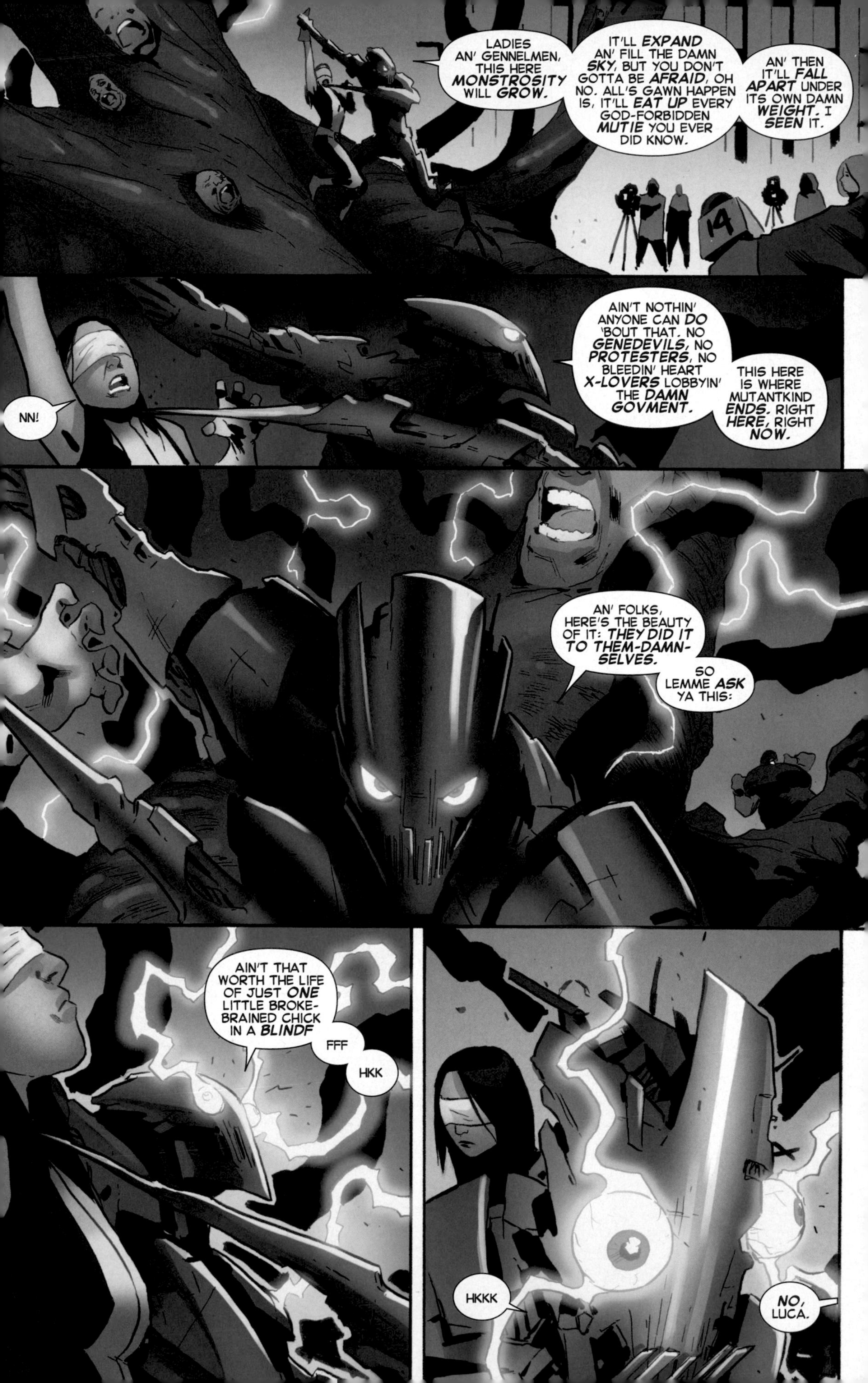
LADIES AN' GENNELMEN, THIS HERE MONSTROSITY WILL GROW.
IT'LL EXPAND AN' FILL THE DAMN SKY, BUT YOU DON'T GOTTA BE AFRAID, OH NO. ALL'S GAWN HAPPEN IS, IT'LL EAT UP EVERY GOD-FORBIDDEN MUTIE YOU EVER DID KNOW.
AN' THEN IT'LL FALL APART UNDER ITS OWN DAMN WEIGHT. I SEEN IT.
14
NN!
AIN'T NOTHIN' ANYONE CAN DO 'BOUT THAT. NO GENEDEVILS, NO PROTESTERS, NO BLEEDIN' HEART X-LOVERS LOBBYIN' THE DAMN GOVMENT.
THIS HERE IS WHERE MUTANTKIND ENDS. RIGHT HERE, RIGHT NOW.
AN' FOLKS, HERE'S THE BEAUTY OF IT: THEY DID IT TO THEM-DAMN-SELVES.
SO LEMME ASK YA THIS:
AIN'T THAT WORTH THE LIFE OF JUST ONE LITTLE BROKE-BRAINED CHICK IN A BLINDF
FFF
HKK
HKKK
NO, LUCA.

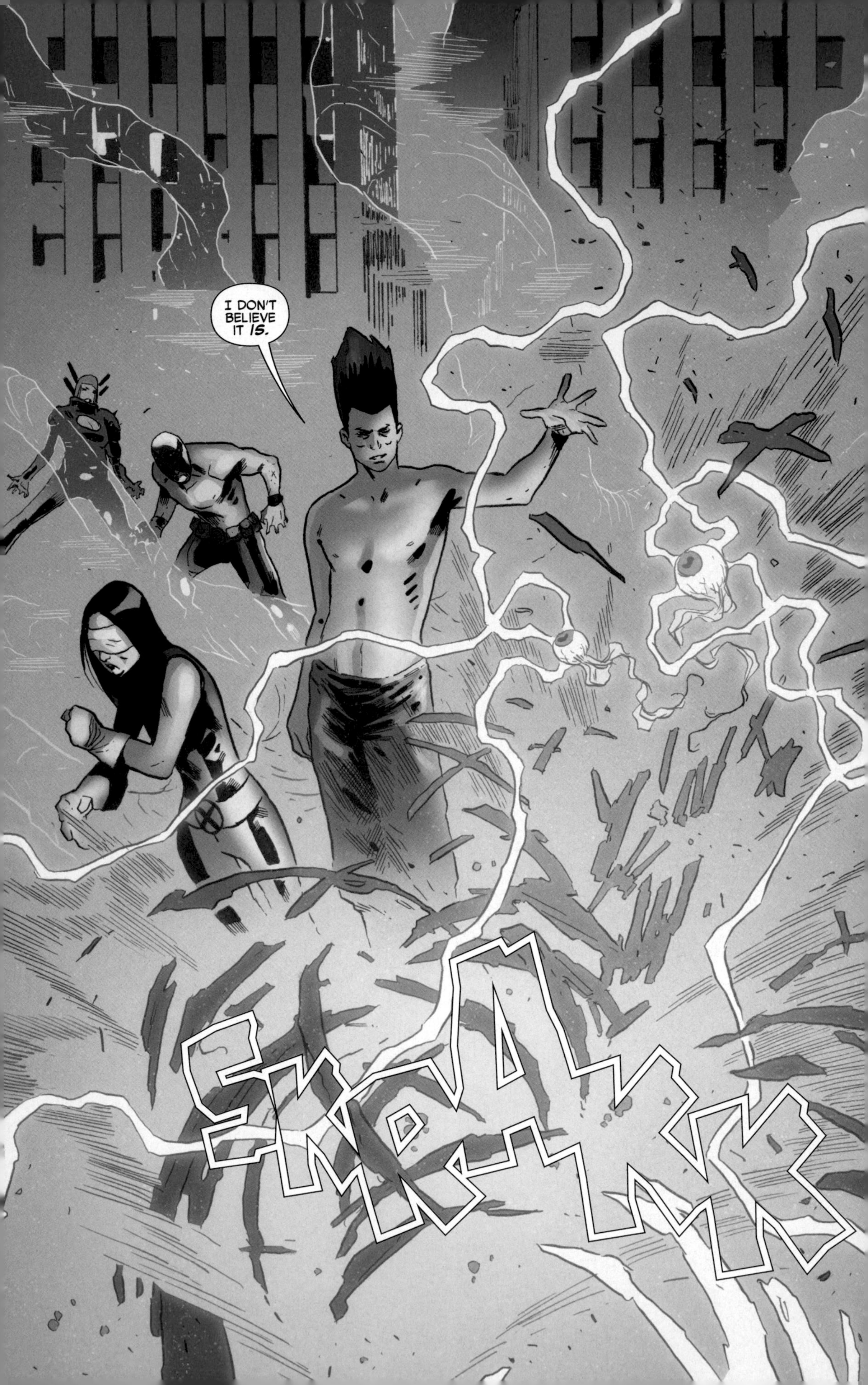

I DON'T BELIEVE IT IS.

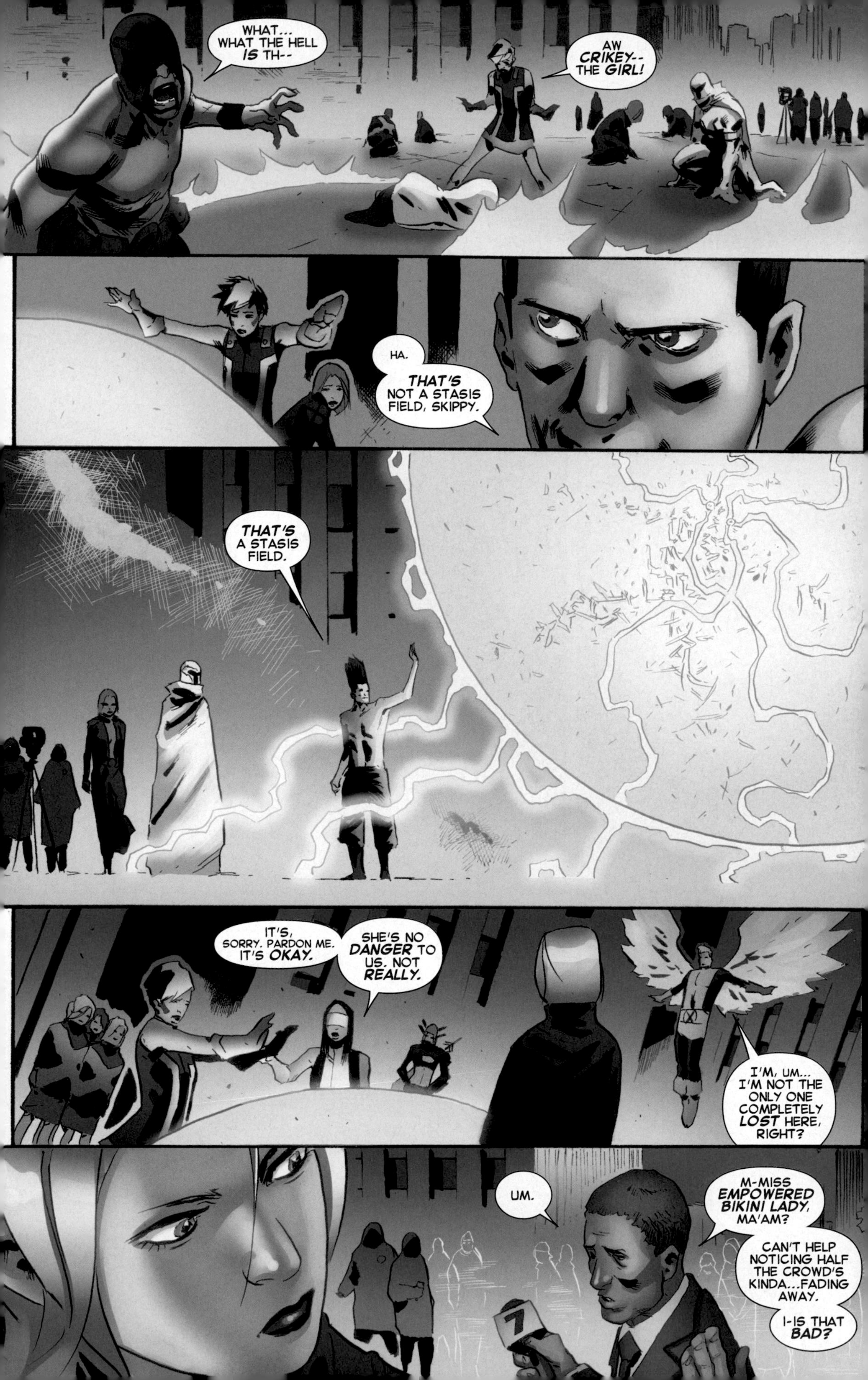
WHAT... WHAT THE HELL IS TH--
AW CRIKEY-- THE GIRL!
HA.
THAT'S NOT A STASIS FIELD, SKIPPY.
THAT'S A STASIS FIELD.
IT'S, SORRY. PARDON ME. IT'S OKAY.
SHE'S NO DANGER TO US. NOT REALLY.
I'M, UM... I'M NOT THE ONLY ONE COMPLETELY LOST HERE, RIGHT?
UM.
M-MISS EMPOWERED BIKINI LADY, MA'AM?
CAN'T HELP NOTICING HALF THE CROWD'S KINDA...FADING AWAY.
I-IS THAT BAD?

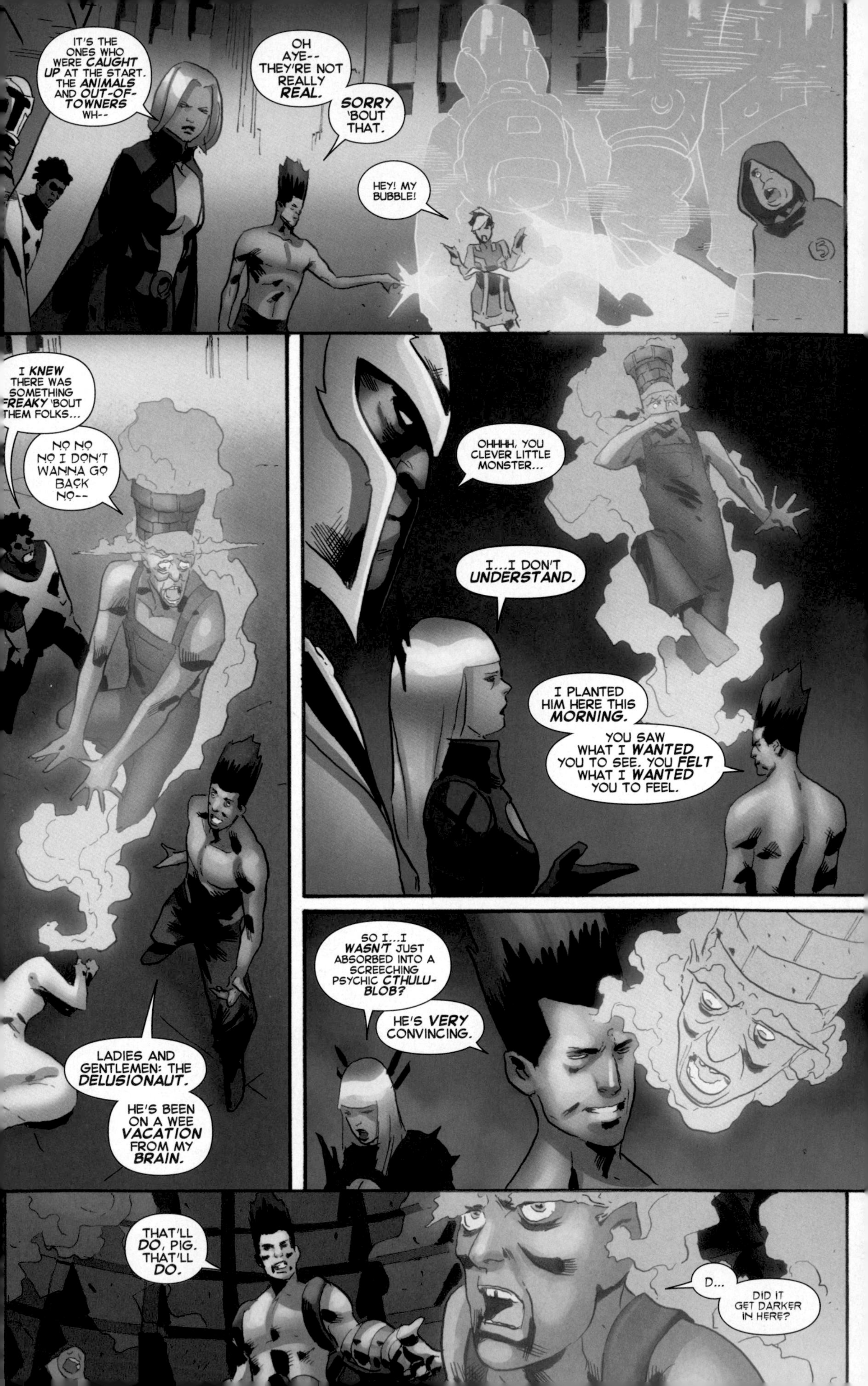
IT'S THE ONES WHO WERE CAUGHT UP AT THE START. THE ANIMALS AND OUT-OF-TOWNERS WH--
OH AYE-- THEY'RE NOT REALLY REAL.
SORRY 'BOUT THAT.
HEY! MY BUBBLE!
5
I KNEW THERE WAS SOMETHING FREAKY 'BOUT THEM FOLKS...
NO NO NO I DON'T WANNA GO BACK NO--
LADIES AND GENTLEMEN: THE DELUSIONAUT.
HE'S BEEN ON A WEE VACATION FROM MY BRAIN.
OHHHH, YOU CLEVER LITTLE MONSTER...
I...I DON'T UNDERSTAND.
I PLANTED HIM HERE THIS MORNING.
YOU SAW WHAT I WANTED YOU TO SEE. YOU FELT WHAT I WANTED YOU TO FEEL.
SO I...I WASN'T JUST ABSORBED INTO A SCREECHING PSYCHIC CTHULU-BLOB?
HE'S VERY CONVINCING.
THAT'LL DO, PIG. THAT'LL DO.
D...
DID IT GET DARKER IN HERE?

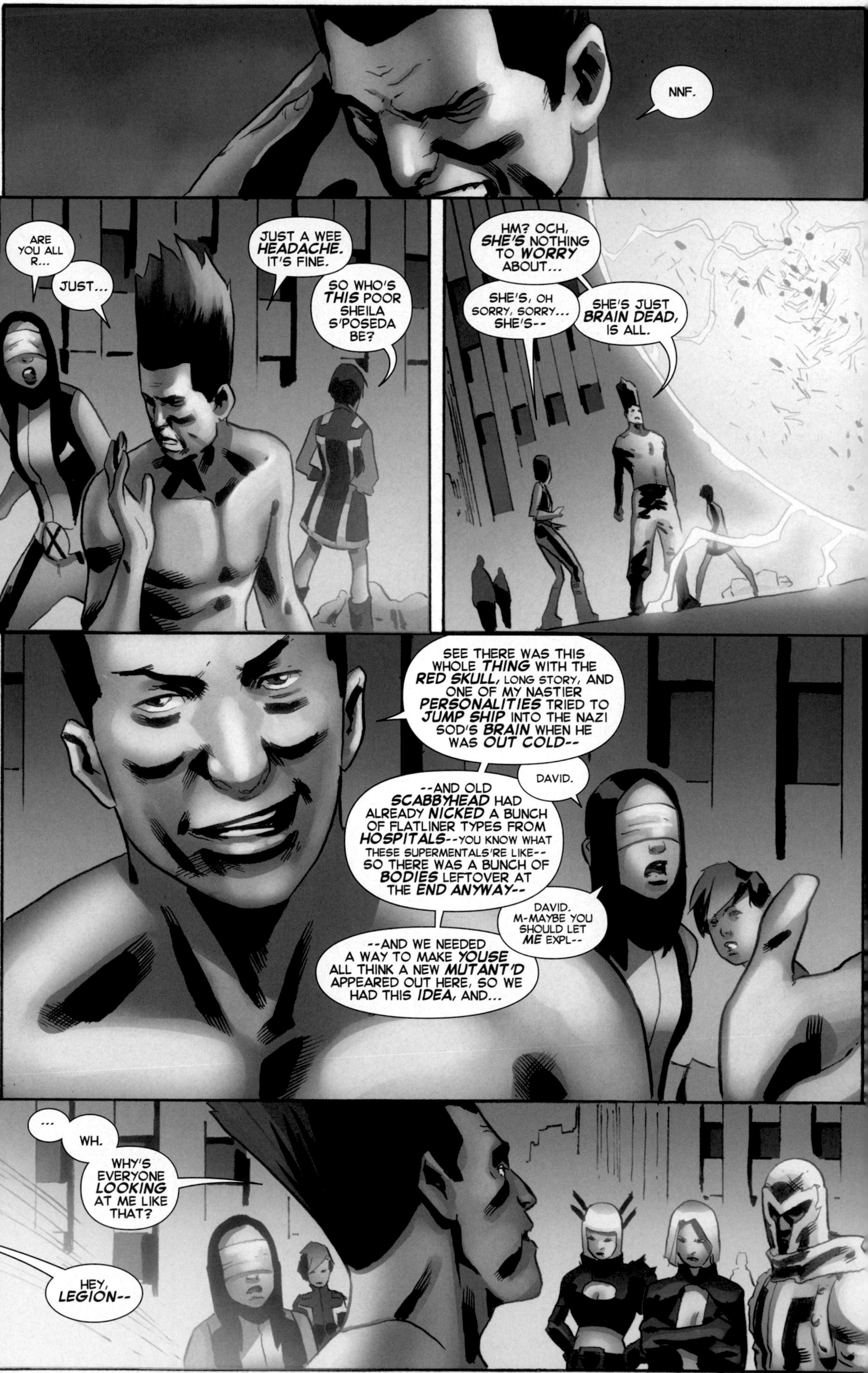
NNF.
ARE YOU ALL R...
JUST...
JUST A WEE HEADACHE. IT'S FINE.
SO WHO'S THIS POOR SHEILA S'POSEDA BE?
HM? OCH, SHE'S NOTHING TO WORRY ABOUT...
SHE'S, OH SORRY, SORRY... SHE'S--
SHE'S JUST BRAIN DEAD, IS ALL.
SEE THERE WAS THIS WHOLE THING WITH THE RED SKULL, LONG STORY, AND ONE OF MY NASTIER PERSONALITIES TRIED TO JUMP SHIP INTO THE NAZI SOD'S BRAIN WHEN HE WAS OUT COLD--
DAVID.
--AND OLD SCABBYHEAD HAD ALREADY NICKED A BUNCH OF FLATLINER TYPES FROM HOSPITALS--YOU KNOW WHAT THESE SUPERMENTALS'RE LIKE--SO THERE WAS A BUNCH OF BODIES LEFTOVER AT THE END ANYWAY--
DAVID. M-MAYBE YOU SHOULD LET ME EXPL--
--AND WE NEEDED A WAY TO MAKE YOUSE ALL THINK A NEW MUTANT'D APPEARED OUT HERE, SO WE HAD THIS IDEA, AND...
...
WH.
WHY'S EVERYONE LOOKING AT ME LIKE THAT?
HEY, LEGION--

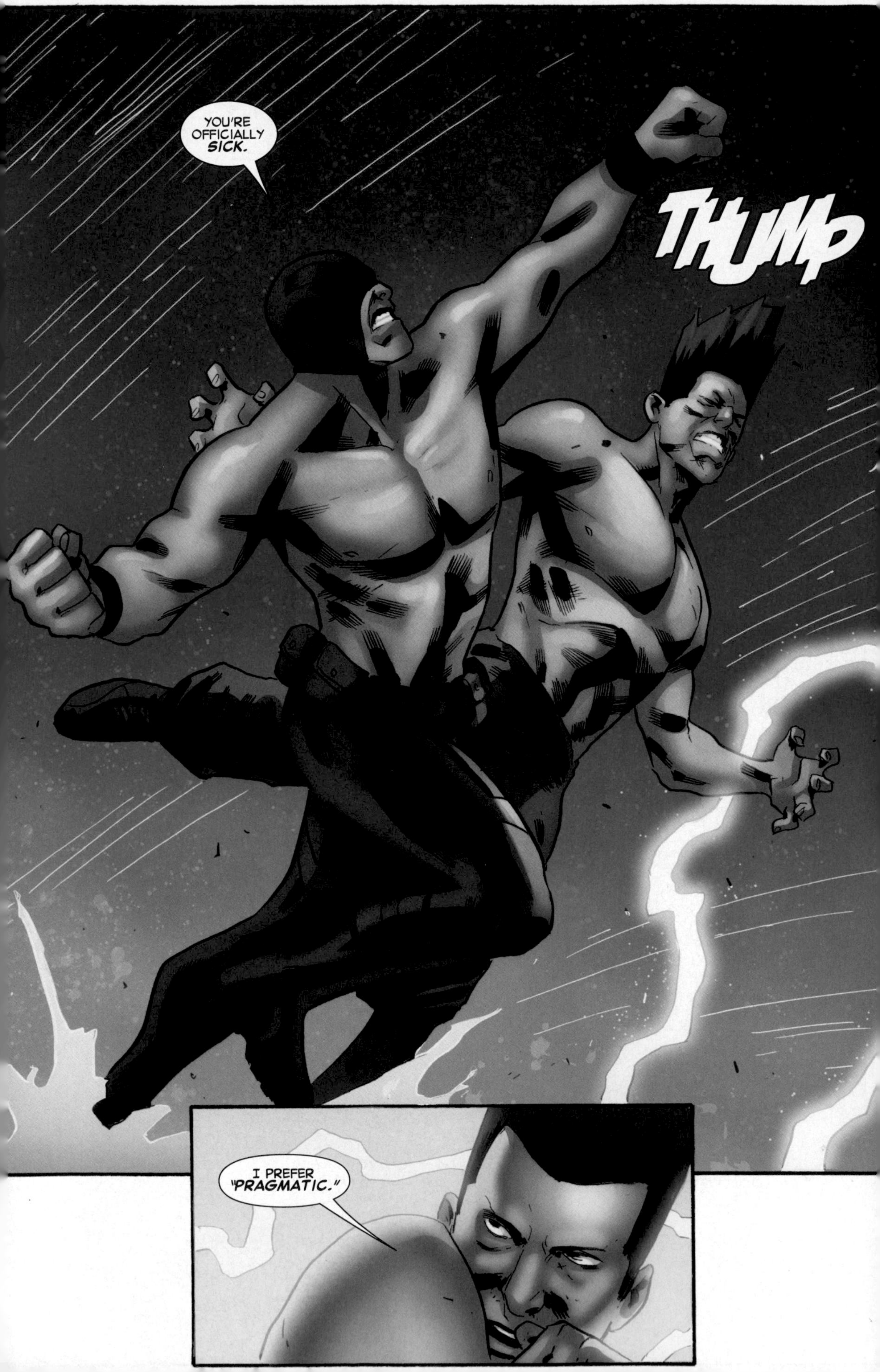
YOU'RE OFFICIALLY SICK.
THUMP
I PREFER "PRAGMATIC."

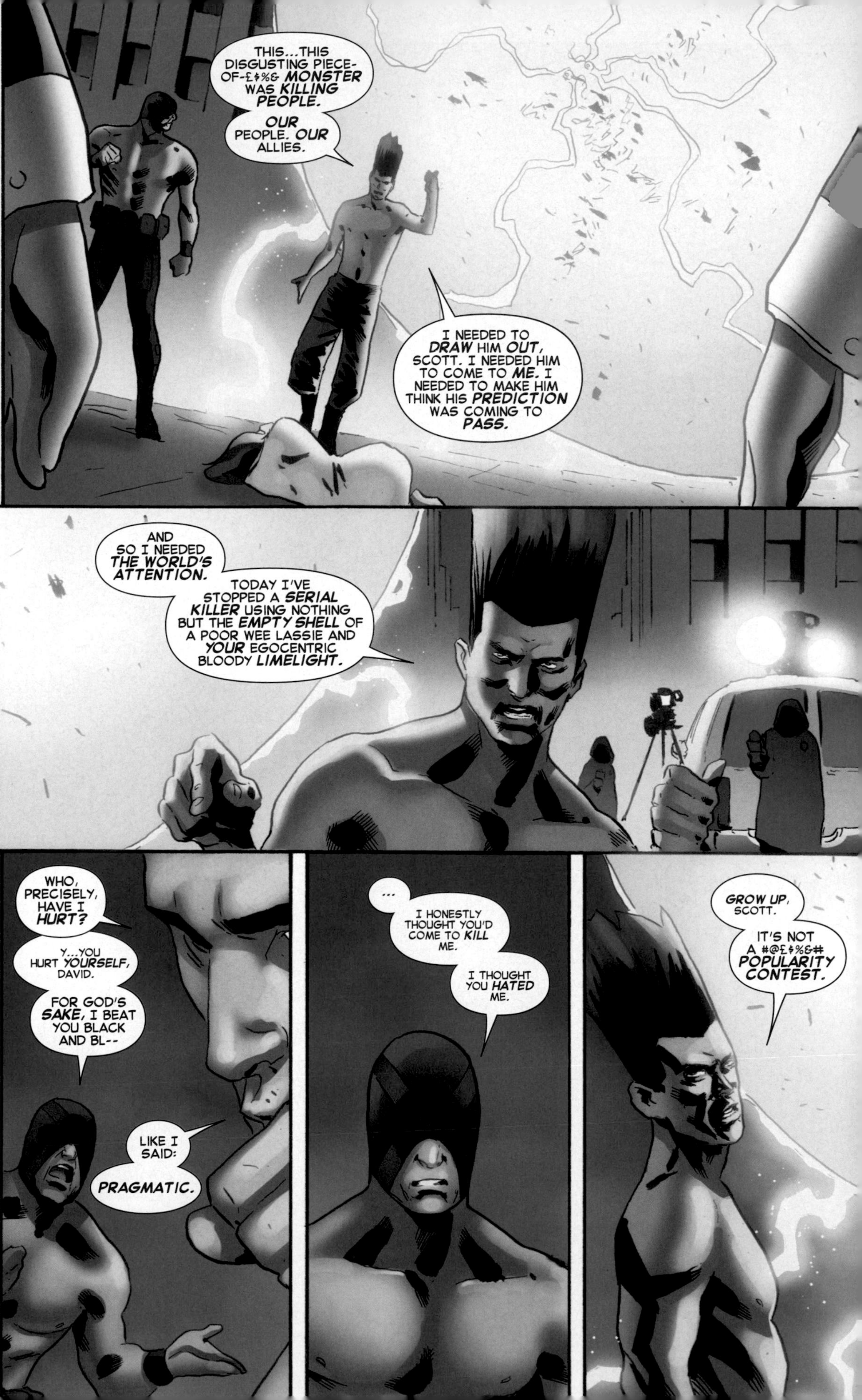
THIS...THIS DISGUSTING PIECE-OF-£$%& MONSTER WAS KILLING PEOPLE.
OUR PEOPLE. OUR ALLIES.
I NEEDED TO DRAW HIM OUT, SCOTT. I NEEDED HIM TO COME TO ME. I NEEDED TO MAKE HIM THINK HIS PREDICTION WAS COMING TO PASS.
AND SO I NEEDED THE WORLD'S ATTENTION.
TODAY I'VE STOPPED A SERIAL KILLER USING NOTHING BUT THE EMPTY SHELL OF A POOR WEE LASSIE AND YOUR EGOCENTRIC BLOODY LIMELIGHT.
WHO, PRECISELY, HAVE I HURT?
Y...YOU HURT YOURSELF, DAVID.
FOR GOD'S SAKE, I BEAT YOU BLACK AND BL--
LIKE I SAID:
PRAGMATIC.
...
I HONESTLY THOUGHT YOU'D COME TO KILL ME.
I THOUGHT YOU HATED ME.
GROW UP, SCOTT.
IT'S NOT A #@£$%&# POPULARITY CONTEST.

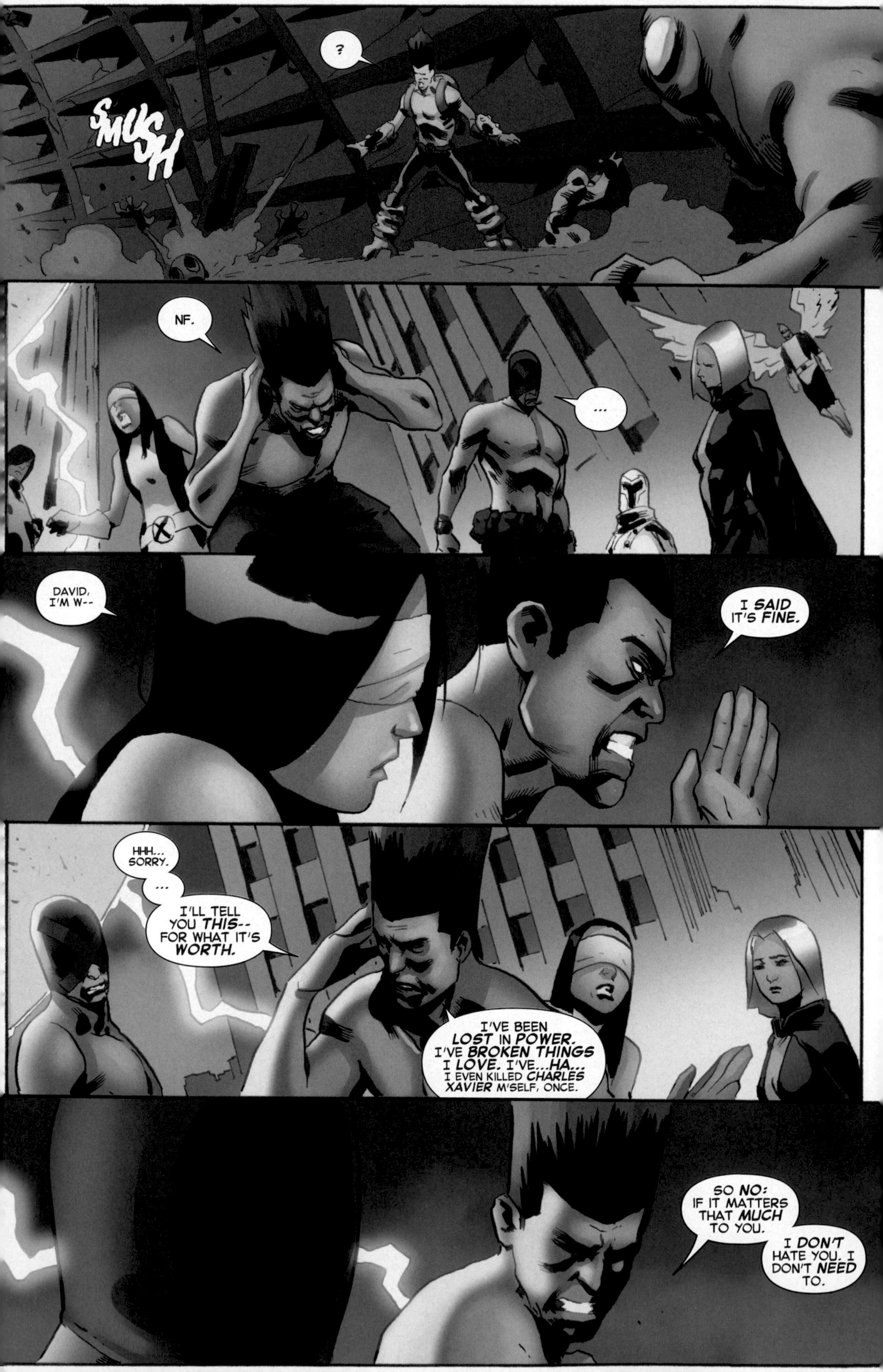
?
SMUSH
NF.
...
DAVID, I'M W--
I SAID IT'S FINE.
HHH... SORRY.
...
I'LL TELL YOU THIS-- FOR WHAT IT'S WORTH.
I'VE BEEN LOST IN POWER. I'VE BROKEN THINGS I LOVE. I'VE...HA... I EVEN KILLED CHARLES XAVIER M'SELF, ONCE.
SO NO: IF IT MATTERS THAT MUCH TO YOU.
I DON'T HATE YOU. I DON'T NEED TO.

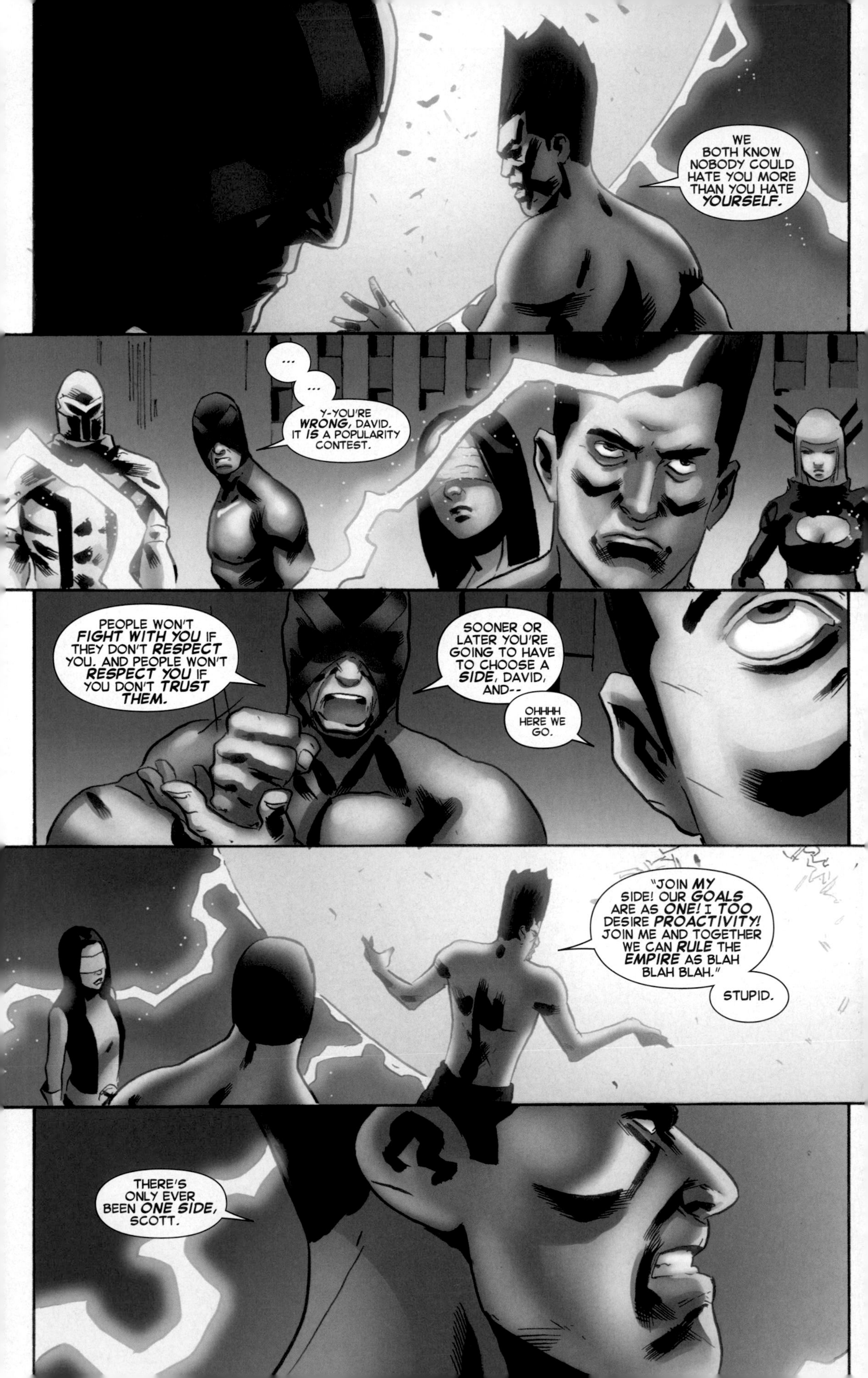
WE BOTH KNOW NOBODY COULD HATE YOU MORE THAN YOU HATE YOURSELF.
...
...
Y-YOU'RE WRONG, DAVID. IT IS A POPULARITY CONTEST.
PEOPLE WON'T FIGHT WITH YOU IF THEY DON'T RESPECT YOU. AND PEOPLE WON'T RESPECT YOU IF YOU DON'T TRUST THEM.
SOONER OR LATER YOU'RE GOING TO HAVE TO CHOOSE A SIDE, DAVID, AND--
OHHHH HERE WE GO.
"JOIN MY SIDE! OUR GOALS ARE AS ONE! I TOO DESIRE PROACTIVITY! JOIN ME AND TOGETHER WE CAN RULE THE EMPIRE AS BLAH BLAH BLAH."
STUPID.
THERE'S ONLY EVER BEEN ONE SIDE, SCOTT.

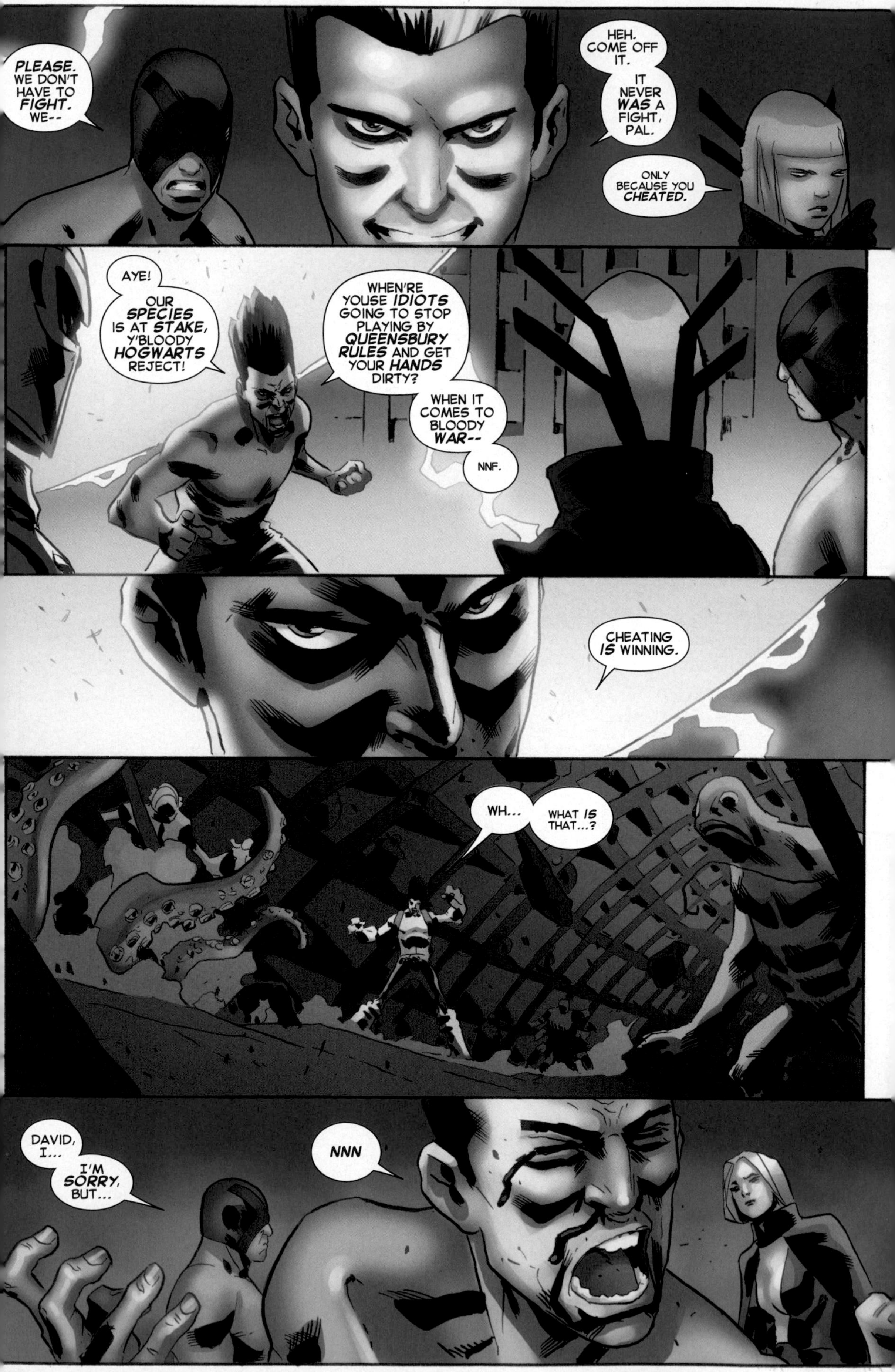
PLEASE. WE DON'T HAVE TO FIGHT. WE--
HEH. COME OFF IT.
IT NEVER WAS A FIGHT, PAL.
ONLY BECAUSE YOU CHEATED.
AYE!
OUR SPECIES IS AT STAKE, Y'BLOODY HOGWARTS REJECT!
WHEN'RE YOUSE IDIOTS GOING TO STOP PLAYING BY QUEENSBURY RULES AND GET YOUR HANDS DIRTY?
WHEN IT COMES TO BLOODY WAR--
NNF.
CHEATING IS WINNING.
WH...
WHAT IS THAT...?
DAVID, I...
I'M SORRY, BUT...
NNN

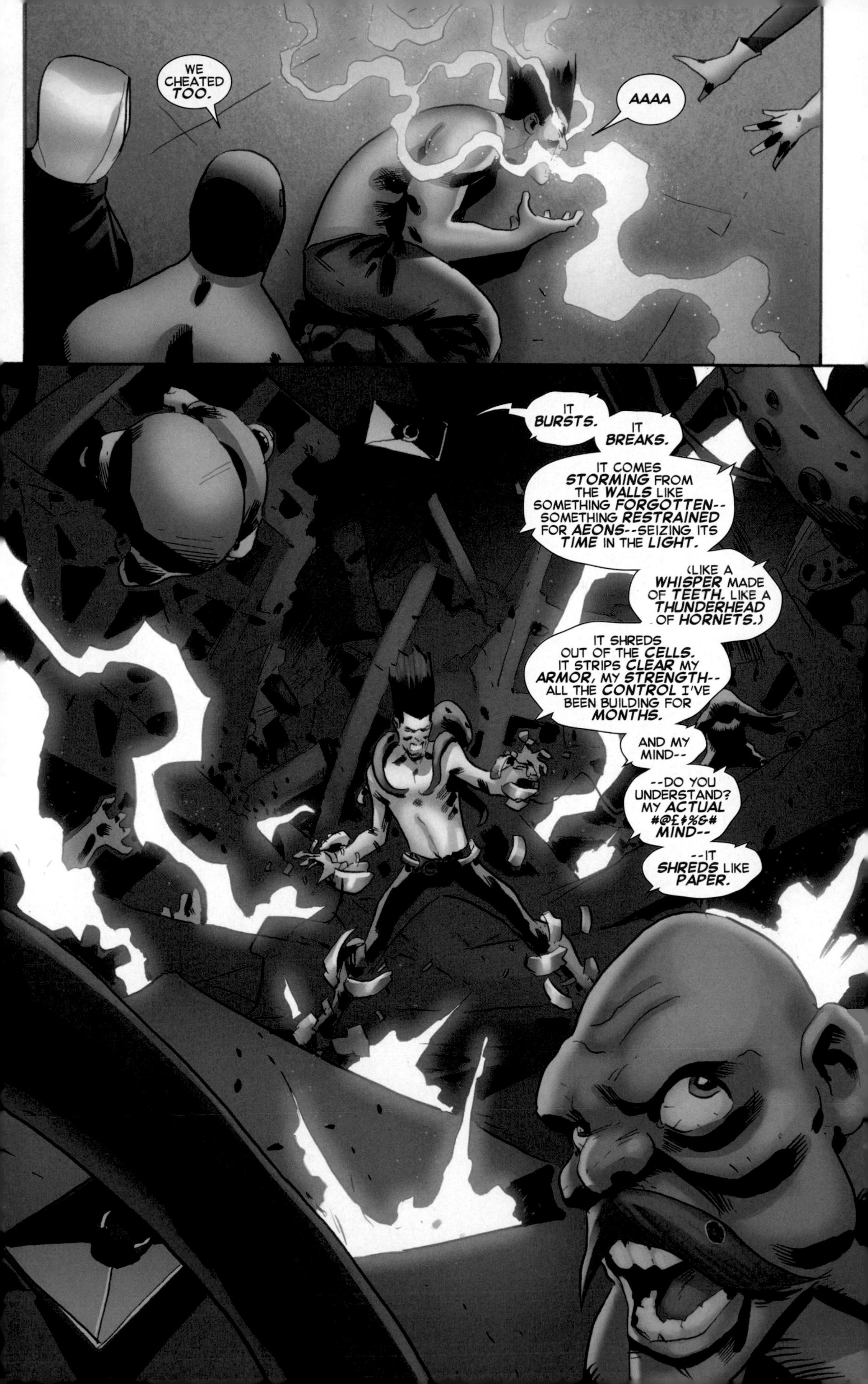
WE CHEATED TOO.
AAAA
IT BURSTS.
IT BREAKS.
IT COMES STORMING FROM THE WALLS LIKE SOMETHING FORGOTTEN--SOMETHING RESTRAINED FOR AEONS--SEIZING ITS TIME IN THE LIGHT.
(LIKE A WHISPER MADE OF TEETH. LIKE A THUNDERHEAD OF HORNETS.)
IT SHREDS OUT OF THE CELLS. IT STRIPS CLEAR MY ARMOR, MY STRENGTH--ALL THE CONTROL I'VE BEEN BUILDING FOR MONTHS.
AND MY MIND--
--DO YOU UNDERSTAND? MY ACTUAL #@£$%&# MIND--
--IT SHREDS LIKE PAPER.

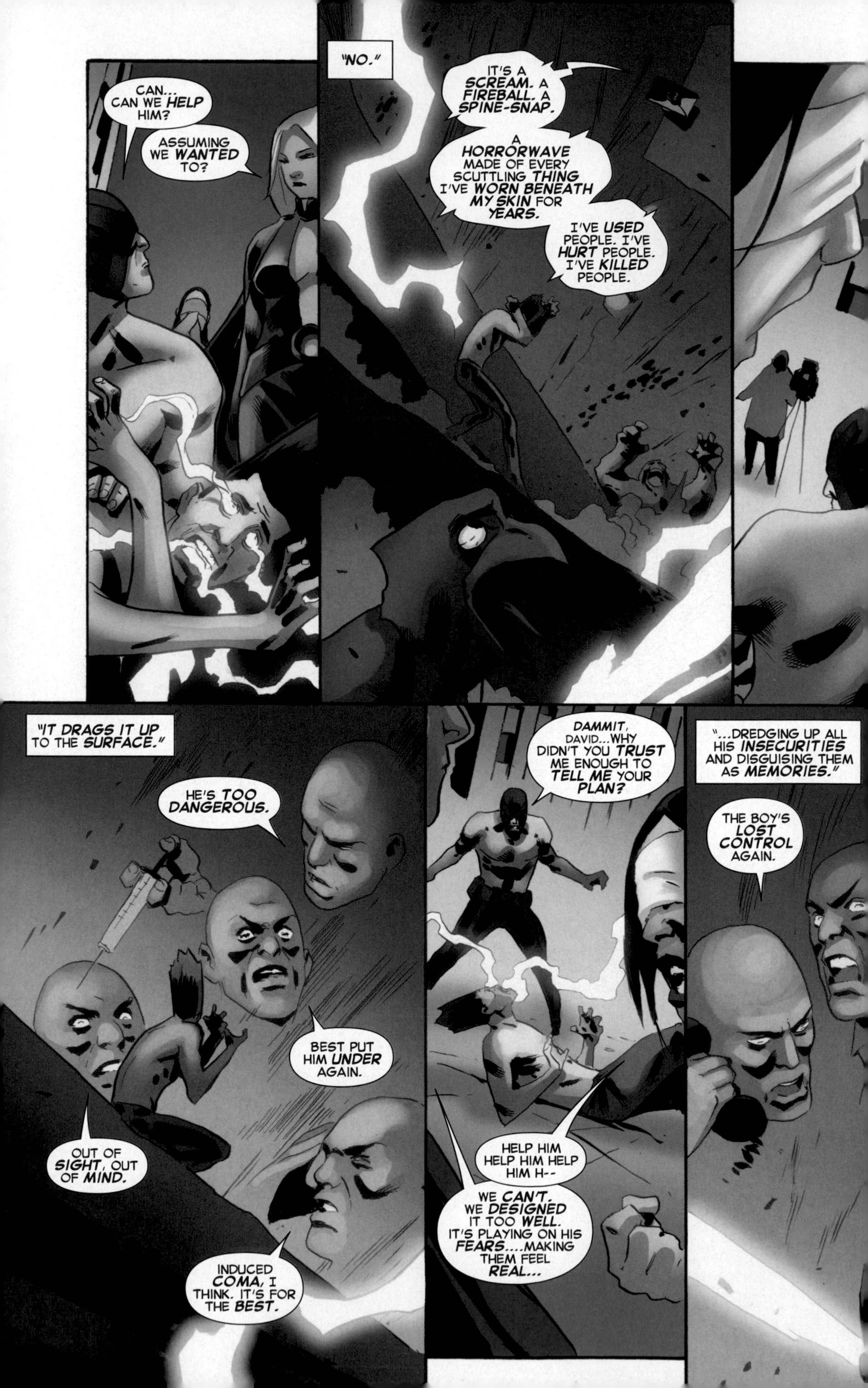
CAN... CAN WE HELP HIM?
ASSUMING WE WANTED TO?
"NO."
IT'S A SCREAM. A FIREBALL. A SPINE-SNAP.
A HORRORWAVE MADE OF EVERY SCUTTLING THING I'VE WORN BENEATH MY SKIN FOR YEARS.
I'VE USED PEOPLE. I'VE HURT PEOPLE. I'VE KILLED PEOPLE.
"IT DRAGS IT UP TO THE SURFACE."
HE'S TOO DANGEROUS.
BEST PUT HIM UNDER AGAIN.
OUT OF SIGHT, OUT OF MIND.
INDUCED COMA, I THINK. IT'S FOR THE BEST.
DAMMIT, DAVID...WHY DIDN'T YOU TRUST ME ENOUGH TO TELL ME YOUR PLAN?
HELP HIM HELP HIM HELP HIM H--
WE CAN'T. WE DESIGNED IT TOO WELL. IT'S PLAYING ON HIS FEARS....MAKING THEM FEEL REAL...
"...DREDGING UP ALL HIS INSECURITIES AND DISGUISING THEM AS MEMORIES."
THE BOY'S LOST CONTROL AGAIN.

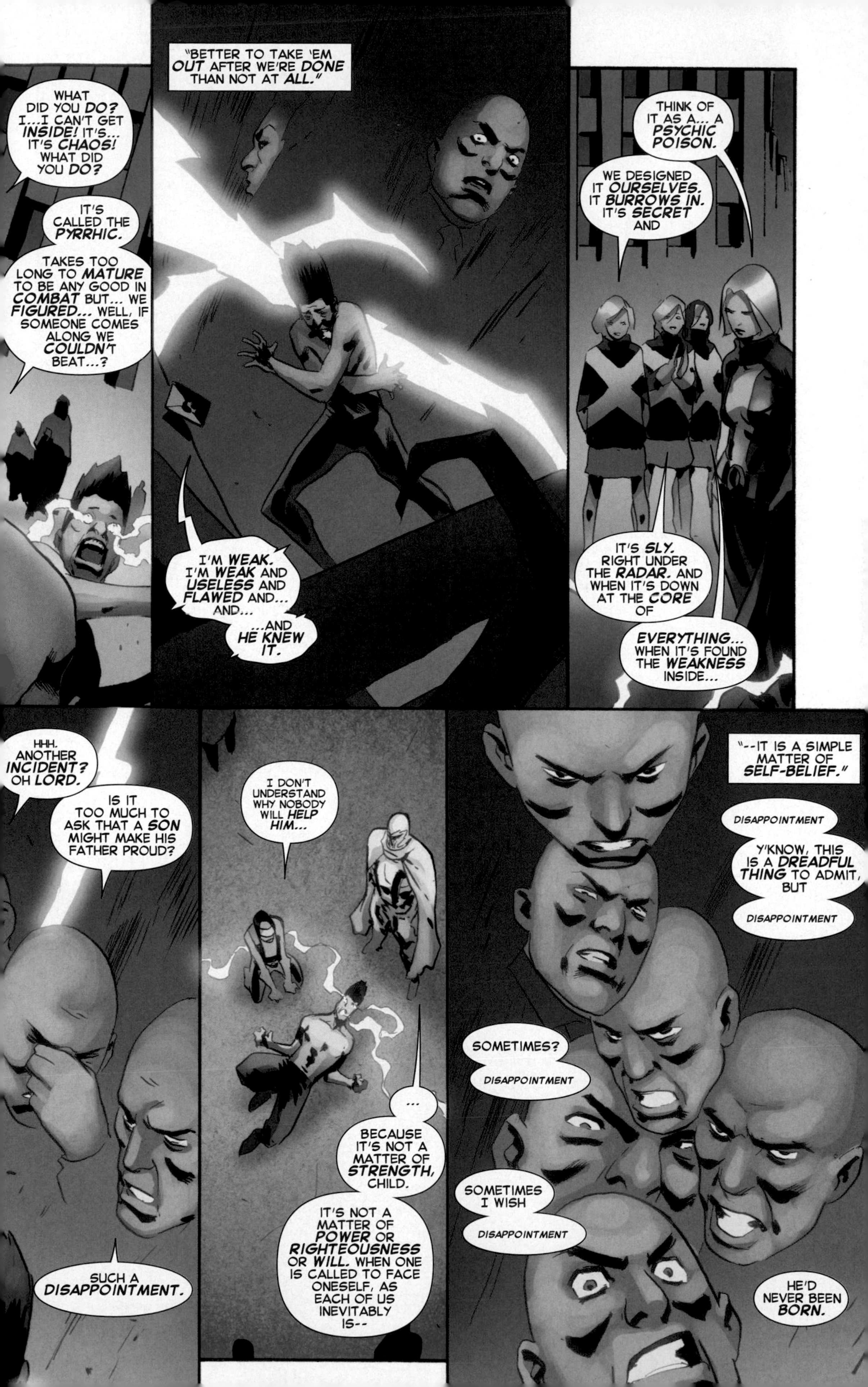
WHAT DID YOU DO? I...I CAN'T GET INSIDE! IT'S... IT'S CHAOS! WHAT DID YOU DO?
IT'S CALLED THE PYRRHIC.
TAKES TOO LONG TO MATURE TO BE ANY GOOD IN COMBAT BUT... WE FIGURED... WELL, IF SOMEONE COMES ALONG WE COULDN'T BEAT...?
"BETTER TO TAKE 'EM OUT AFTER WE'RE DONE THAN NOT AT ALL."
I'M WEAK. I'M WEAK AND USELESS AND FLAWED AND... AND...
...AND HE KNEW IT.
THINK OF IT AS A... A PSYCHIC POISON.
WE DESIGNED IT OURSELVES. IT BURROWS IN. IT'S SECRET AND
IT'S SLY. RIGHT UNDER THE RADAR. AND WHEN IT'S DOWN AT THE CORE OF
EVERYTHING... WHEN IT'S FOUND THE WEAKNESS INSIDE...
HHH. ANOTHER INCIDENT? OH LORD.
IS IT TOO MUCH TO ASK THAT A SON MIGHT MAKE HIS FATHER PROUD?
SUCH A DISAPPOINTMENT.
I DON'T UNDERSTAND WHY NOBODY WILL HELP HIM...
...
BECAUSE IT'S NOT A MATTER OF STRENGTH, CHILD.
IT'S NOT A MATTER OF POWER OR RIGHTEOUSNESS OR WILL. WHEN ONE IS CALLED TO FACE ONESELF, AS EACH OF US INEVITABLY IS--
"--IT IS A SIMPLE MATTER OF SELF-BELIEF."
DISAPPOINTMENT
Y'KNOW, THIS IS A DREADFUL THING TO ADMIT, BUT
DISAPPOINTMENT
SOMETIMES?
DISAPPOINTMENT
SOMETIMES I WISH
DISAPPOINTMENT
HE'D NEVER BEEN BORN.

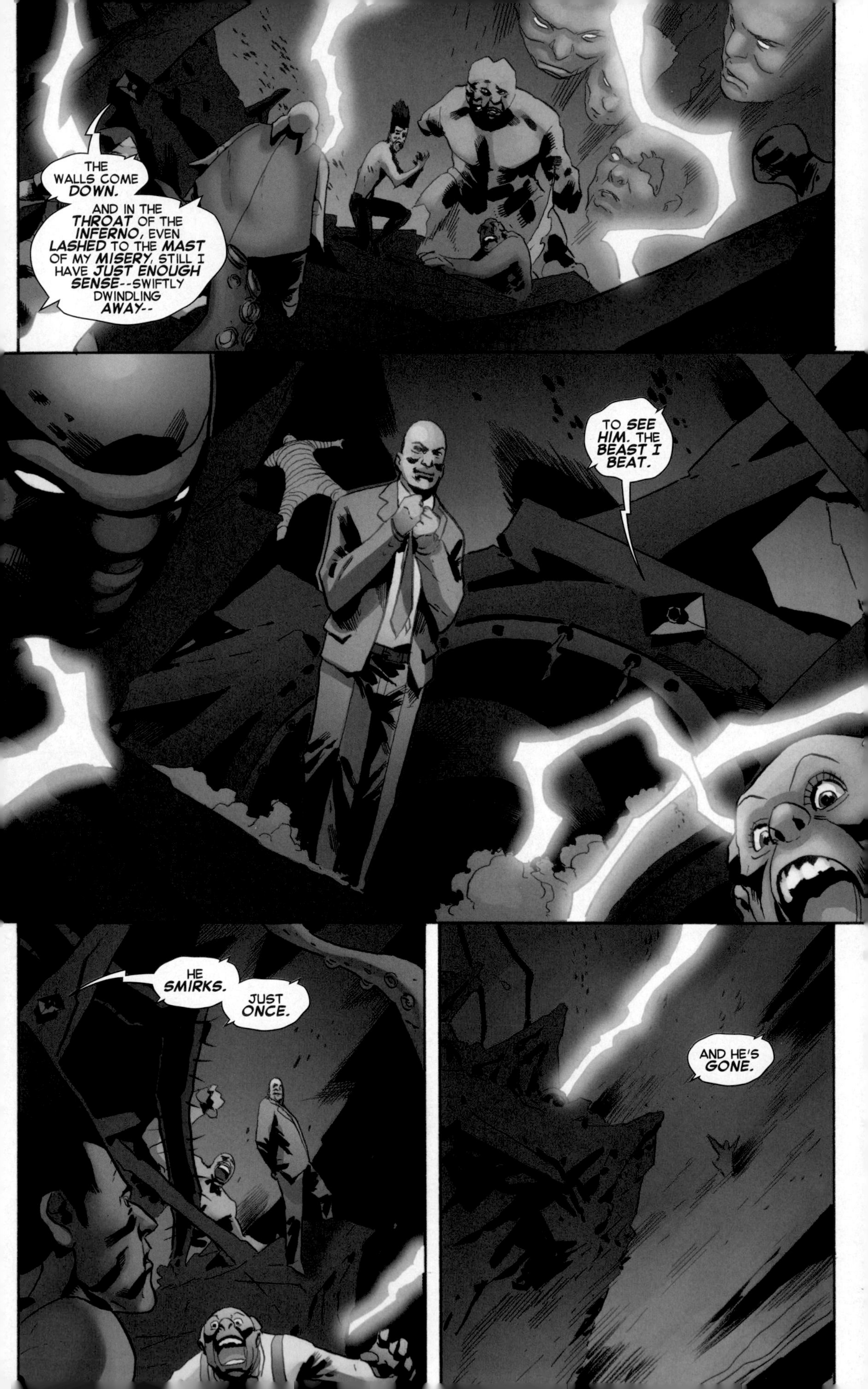
THE WALLS COME DOWN.
AND IN THE THROAT OF THE INFERNO, EVEN LASHED TO THE MAST OF MY MISERY, STILL I HAVE JUST ENOUGH SENSE--SWIFTLY DWINDLING AWAY--
TO SEE HIM. THE BEAST I BEAT.
HE SMIRKS.
JUST ONCE.
AND HE'S GONE.

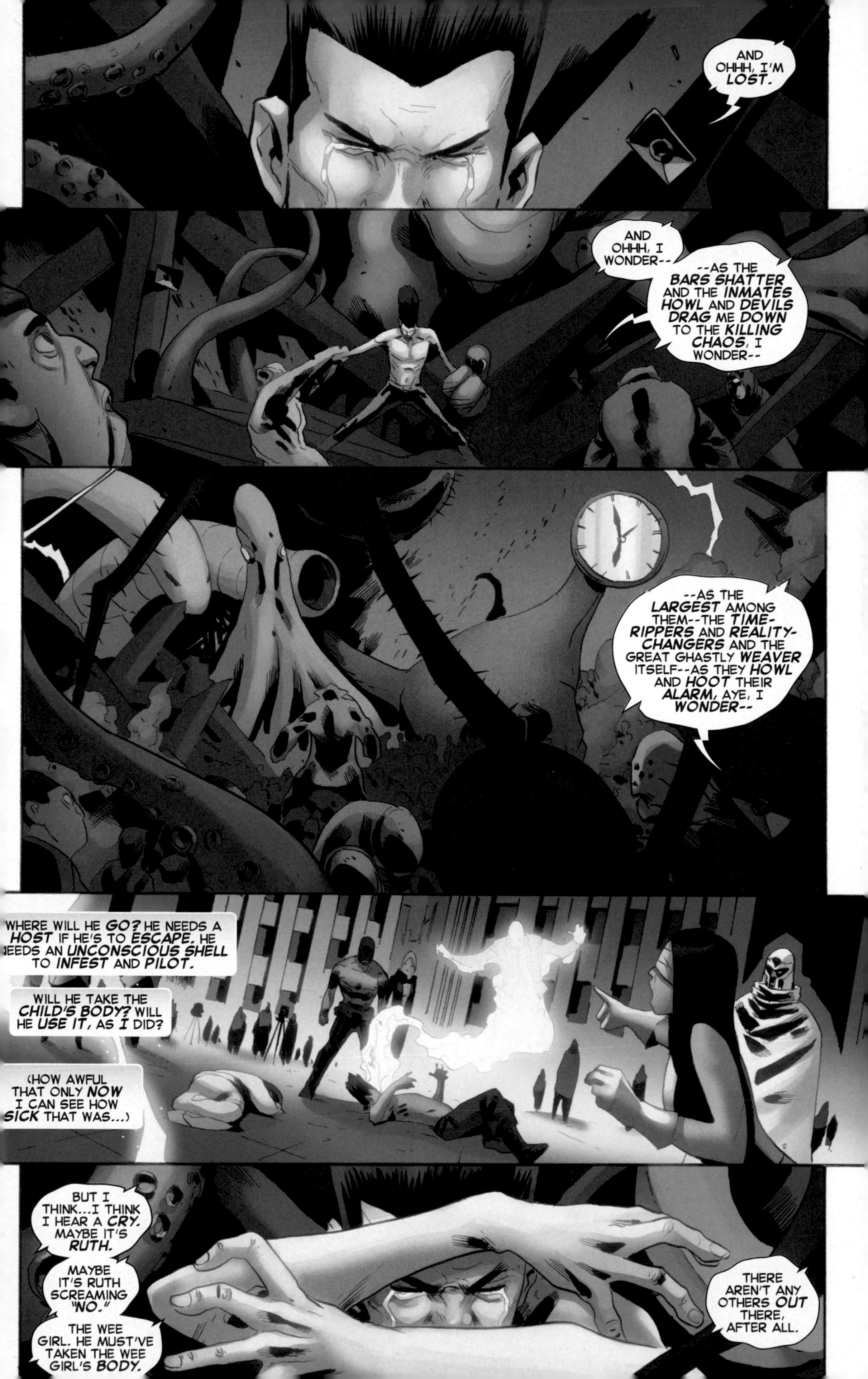
AND OHHH, I'M LOST.
AND OHHH, I WONDER--
--AS THE BARS SHATTER AND THE INMATES HOWL AND DEVILS DRAG ME DOWN TO THE KILLING CHAOS, I WONDER--
--AS THE LARGEST AMONG THEM--THE TIME-RIPPERS AND REALITY-CHANGERS AND THE GREAT GHASTLY WEAVER ITSELF--AS THEY HOWL AND HOOT THEIR ALARM, AYE, I WONDER--
WHERE WILL HE GO? HE NEEDS A HOST IF HE'S TO ESCAPE. HE NEEDS AN UNCONSCIOUS SHELL TO INFEST AND PILOT.
WILL HE TAKE THE CHILD'S BODY? WILL HE USE IT, AS I DID?
(HOW AWFUL THAT ONLY NOW I CAN SEE HOW SICK THAT WAS...)
BUT I THINK...I THINK I HEAR A CRY. MAYBE IT'S RUTH.
MAYBE IT'S RUTH SCREAMING "NO."
THE WEE GIRL. HE MUST'VE TAKEN THE WEE GIRL'S BODY.
THERE AREN'T ANY OTHERS OUT THERE, AFTER ALL.

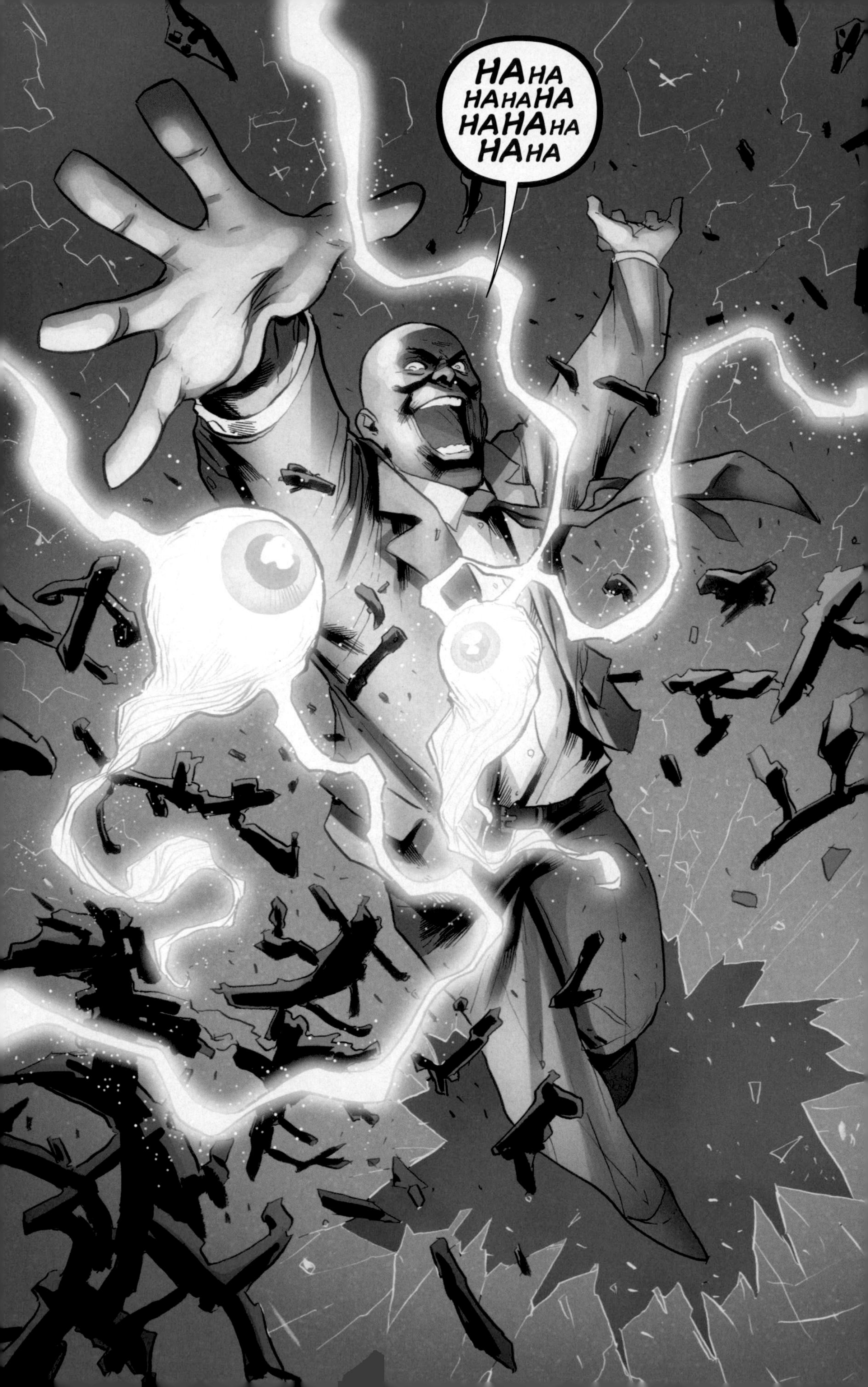
HAha HAhaHA HAHAha HAha

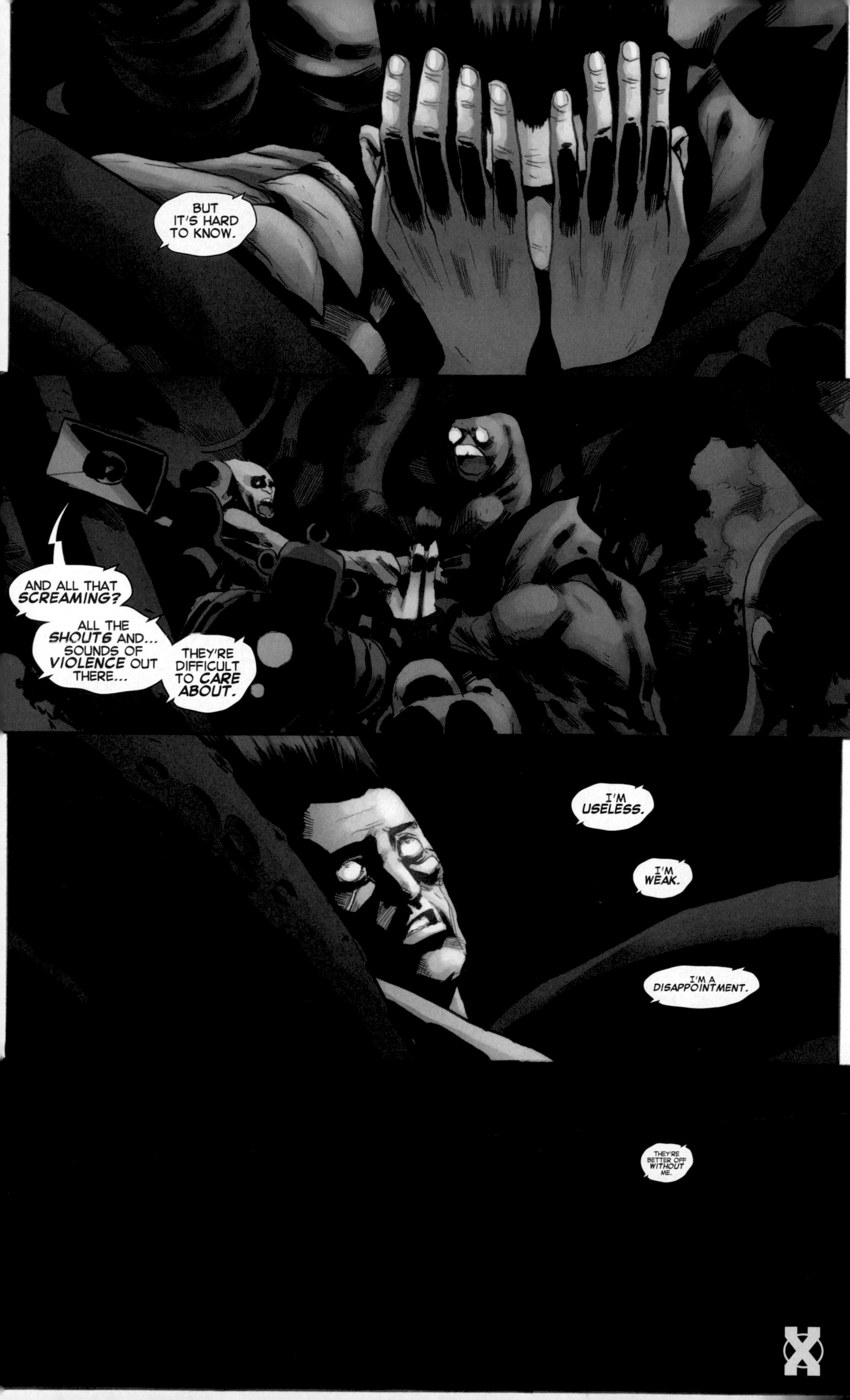
BUT IT'S HARD TO KNOW.
AND ALL THAT SCREAMING?
ALL THE SHOUTS AND... SOUNDS OF VIOLENCE OUT THERE...
THEY'RE DIFFICULT TO CARE ABOUT.
I'M USELESS.
I'M WEAK.
I'M A DISAPPOINTMENT.
THEY'RE BETTER OFF WITHOUT ME.

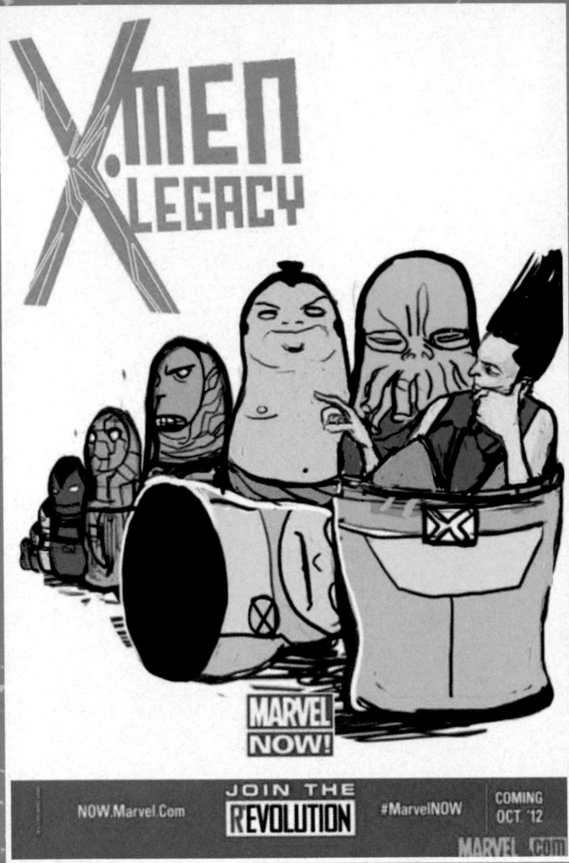
X-MEN LEGACY
MARVEL NOW!
NOW.Marvel.Com
JOIN THE REVOLUTION
#MarvelNOW
COMING OCT. '12
MARVEL.com

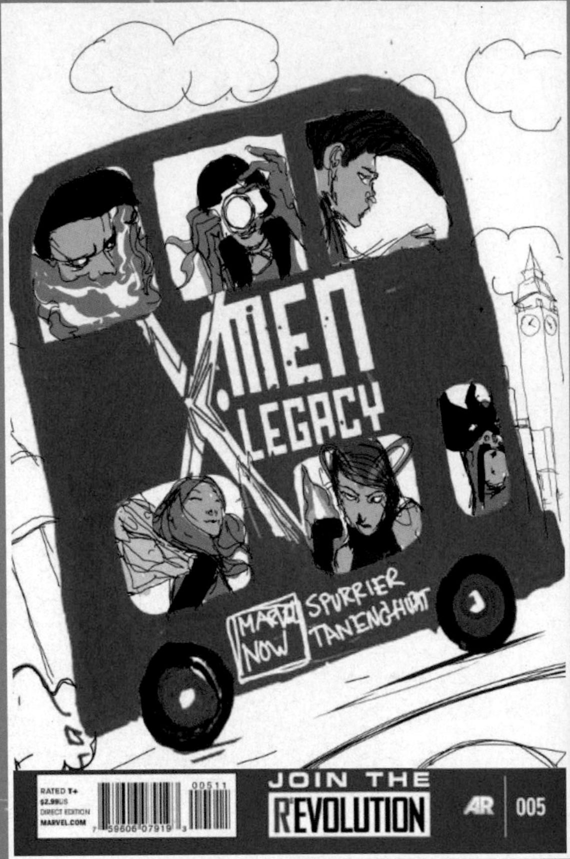
X-MEN LEGACY
NOW
SPURRIER
TAN ENG HUAT
RATED T+
$2.99US
DIRECT EDITION
MARVEL.COM
JOIN THE REVOLUTION
005

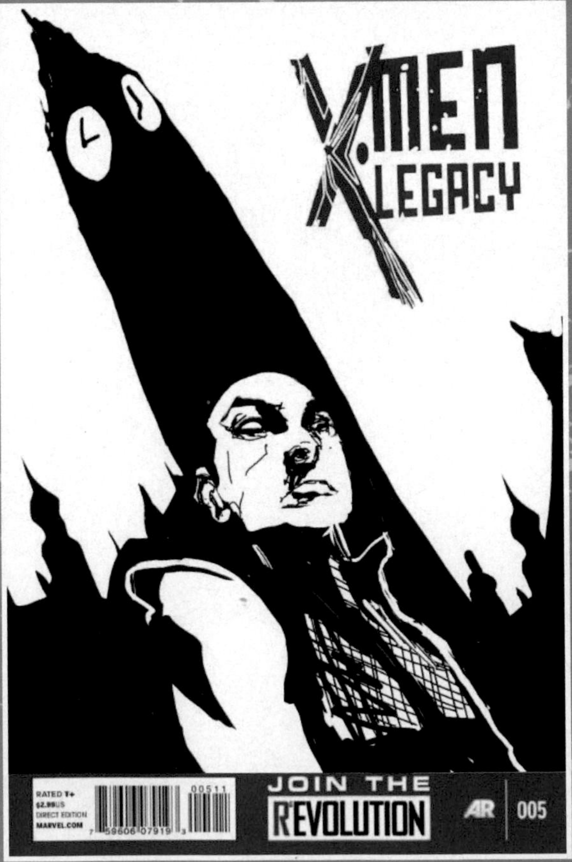
X-MEN LEGACY
RATED T+
$2.99US
DIRECT EDITION
MARVEL.COM
JOIN THE REVOLUTION
005

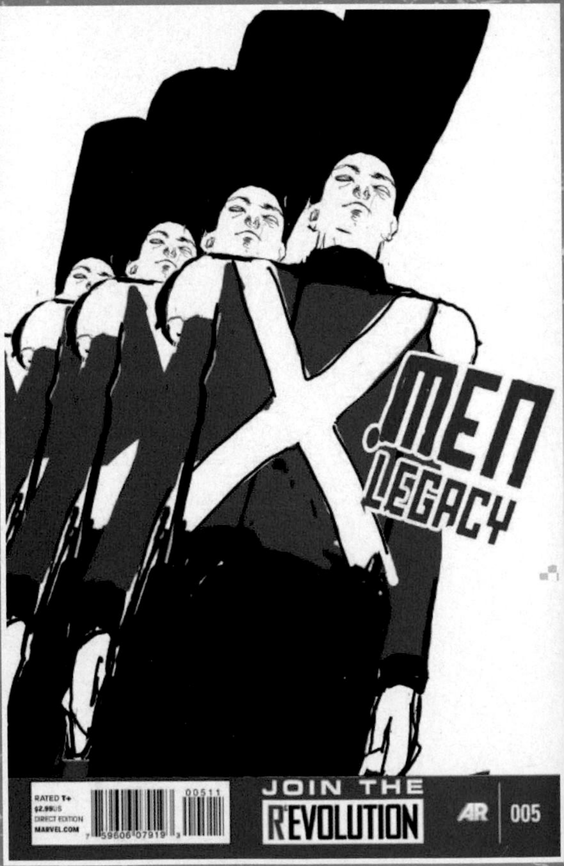
X-MEN LEGACY
RATED T+
$2.99US
DIRECT EDITION
MARVEL.COM
JOIN THE REVOLUTION
005

COVER CONCEPTS by Mike del Mundo

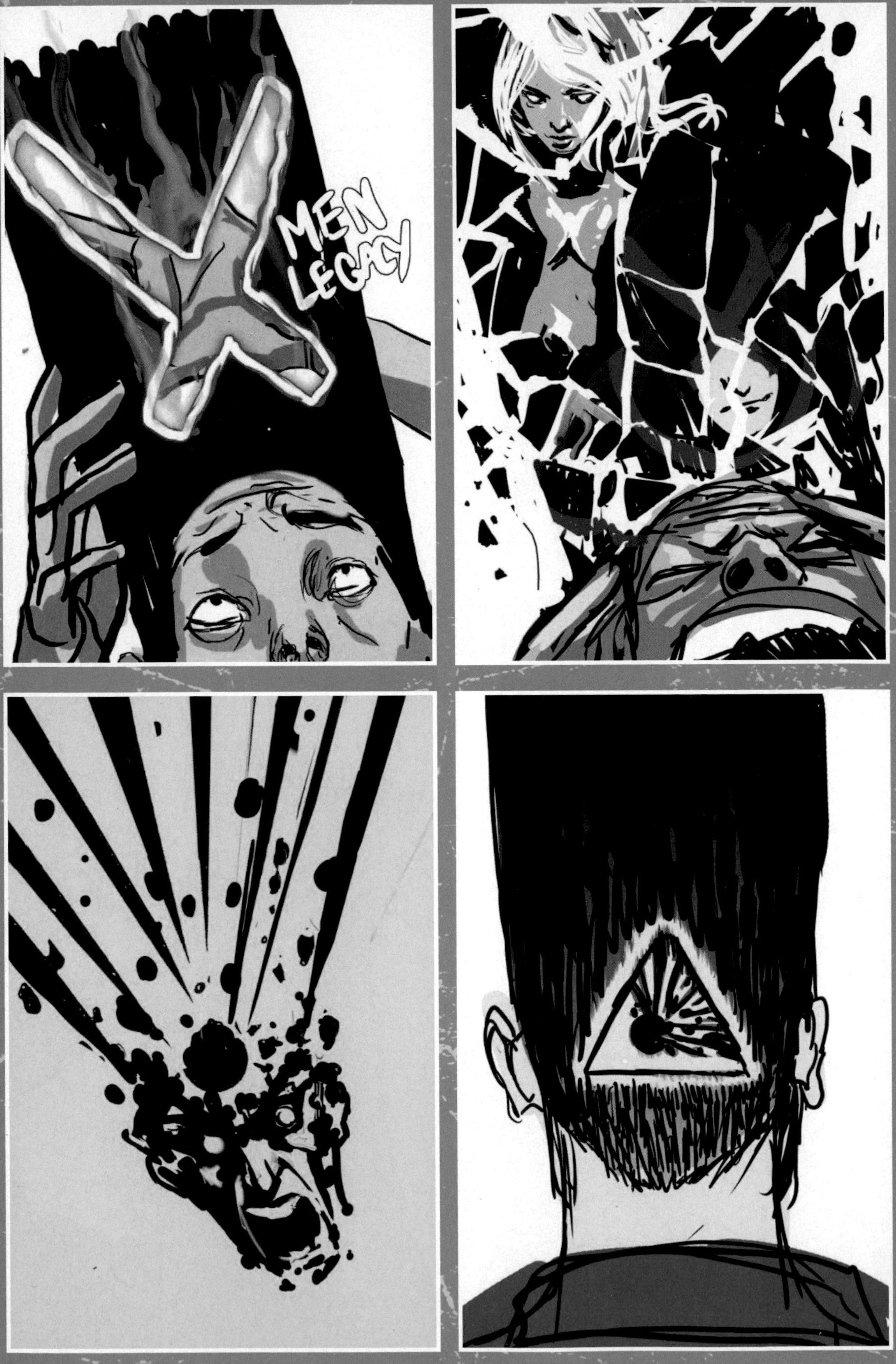
X MEN LEGACY